**THE STAGE IS SET
FOR A NEW ADVENTURE
INTO UNCHARTED FIELDS.**

I had started out as an outright "debunker," taking great joy in cracking what seemed at first to be puzzling cases. I was the arch enemy of those "flying saucer groups and enthusiasts" who very dearly wanted UFOs to be interplanetary. My own knowledge of those groups came almost entirely from what I heard from Blue Book personnel: they were all "crackpots and visionaries." It was useless to remonstrate with the staff of Blue Book personnel; it would have been a clear-cut case of "fighting City Hall."

My transformation was gradual but by the late sixties it was complete. Today I would not spend one further moment on the subject of UFOs if I didn't seriously feel that the UFO phenomenon is real and that efforts to investigate and understand it, and eventually to solve it, could have a profound effect—perhaps even be the springboard to a revolution in mankind's outlook on the universe.

—DR. J. ALLEN HYNEK

THE HYNEK UFO REPORT

DR. J. ALLEN HYNEK

A DELL BOOK

Published by
Dell Publishing Co., Inc.
1 Dag Hammarskjold Plaza
New York, New York 10017

Dell ® TM 681510, Dell Publishing Co., Inc.

ISBN: 0-440-19201-3

Printed in the United States of America
First printing—December 1977
Second printing—January 1978

CONTENTS

PROLOGUE

Under the Freedom of Information Act, much government material that for years had been considered "classified" and otherwise restricted—material from the judiciary, foreign relations, and the FBI and CIA files—has been made available to the public. Only those matters that might jeopardize national security or involve an individual's constitutional rights continue to remain withheld.

Project Blue Book, the Air Force's project on UFOs, was always regarded officially as "unclassified," but this amounted to a standing joke among those who knew better. Not only were many of the reports labeled "Confidential" or "Secret," but the citizen who tried to examine Blue Book files was given a polite runaround or an outright refusal on various grounds. Those who sought to find out about the Air Force's investigation of UFOs were usually brushed off on the basis that the UFO files contained information that might reveal secrets about experimental military aircraft and hardware, new and advanced radar equipment and its secret locations, missiles, and military bases and installations.

In short, what was true in theory was not true in practice. Blue Book files *were not* open to the public, even though the Air Force claimed publicly that Blue Book was an open book.

Well, finally it is. The essentially complete files are available at the National Archives in Washington, D.C. For a price, one can obtain rather poor quality reels of microfilm of the files extant.* Or, one can examine the files in

* I say they are "essentially" complete because over the course of twenty-two years some cases were partially or completely lost or misplaced. Photographs and supplementary material like telephone notes, teletype messages, etc., were "borrowed" from the files and

person at the National Archives. Either approach involves hours of tedious work.

The Center for UFO Studies, in Evanston, Illinois, of which I am the Scientific Director, has obtained a complete set of the microfilms, and these are available for serious students of the UFO phenomenon. I have written much of the present book from these films, adding material from my own personal experience as scientific consultant to Project Blue Book. Therefore, the reader will find in this book material that cannot be found in the files themselves.

In all, there are 13,134 reports in the Air Force files. A simple catalogue of these cases, giving only their geographical locations, dates, Air Force evaluation (and the revised evaluation suggested by my associates at the Center for UFO Studies and myself) represents a pile of sheets on my desk nearly a foot high! And these cases themselves represent only a fraction of the total number of UFO reports that have come to the attention of the Center, where a computerized data bank (called UFOCAT) of over 50,000 individual entries from all over the world is located.

It is very important to remember that the "raw materials" for the study of the UFO phenomenon are not the UFOs themselves but the *reports* of UFOs. These reports include the total circumstances surrounding each case and the caliber and reputations of the witnesses—information that will allow us to make a logical and rational judgment about the nature of the UFO phenomenon, if such judgment is at all possible.

In the public mind, UFOs seem to be synonymous with spaceships and visitors from outer space. Certainly a careful study of the more extraordinary and unexplained UFO cases, not only from the Air Force files but from the more extensive files at the Center for UFO Studies, leaves little doubt that an "intelligence" of some sort is operating. But what kind and where from?

We must be extremely careful not to be too self-centered about this question. It is only too natural for us to think that all intelligence must necessarily be like our own—that

---

never returned, often probably through carelessness. The files were not kept in apple-pie order, a fact I both observed and deplored.

visitors, if these they be, must think and act as we do. Indeed there are people in other nations whose actions we sometimes find difficult to understand; why, then, presume that the intelligence that appears to manifest itself in one way or another through the UFO phenomenon must be akin to ours? Or why assume that it necessarily operates under the conditions we are accustomed to? And, whence this intelligence? Does it really hail from afar, or is it perhaps much closer to us than popularly supposed? Is it *meta*terrestrial rather than extraterrestrial? Or, going even further afield, is it in some way, as the psychologist Jung held, a strange manifestation of the human psyche?

This overall concern has even invaded Hollywood, a sure index of its pervasiveness and popular appeal. It is the central theme of the motion picture *Close Encounters of the Third Kind* (the title of which comes directly from the author's previous book, *The UFO Experience*) whose director, Steven Spielberg, has had an intense interest in the subject of UFOs for many years. Spielberg has succeeded in capturing on film the essence of the UFO enigma, the mounting evidence that intelligence other than our own not only exists, but, in a manner peculiarly its own, is making itself known to the human race.

In this vein, I am reminded of a conversation I once had with U Thant, the late Secretary General of the United Nations, during my days as a skeptic. We had been discussing UFOs and interstellar travel, and he asked me whether I thought extraterrestrials might possibly visit our world. I responded that as an astronomer I found the distances and the times necessary to make the journey so great as to preclude it entirely. U Thant looked at me, arched his eyebrows, and said: "You know, I am a Buddhist, and we believe in life elsewhere." I told him that as an astronomer I did too, but that the physical conditions, especially the length of time involved in journeys from outer space, seemed insuperable. The Secretary General paused, leaned back in his chair, and said, "Ah, but what may seem like years to us, may be just a day or two to others."

And so it may. We know so little about the vast universe, poised as we are on our tiny vantage point, the earth, that things far beyond our imagination may indeed be possible.

In the meantime, we must satisfy ourselves by studying

UFO *reports*, not UFOs. Reports are made by people and people are often mistaken about what they observe. Therefore, reports made by several witnesses very probably should be given greater weight, for each account can be measured against the others for accuracy. Still, it is impossible to vouch for the validity of each of the puzzling reports listed in Project Blue Book, even for those cases which I investigated and in which I became personally involved. The witnesses I interviewed *could* have been lying, *could* have been insane, or *could* have been hallucinating collectively—but I do not think so. Their standing in the community, their lack of motive for perpetration of a hoax, their own puzzlement at the turn of events they believed they witnessed, and often their great reluctance to speak of the experience—all lend a subjective reality to their UFO experience.

The question we must puzzle over is simply this: What level of *objective* reality?

So, here now, is the gist of what you will find if you take the trouble to spend weeks at the National Archives or wade through more than a mile of microfilm at home—plus what I have been able to add from my long personal association with Blue Book.

I leave you to judge for yourself.

—J. ALLEN HYNEK

1

BLUE BOOK IS NOT A BOOK

Please send me a copy of the Air Force Blue Book.
—from a letter by a student

There is not now nor was there ever an Air Force Blue Book. The Air Force never published a comprehensive compilation of the work of their Project Blue Book, which was the name given to the project concerned with the receipt and analysis of thousands of individual UFO reports recorded over a span of some twenty years.*

Strange apparitions in the sky and on or near the ground have been reported on occasion throughout history. There was a "UFO flap" of considerable proportions in the United States in 1897–98, and in Europe during World War II "foo fighters" (luminous balls that followed airplanes) were reported by pilots on both sides. There was also a rash of "ghost rockets" in the Scandinavian countries in 1946. But the year 1947 is generally credited as the year in which the modern wave of "flying saucer" or UFO reports began.

The early reports of UFOs were largely of discs observed during the daytime or of strange lights seen at night. "Close Encounters" or reports of UFO experiences in close proximity to the witness or percipient—as close as a few hundred feet or less—do not occur frequently in Blue Book files. The discs, oval, ellipsoid, or "egg"-shaped objects

---

*From time to time the Air Force did issue news releases and short summaries—generally called "Fact Sheets"—as well as a series of Project Blue Book reports. One of these, Special Report No. 14, did contain a statistical study of 2,199 reports made through 1952. This report is well worth reading for the things it says—and does not say (see Chapter 12).

were "flying saucers" because they generally looked somewhat like saucers, or more specifically, like two saucers—one overturned upon the other—to most observers reporting them. And although other terms were used to describe them, the term flying saucer soon became popular with both press and public alike.

Actually, the term flying saucer had been coined a half-century before by a farmer named Martin (see Vallee, p. 1)* But it wasn't popularized in the modern press until the widely publicized sighting of Kenneth Arnold, a private pilot, on June 24, 1947 (see p. 99).

The United States Air Force, the military arm charged with protecting us from any mechanical device that flies (outside of our own), naturally was given the responsibility of investigating this bizarre and—for all the government knew—potentially fearsome aerial weapon. It was only because "flying saucers" might pose a serious threat to the national security that the Air Force regarded them in the beginning as a priority matter; it wasn't important whether their origin was some country here on Earth, some other planet, or even some distant solar system. The fact was, they might be dangerous.

Thus, although the Air Force paid lip service to the "potential scientific advances" that might derive from a study of UFOs, there were only two aspects of the UFO problem that ever really concerned them: whether or not UFOs were a threat to national security, and whether or not they were extraterrestrial. The Air Force satisfied itself rather quickly that UFOs posed no threat to the United States, and after much internal and, at times, bitter controversy (not reported in the press), it was also decided that there was no compelling evidence that UFOs were extraterrestrial. Therefore, most of its job was done.

At that point it would have been well had the vexing problem of dealing with the continued flow of UFO reports been turned over to a scientifically oriented organization. In all fairness to the Air Force, its primary responsibility to the nation is national defense and not abstract scientific research. Instead, the Air Force was stuck with the job, although it tried, repeatedly, down through the years, to

*Anatomy of a Phenomenon, Henry Regnery, Chicago, 1965.

foist this most unwelcome task onto some other governmental agency.*

In 1947–48, the first UFO reports were channeled to the Air Technical Intelligence Center (ATIC) at Wright-Patterson Air Force Base in Dayton, Ohio—the agency responsible for analyzing intelligence information of interest to the Air Force.

When I became personally involved nearly a year later, I learned that there had been great consternation in the intelligence division over the sudden and seemingly preposterous series of reports that were coming in from both civilian and military quarters. ATIC could easily have discounted the civilian reports (and they generally did), but they could not discount outright their own trained personnel—the military witnesses.

In the beginning, UFO reports were vague and sketchy, as I was to learn when I took on the responsibility of trying to explain as many as I could astronomically. ATIC just couldn't get the kind of "hard data" the military was used to getting; they wanted close-up photos, pieces of hardware, detailed descriptions, and so forth. Instead, a military pilot would report that he saw a metallic-looking object, possibly "disc-shaped"; a wingless craft which "buzzed" him and then shot away at incredible speed—and that was about all.

The Air Force was baffled. A wingless craft? Nonsense! It couldn't be. Perhaps the pilot had seen a meteor or had hallucinated. Undoubtedly the airman had been confused, perhaps inhaling too much, or too little, oxygen. Besides, since no one else had reported it, why not just write it off as a misperception of a natural event or phenomenon, or perhaps as a full-fledged hallucination?! Within the confines of the Pentagon, where precision reports and snappy decisions were the rule, ATIC's bewilderment about UFOs was not very highly regarded.

In the meantime, two schools of thought about UFOs quickly developed at ATIC in Dayton, and in intelligence circles elsewhere. One school felt that UFOs should be taken very seriously. Their belief was so strong that a top-secret "Estimate of the Situation" was sent to Washington, stating that flying saucers were probably interplanetary and

---

*Jacobs gives a fine account of these maneuvers.

that the military should be put on an "alert" footing. Some didn't go as far as that, but were ready to accept that flying saucers were real. Ineed, in a letter to the Commanding General of the Army Air Forces General Twining wrote:

> As requested . . . there is presented below the considered opinion of the Command concerning the so-called "flying discs" that:
>   a. the phenomenon reported is something real and not visionary;
>   b. there are objects probably approximating the shape of a disc, of such appreciable size as to appear to be as large as man-made aircraft.*

The other school of thought took the much easier way out and summarily dismissed the entire subject as misperceptions, a fad, postwar nerves, or the effects of a "silly season," particularly when the reports came from civilians.

The top brass in Washington chose to adopt the latter view. It was much simpler. And, after all, their Scientific Advisory Board composed of reputable and highly placed scientists had said such things just couldn't be—they had to be mirages or the result of plain good old-fashioned imagination. It was against all known science that a craft could behave in the manner attributed to UFOs: amazing accelerations from a standing start, right-angled turns, rapid, noiseless disappearances after seemingly and openly defying gravity by hovering effortlessly above the ground.

Science had said that it was impossible and the Air Force theorem which was to cause so much trouble later on was born: "It can't be, therefore it isn't."

Still, reports of unusual sightings persisted (that was to be one of the very annoying things about UFOs—fads, after all, disappear in time). Reports continued to pile up at Wright-Patterson in Dayton. Finally ATIC recommended, and Washington agreed, that a separate and formal project be set up to evaluate the situation and get to the bottom of the problem once and for all.

In February of 1948, Project Sign was born. It lived

---

*Lt. Gen. Nathan Twining, Commander of the Air Matériel Command, to Commanding General, Army Air Forces, September 23, 1947.

for almost one year. But as the forerunner of Projects Grudge* and Blue Book, it started the Air Force down a long path of dealing with one of the most prolonged and controversial issues in its history.

Shortly after Sign had been started, I was asked, as an astronomer (a point I always emphasize), to join the project as technical consultant. I was to see how many of the reports up to that time could be explained rationally and astronomically as meteors, twinkling stars, and bright planets. Obviously, few of the many daylight discs could be so explained. No astronomical object appears as a metallic flying disc violently cavorting through the daytime sky. But there were many others that could and did have astronomical explanations. Here are some examples of reports that I evaluated as astronomical:

> On October 13, 1947, many witnesses in Dauphin, Manitoba, reported an object, blue in color, which appeared to be the size of a softball and to have the shape of a meteor. It pursued a straight course at low altitude and was seen for a duration of three seconds.

My evaluation statement read:

> The reports of this incident answer to the description of a large meteor or fireball. The trajectory, speed, color, and explosion are particularly convincing evidence.

> On July 11, 1947, in Codroy, Newfoundland, two people noted a disc-shaped object moving at a very high velocity and having the size of a dinner plate. The object was very bright and had an afterglow behind it that made it look like a cone.

My evaluation statement reads:

> The descriptions given by the observers of this object answer quite closely to that of a typical bright, "slow-

*While there probably was some significance to the names given the Air Force's official investigations of the UFO problem (Capt. Ruppelt indicated that there was), no official explanations of the code name were ever offered.

moving" bolide. It is extremely unlikely that the object was anything more than a fireball.

On October 8 or 9, 1947 in Las Vegas, Nevada, an ex–Air Force pilot and others reported observing a trail apearing high in the sky at an estimated speed of 400–1000 MPH. The object producing the trail was not visible. The trail was as white as a cloud and dissipated in fifteen to twenty minutes. The object proceeded in a straight line and then made an approximate 180-degree turn of radius 5–15 miles and proceeded away towards the direction of the first appearance. The weather was "almost cloudless."

My evaluation statement reads:

In everything except the course flown, the description given answers to that of a fireball. The course indicated, however, appears fatal to this hypothesis. No fireball on record, to this investigator's knowledge, has ever been known to turn back on itself.

The planet Venus was a frequent culprit:

On March 7, 1948 USAF officers in Smyrna, Tennessee, watched an oval object in a direction WNW from Smyrna. It was yellow-orange in color and moved very slowly until about five degrees above the horizon. They watched it for about forty-five minutes until it faded away.

My evaluation stated:

The object sighted here was undoubtedly the planet Venus. The stated position checks exactly (within allowable observational error) with the computed position of Venus. Description of color, speed, and setting time all check closely.

In both World Wars, I have learned, many rounds of ammunition were fired at Venus, each side thinking this bright planet was a device of the enemy. Even comets were occasionally reported as UFOs:

On November 8, 1948 a weather observer in Panama observed a spherical object with a tail like a comet for forty minutes. He stated that it was larger than Venus, had the color of a star, and was apparently at a high altitude.

My evaluation stated:

It seems entirely probable that the object sighted was the comet 1948L, which had been discovered two days earlier in Australia . . . There is no single statement in the limited report that contradicts the comet hypothesis.

Sometimes, even the setting sun and moon, or the moon seen through scudding clouds, was reported as a UFO.

It may be that my interim reports helped the transformation of Project Sign into the extremely negative Project Grudge, which took as its premise that UFOs simply *could not be*. I tried hard to find astronomical explanations for as many cases as I could, and in those that I couldn't I reached to draw out as many natural explanations as possible. Sometimes, I stretched too far.

Clearly, I, too, thought at the time that UFOs were just a lot of nonsense. I enjoyed the role of debunker even though I had to admit that some of the original 237 cases I studied *were* real puzzlers.

The final tally or box score that I turned in to the Air Force on April 30, 1949, after nearly a year (by no means full-time) of attempting to force-fit normal explanations to these cases is of sufficient interest to reproduce here.

Class	Number of Incidents	Approx. %
1. Astronomical		
a. High probability	42	18
b. Fair or low probability	33	14
Total	75	32
2. Non-astronomical but suggestive of other explanations		

a. Balloons or ordinary aircraft	48	20
b. Rockets, flares, or falling bodies	23	10
c. Miscellaneous (reflections, auroral streamers, birds.) etc.		
Total	84	35

3. Non-astronomical, with no evident explanation

a. Lack of evidence precludes explanation	30	13
b. Evidence offered suggests no explanation	48	20
Total	78	33

After having submitted the above report, I returned to full-time astronomical research and teaching.

On December 27, 1949, the Air Force announced that Project Grudge had been terminated, its investigations of the UFO phenomenon completed. Within several days, a report was issued. It was entitled "Unidentified Flying Objects—Project Grudge," Technical Report No. 102-AC-49/15-100, and was aptly abbreviated by some as "The Grudge Report."

My work figured in one of the appendices of the report. After studying, analyzing, and evaluating 237 of the best reports, my assistant and I had found that 32 percent could be explained astronomically. Others who worked on the report found 12 percent to be balloons. Another 33 percent were listed as misidentified aircraft, hoaxes, or reports too sketchy to attempt evaluation. That left 23 percent that could not be identified or classified in any of the previously mentioned categories. They were "Unknowns."*

*One must bear in mind that these statistics were based on only 237 cases. Where the full 13,134 cases are (see Chapter 11) critically appraised, the percentages of unknowns falls to some 5 percent. The high percentage of "unknowns" in the "early returns" may have been because, in the beginning, the public was "new" to reporting sightings and hence tended toward reporting only the more unusual cases.

Twenty-three percent unknowns! That could have been considered extremely newsworthy. But hardly a peep out of the press. Why? According to Ruppelt, the newsmen who got copies of the report felt that it was ambiguous and possibly misleading. "Since the press had some questions about the motives behind releasing the Grudge Report, it received very little publicity while the writers put out feelers. Consequently, in early 1950 you didn't read much about flying saucers."

Perhaps the reason the press failed to grasp the significance of the 23 percent unknowns was that one of the Grudge Report's main recommendations called for the project to be *reduced* in scope, rather than *increased*. This in the face of nearly one-quarter of the report unexplained! Further, a note following the Grudge Report recommendations stated that: "It is readily apparent that further study along the present lines would only confirm the findings herein." While ambiguous, the statement seemed to firm up the position that there was nothing of importance to investigate, the high percentage of "Unknowns" notwithstanding.

So, for all intents and purposes, Project Grudge no longer existed and UFOs were a dead issue. ATIC in Dayton continued to receive and record reports, but hardly anyone showed any interest and there was little if any investigation going on.

UFOs, however, did not cease *their* activities. On the contrary, 1950 was a fairly good year for UFO reports, with 210 compiled before year's end; twenty-seven, or 13 percent, of these were unidentified.

But UFOs weren't a very good story in 1950. They were being swept aside by the really big news—the advance of the North Korean armies on the 38th Parallel. The Korean War was a reality and UFOs were not (at least as far as the U.S. Air Force was concerned).

So it went until 1952. The year began with only a trickle of reports coming in to ATIC, bolstering the beliefs of those who predicted that UFOs, like old soldiers, would just fade away. But in July of that year, a major UFO "flap" occurred. It occurred in, of all places, Washington, D.C.

Capt. Ruppelt, who was on hand when the now historic

incident took place, described the situation in his book, *Report on Unidentified Flying Objects*:

> When radars at the Washington National Airport and at Andrews AFB, both close to the Nation's capital, picked up UFOs, the sightings beat the Democratic National Convention out of headline space. They created such a furor that I had inquiries from the office of the President of the United States and from the press in London, Ottawa, and Mexico City. A junior-sized riot was only narrowly averted in the lobby of the Roger Smith Hotel in Washington when I refused to tell the U.S. newspaper reporters what I knew about the sightings.
>
> Besides being the most highly publicized UFO sightings in the Air Force annals, they were also the most monumentally fouled-up messes that repose in the files.

The great "Washington flap" of 1952 and the tremendous wave of UFO reports that swamped the Blue Book office that summer was a true source of worry to the Air Force and to the government—from two entirely different standpoints. There was the question, "What are they?"; but the CIA was even more interested in the possibility that enemy agents might clog military communications with a barrage of false flying-saucer reports, thus camouflaging a real attack on the country.

The second concern took overriding precedence. On December 4, 1952, the Intelligence Advisory Committee recommended that: "The Director of Central Intelligence will 'enlist the services of selected scientists to review and appraise the available evidence in the light of pertinent scientific theories. . . .'" But this was only the official reason, as is clearly indicated by the recommendations of the "selected scientists," convened under the chairmanship of Dr. H. P. Robertson, a noted physicist and relativity expert. The true purpose of the panel was to "defuse" a potentially explosive situation from the standpoint of national security. In short, in convening the panel, the CIA was fearful not of UFOs, but of UFO *reports*. So, under the guise of a symposium to review the physical nature of UFOs, the meetings of the scientists, who already subscribed to the "It can't be, therefore it isn't" philosophy, got underway on January 14, 1953. I sat in on three of the five day-long meetings as an associate panel member.

The other question, "What are they?," was already being studied intensively at the Battelle Memorial Institute, in Columbus, Ohio. The rising tide of reports in 1952 had caused the Air Force to contract with Battelle, a most prestigious scientific institution, to study secretly all reports through the end of 1952 to determine primarily whether the "Unknowns" differed in basic characteristics from the "Knowns." (For the surprising results of this study, see p. 253.)

When Battelle heard of the CIA's intent to convene the Robertson panel, an urgent letter, classified SECRET (and therefore not part of the Blue Book files), was dispatched to the CIA via the Blue Book office. It strongly recommended that the scientific panel be postponed until the Battelle study was completed. Even Battelle did not realize that the primary issue was not science but national security! Predictably, the CIA went ahead with its plans.

On the three days I sat in on the series of meetings I was negatively impressed by the relatively few cases examined by the panel. Several now classic UFO reports were discussed: the famous Tremonton, Utah (p. 235), and Great Falls, Montana (p. 251), films were reviewed and summarily dismissed as "seagulls" and "jet aircraft," respectively. But only five other cases were discussed in any detail, one of which (Bellfontaine, Ohio, August 1, 1952) has disappeared from the Blue Book files. The others were the Yaak, Montana (August 1, 1952); the great Washington flap of July 19, 1952 (which was dismissed as "effects of inversion," even though the weather records showed only a trivial inversion of one and a half degrees—on many nights that summer the inversion was greater but no radar UFOs appeared); the Haneda AFB case (August 5, 1952), and the Presque Isle, Maine case (October 10, 1952). Some fifteen other cases were briefly reviewed, in contrast to the 2,199 cases then under detailed study at Battelle. Scarce wonder that Battelle considered the convening of a mere five-day panel, no matter how prestigious the panel members, both premature and hardly to be compared with the study of many months they were then engaged in.

The Robertson Panel Report* begins thusly: "Pursuant to the request . . . the undersigned panel [Dr. H. P. Robertson, Dr. Luis Alvarez, Dr. Lloyd Berkner (who was present on the last two days of the meeting only), Dr. S. A. Goudsmit, and Dr. Thornton Page] . . . has met to evaluate any possible threat to the national security posed by Unidentified Flying Objects, and to make recommendations thereon." It is clear that the panel understood its true purpose from the outset.

The report continues: "As a result of its considerations, the Panel concludes: That the evidence presented . . . shows no indication that these phenomena constitute a direct physical threat to national security . . . and that there is no evidence that the phenomena indicate a need for the revision of current scientific concepts."

The main thrust of the panel, and the dictum that set the Pentagon policy on UFOs for all the remaining sixteen years of the existence of Blue Book was: "The Panel further concludes . . . that the continued emphasis on the reporting of these phenonmena does, in these parlous times, result in a threat to the orderly functioning of the protective organs of the body politic." This was followed by: "We cite as examples the clogging of channels, the danger of being led by continued false alarms to ignore real indications of hostile actions, and the *cultivation of a morbid national psychology in which skillful hostile propaganda could induce hysterical behavior and harmful distrust of duly constituted authority*." [Italics added].

The report ended with the recommendation that "national security agencies take immediate steps to strip the Unidentified Flying Objects of the special status they have been given and the aura of mystery they have unfortunately acquired."

Blue Book was now under direct orders to debunk, and what captain, or even major, would go against the recommendations of such an august body of scientists as was relayed through the Pentagon?

Because of the very great secrecy surrounding the Battelle study (for years, the rule around Blue Book was that the name Battelle must never be mentioned!) it is unlikely that any of the Robertson panel members were even aware

*Obtainable through the Center for UFO Studies.

that the expensive study was in progress; indeed, had they known, they might well have recommended that it be stopped in the interests of national security. The implication in the Panel Report was that UFOs were a nonsense (non-science) matter, to be debunked at all costs. I remember the conversations around the conference table in which it was suggested that Walt Disney or some educational cartoon producer be enlisted in this debunking process.

The Robinson Panel report was signed by the five principal panel members. As an associate member I was not asked to sign, but I remember clearly resolving well in advance that were I asked, I would refuse. Even at that early date, when I was still much of a skeptic, I remember feeling that short shrift was being made of UFOs from a scientific standpoint. In retrospect, it is now clear that indeed it was.

At about this time, I was asked by Battelle to undertake a particularly interesting study: poll astronomers to find out how they feel about flying saucers! To initiate this survey, I was to seize the opportunity afforded by a national astronomical meeting, after which I was to travel to various observatories and query astronomers directly. I was to bring up the subject casually, and not in an argumentative form, so as to discover what each scientist thought about the subject—privately.

I did feel somewhat like an intelligence operative, but since I knew that the quest was for a good cause, and would result in no embarrassment to my fellow astronomers, I went along with it.

It may come as a surprise to the reader that 41 percent of those I queried were sufficiently interested in the whole subject to go so far as to offer their services if ever they were really needed. Twenty-three percent felt that UFOs represented a problem that was more serious than people recognized. Only 36 percent were not interested at all or were totally hostile to the subject.*

*A recent survey of professional astronomers, ("Report on a Survey of the Membership of the American Astronomical Society Concerning the UFO Problem," P. A. Sturrock. Report #681, Institute for Plasma Research, Stanford University, Stanford, California; January 1977) showed a marked increase in their interest in the UFO phenomenon. In answer to one of the twelve questions submitted

The 41 percent figure—those that were sympathetic or more than sympathetic—deserves comment. I have heard some of these men disavow any interest at all in the subject of UFOs when engaging in a group discussion with their peers; yet when talking privately, they admitted the opposite. I have observed this phenomenon so often that I am led to call it the "committee complex." It might be stated as a theorem: *A scientist will confess in private to interest in a subject which is controversial or not scientifically acceptable but generally will not stand up and be counted when "in committee."*

Scientists are deathly afraid of voicing support for anything that might make them look foolish in the eyes of their peers, anything that might be considered "unscientific." Thus, the decisions reached by the various panels and committees which have met from time to time to consider UFOs were, in a sense, predictable. The panel members voted for the "safe" decision every time, which was, of course, anti-UFO.

A striking corroboration of this "theorem" is found in the Sturrock survey mentioned below: of the 1,356 astronomers replying to the questionnaire, only two waived anonymity as far as publication was concerned, yet all but 34 were willing to sign their names to the questionnaire itself. Clearly, astronomers are not yet willing to let their peers know that they even *think* about UFOs!

As Blue Book got going in late 1952 I was quite happy to be called back to active duty, so to speak, and enjoyed my regular visits to Dayton to look over incoming reports. My task was still to seek astronomical explanations for as many cases as I could, and I took pleasure in finding them whenever possible.

Capt. Ruppelt, the first director of Project Blue Book, had a most difficult task. The intra–Air Force controversy on UFOs had by no means died down and Ed Ruppelt was called on to be a UFO spokesman in handling the many queries from Washington and the requests for "briefings" from generals and legislators. It seemed that he was out of

to them, asking whether the UFO problem deserved scientific study, 23 percent replied "certainly," 30 percent "probably," 27 percent "possibly," 17 percent "probably not," and only 3 percent "certainly not." Fifty-two percent of the questionnaires were returned, comprising 1,356 members of the Society.

DR. J. ALLEN HYNEK   25

the office a great deal of the time—tracking down cases or
appeasing Washington. Ruppelt was, in my opinion, a
prime victim of the "committee complex." He was there
to tell the brass what UFOs were—not to perpetuate a
mystery. Generals don't like mysteries; they want hard,
crisp answers. "We showed that it was a balloon" or "it
was definitely Venus" won more acclaim that "we don't
know what it is; it might be extraterrestrial but we are
puzzled."

The term of office of each of the directors of Project
Blue Book was never very long; turnover was frequent. The
rank of the officers was relatively low—a further indication
of the low level of priority given the project.

With each new director there came some new viewpoint
and methodology. But in the Air Force, or the military in
general, one takes orders, and the unspoken orders from
the Pentagon, stemming from the recommendation of the
Robertson Panel, seemed clearly to be to "hold the fort,"
to "play down the UFO subject," and not to "rock the
boat." And these directors were all, in turn, good officers:
they knew what the orders were and they followed them
well—perhaps too well.

The following is a list of the successive directors of
Project Blue Book:

Mar. 1952–Feb. 1953	Capt. E. J. Ruppelt
Feb. 1953–Jul. 1953	1st Lt. Bob Olsson
Jul. 1953–May 1954	Capt. E. J. Ruppelt
Mar. 1954–Apr. 1956	Capt. Charles Hardin
Apr. 1956–Oct. 1958	Capt. George T. Gregory
Oct. 1958–Jan. 1963	Maj. (later Lt. Col.) Robert Friend
Jan. 1963–Dec. 1969	Maj. (later Lt. Col.) Hector Quintanilla

I knew all of these men quite well, lunching with them
regularly on my visits to Dayton, sometimes at the Officers' Club and sometimes at nearby restaurants. Occasionally, when one of the junior officers or a secretary
had a birthday, I joined in celebrating it with a longer
lunch than usual. But I knew my place; I was a consultant,
not a director or policy setter. I knew, too, that to run
counter to what I had observed to be their "orders" would

render me very shortly a *persona non grata*. This I did not want: it was important to me to maintain my status on Blue Book, for I was beginning at this time to suspect that there might just be something to the UFO phenomenon after all and I wanted to be on hand when "good" cases came along. There was no other way I could gain access to the military reports, which weren't being made public. So, I bided my time.

Meanwhile, my attitude continued to change. I had started out as an outright "debunker," taking great joy in cracking what seemed at first to be a puzzling case. I was the archenemy of those "flying saucer groups and enthusiasts" who very dearly wanted UFOs to be interplanetary. My own knowledge of these groups came almost entirely from what I heard from Blue Book personnel: they were all "crackpots and visionaries." It was not until considerably later that I learned from direct contact with such groups as APRO (Aerial Phenomena Research Organization) and NICAP (National Investigations Committee on Aerial Phenomena) that they counted among their members many dedicated, rational people who were earnestly and independently trying to gather and evaluate UFO reports, and who felt that Blue Book was not exactly a scientific effort.

As time went on and reports accumulated, so that my data base was far more extensive than it had been in Project Sign days, I came to realize that inherent in the better UFO reports there was much more than "fooled the eye or deluded the fool." There was a phenomenon consisting of new empirical observations that demanded far more serious attention than Blue Book was giving it. It was useless to remonstrate with the staff of Blue Book; it would have been a clear-cut case of "fighting City Hall." I made many recommendations during my tenure of office but generally to no avail.* When at last the Condon Committee (see Chapter 12) was created, I thought the atmosphere would change. But the "committee complex" once again operated in full force (a few members of the committee who dared buck the committee complex were summarily fired as "incompetent").

The transformation from skeptic to—no, not believer

*See Jacobs for further discussion of these matters.

because that has certain "theological" connotations—a scientist who felt he was on the track of an interesting phenomenon was gradual, but by the late '60s it was complete. Today I would not spend one additional moment on the subject of UFOs if I didn't seriously feel that the UFO phenomenon is real and that efforts to investigate and understand it, and eventually to solve it, could have a profound effect—perhaps even be the springboard to a revolution in man's view of himself and his place in the universe.

2

THE UFO EXPERIENCE:
THE PHENOMENON ITSELF

"Incredible tales told by credible persons . . ."
— General Samford

Blue Book wasn't interested in the broader philosophical and sociological questions implied by the very existence of UFO reports; but then, that wasn't their job.

It does seem odd, however, that no one in the higher echelons of the military evinced any curiosity about the continued flow of UFO reports and about the nature of those reports. Why "flying saucers"? Why not flying cubes or flying pyramids, or for that matter, why not flying pink elephants or even flying buildings, reported from a hundred different countries? Indeed, if UFO reports were entirely the result of excited imaginations, why not hundrds, possibly thousands, of totally and radically different types of reports as people of different cultures let their locally conditioned imaginations loose? But no. Instead, a continued flow of reports of fairly similar things which could be roughly classified into just a few categories.

A number of years ago I devised a simple classification system based solely on what was reported as observed and not on any preconceived idea of what the actual nature of UFOs might be. It was purely an observational classification system, much like an astronomer might use to classify different types of stars or a zoologist different types of beetles that he came across in his explorations.

Since the most frequently reported sightings are those of strangely behaving lights in the night sky, I called these, simply, *Nocturnal Lights*. This doesn't include just *any* lights that puzzle the observer (many people are puzzled by bright planets, twinkling stars, and aircraft at night), but those which are *truly* puzzling, even to experts, because their behavior does not fit the pattern of lights from known sources. One must always keep in mind that the "U" in UFO simply means "unidentified"—but unidentified to *all*, not just to the witnesses.

Then there are the UFOs sighted in the daytime. Since the majority (but not all) of these have an oval shape and are often reported as metallic-looking, these are simply called *Daylight Discs*. Most UFO photographs made in the daytime portray such discs (see p. 95). It could be that *Nocturnal Lights* observed in the daytime would appear as *Daylight Discs*—we don't know. But observationally the distinction is useful.

A separate category is also needed for UFOs that are indicated by radar. An important subdivision in this category are radar findings that are supported by visual observations. If it can be established with reasonable assurance that a radar sighting confirms a visual sighting, or vice versa, then obviously this sighting is of major importance.

A broad category of utmost importance consists of those UFO sightings, regardless of type, that occur very close at hand, say within a few hundred feet, or at least close enough so that the witness is able to use his stereoscopic vision and discern considerable detail. These sightings are, so to speak, in the immediate reference frame of the observer—they are not "someone else's UFO," but very much this observer's UFO, a sort of very personal UFO experience.

I have termed this broad category of UFOs the *Close Encounters*. There are three obvious kinds of Close Encounters, and it will be helpful to define them separately. Again the distinction lies in what is *observed* rather than in any certain fundamental difference.

Close Encounters of the First Kind (CE I)

Here we have a close encounter with a UFO but there is no interaction of the UFO with either the witness or the environment, or at least none that is discernible. The encounter must be close enough, however, so that the UFO is in the observer's own frame of reference and he is able to see details. The chance, therefore, of this sighting being a misidentification of Venus or a conventional aircraft, etc., is quite small, particularly if the sighting is made by several persons.

Close Encounters of the Second Kind (CE II)

Here the UFO is observed interacting with the environment and frequently with the witness as well. The interaction can be with inanimate matter, as when holes or rings are made on the ground, or with animate matter, as when animals are affected (sometimes becoming aware of the presence of the UFO even before human witnesses). People, too, can be affected, as in the many reported cases of burns, temporary paralysis, nausea, conjunctivitis, etc. But in order for a CE-II to have taken place, the presence of the UFO must be established at the same spot in which the physical effects are noted. That is, if a burnt ring on the ground is noted, it must be at the exact place where the UFO was sighted hovering, or if an automobile ignition system is interfered with, such interference must have occurred at the time and place of the UFO sighting.

The observed physical effects in these cases (often called "physical trace cases") must not be explainable in some other obvious way. That is, if holes in the ground ("landing marks") are found, these marks must be unique, and not like marks found elsewhere in the vicinity.

Close Encounters of the Second Kind are of particular interest to scientists who can, in a sense, bring the UFO "into the laboratory." Burnt grasses, samples of disturbed soil, etc., can be tested with a view toward determining what caused the burn, what pressures were necessary to produce the imprints on the ground, and to finding what chemical changes occurred in the soil samples by comparing the affected soil with control samples from the vicinity. To this day, no "piece" of an actual UFO has ever been authenticated but the effects of the presence of UFOs have been amply attested to. A catalogue of over eight hundred cases in which the UFO was both seen and left physical traces has been compiled by Mr. Ted Phillips* and the catalogue continues to grow.

*Available through the Center for UFO Studies, Evanston, Ill., 60202

Close Encounters of the Third Kind (CE III)

Here there is not only a close encounter with the UFO, but with its apparent "occupants" or "UFOnauts." Close Encounters of the Third Kind bring us to grips with the most puzzling aspect of the UFO phenomenon: the apparent presence of intelligence other than our own, intelligence we can recognize but not understand. Hundreds of Close Encounters of the Third Kind have been reported all over the world in the past decades. A catalogue of over one thousand cases has been compiled by Bloecher; it, like other UFO catalogues, continues to grow.

UFOs of other categories seem to demonstrate intelligent action. Certainly this action does not appear to be random, but seems almost programmed or planned. As reported, UFOs buzz airplanes and cars, prefer the lonely hours of the night, usually but by no means exclusively avoid crowds and urban areas, and make singularly "local" appearances rather than moving about a wide area of the country.

In Close Encounters of the Third Kind, where the occupants make their presence known, we find reported creatures who resemble humans but are predominantly shorter and slimmer, capable of communication in their own way and on their own terms. Their interaction with humans has been reported to be largely impersonal, neither overtly friendly nor hostile. There have been instances, reported in all seriousness, of "abductions" of humans, ostensibly for "testing purposes." The details of such abductions have almost always been obtained through regressive hypnosis since it appears that the abduction experience, whatever its physical reality, has proved so traumatic to the witness or witnesses that the conscious memory retains only a mere skeleton of the total experience. The details must generally be obtained from the subconscious.

Clearly, Close Encounters of the Third Kind hold the most fascination for us because they bring into focus most sharply our fear of the unknown, the concept of other intelligences in space, and the possibility of intelligent contact with such beings, with all that such contact might imply for the human race.

These, then, are the six categories into which UFO sightings may be divided for the sake of convenience. It is important to note that this simple classification system carries with it no implication of a theory of UFOs, either of their origin or their nature. It simply differentiates the manner in which the UFO is perceived and what is perceived. The same classifications apply equally if UFOs are indeed an objective physical reality or if they should prove to be something totally different.

Blue Book contains examples of all six categories, although with the Air Force philosophy operative (*all* UFO reports *must*, from the nature of things, be misidentifications of normal, conventional things) we can expect that short shrift would be made of the Close Encounter cases, especially those of the Second and Third Kind. Since Air Force files were arranged according to no system whatsoever (not even the simplest cross-indexing of cases, or intercomparison, or classification, was employed), knowledge of these six categories should be of tremendous assistance as we make our way through the maze of Blue Book files in the pages that follow.

3

IT CAN'T BE:
THEREFORE IT ISN'T

*"The powers-that-be are anti-flying saucer and to
stay in favor, it behooves one to follow suit."*
—*Air Force officer quoted by Capt. E. J. Ruppelt,
first Director of Project Blue Book, in* The Report
on Unidentified Flying Objects.

In the earliest days of the modern era of "flying saucers,"
at the very inception of Project Sign—forerunner of
Projects Grudge and Blue Book—there were two factions
within the Air Force Intelligence system: those who believed that the mounting evidence was sufficient to take
"flying saucers" very seriously—even to the belief that they
were interplanetary spaceships—and those who believed
that by no stretch of the imagination could the evidence
be taken seriously. The latter group argued that with our
advanced knowledge of the physical world around us, by
the very nature of things these reports *had to be* nonsense.
Rather quickly, probably because of the matter-of-fact
nature of the military mind, the latter group won favor,
and when Project Grudge replaced Sign late in 1948, the
"anti-UFO policy" was set for all time. In the end, the
Air Force "got rid" of UFOs altogether with a most helpful assist from the Condon Committee at the University of
Colorado (see Chapter 12).

Once the decision was made that UFOs had to be fig-
ments of the imagination, the Air Force policy on UFOs
never changed direction. "It can't be, therefore it isn't"
became the guiding principle, and anyone associated with
Blue Book, from Director down, learned to follow suit or
else. . . . Even though the shifting winds of public opinion
about UFOs often reached gale proportions (especially at
such times of great concern as the great UFO scare over

Washington, D.C. in 1952 and the Michigan "swamp gas" episode in 1966), the Air Force held firm, like a rusted weather vane that stubbornly points in one direction only.

When it became clear to me and others within the project (as a result of personal conversations with officers of colonel rank and higher) that the official Pentagon policy was to debunk UFO sightings, intelligence analysts and investigators alike (myself included, since at that time I felt the lack of "hard" evidence justified the practical "it just can't be" attitude) did their best to come up with "commonsense" explanations for each new UFO report. I stress the word "each," for there was no attempt to look for patterns in the reports; each report was regarded as though it were the only UFO report in the world. This made it easier to find some individual explanation, even though it was sometimes far-fetched. It might even be stated as a sort of theorem: "For any UFO report, when regarded by itself and without reference to similar or related reports, there can always be found a *possible* commonsense explanation, even though its probability may be small." There is safety in doing this because it is quite true that the great majority of UFO reports turn out to be ordinary things like balloons and aircraft that people misidentify, very often honestly. In a country where it rarely ever rains, the weather forecaster is quite safe in predicting fair weather!

When I first became associated with Project Sign, I too was eager to do my part in dispelling what I sincerely thought at the time to be a public fantasy, a popular craze. I "distinguished" myself by dismissing the following reported UFO as an "atmospheric eddy"! Let us look at the report itself, first as it was reported by John Brosman in the Twin Falls, Idaho, *Times News* of August 15, 1947, and then as it appears in the Project Sign files:

> Just as Magic Valley and the nation were starting to let go of lamp posts after reeling under a welter of flying saucer reports, two more Twin Falls County men revived speculation on the mystery with vivid descriptions of discs they saw.
>
> From A. C. Urie, who operates the Auger Falls Trout Farm six miles west of Blue Lake Ranch in Snake River Canyon, came perhaps the most detailed

account of the fast flying object the nation has yet produced.

The flying saucer Urie saw was skimming through Snake River Canyon at a height of about 75 feet at 1 P.M. Wednesday. At 9:30 A.M. the same day, L. W. Hawkins, Twin Falls County Commissioner, and former county sheriff from Filer, also saw two circular objects soaring along at a great height near Salmon Dam twenty miles southwest of Twin Falls.

Here is Urie's eyewitness description of the flying disks seen by him and his sons Keith, 8, and Billy, 10: "I obtained a close-up view of the flying saucer as it passed by the trout farm at 1 P.M., Aug. 13, down Snake River Canyon at a height of about 75 feet from the canyon floor. I would estimate the speed at about 1,000 miles per hour." Urie explained that the incident occurred while the two boys were coming across the river from the north side in a boat. He had become concerned about what was delaying them and had walked down toward the river to see if they were all right. "I had a side view at a distance of about 300 feet and almost on a level with the thing," Urie continued. "Two of my boys, Keith and Billy, were below me and they also saw it at about a 45-degree angle. They both got a bottom and a side view, and we were all looking at it from the south side of the canyon. . . . It was all one color, sort of a light sky blue with a red tubular fiery glow at the side of the top, or hood," Urie continued. "The canyon floor is rough at that particular point and it rode up and down over the hills and hollows at a speed indicating some type of control faster than the reflexes of man. It is my opinion that it is guided by instruments and must be powered by atomic energy as it made very little noise, just a s-w-i-s-h as it passed by." Urie described the size as about 20 feet long by 10 feet high and 10 feet wide, giving it an oblong shape. It might be described as looking like an inverted pie plate or a broad-brimmed straw hat that had been compressed from two sides. Pressed for his candid opinion of just what it was, Urie said that he was convinced that there was something to this flying saucer situation. "I know a number of people who have also seen them and I know that they're not just imagining something or trying to get their names in the paper," Urie commented. "I do know that it scared the boys and made me feel pretty uneasy," he added.

Tracing down a rumor that County Commissioner Hawkins had seen an unusual object in the air on the same day as Urie's experience, the *Times News* called him at his Filer home. "Yes, I did," he replied, without hesitation. "I'll have to admit I've been skeptical all along until I saw it with my own eyes. I can't say what it was but I can say there's something in the air." Hawkins related that while at Salmon Dam Wednesday morning a sound resembling the echo of a motor caused him to look upward and there he saw two circular objects that reflected light. They were traveling at a great speed and higher than most airplanes, according to Hawkins. Aside from this he declined to add details except to say, "There's something in the air." His general description, however, corresponded closely to those of hundreds of persons who reported seeing flying saucers. . . .

Both the Idaho paper and the Sign account give almost identical sketches of the object (see below):

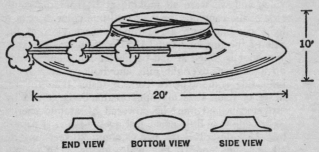

Reproduction of original sketch of the object seen by Mr. A. C. Urie and sons in Snake River Canyon, as it appeared in the Twin Falls, Idaho, *Times News*, August 15, 1947.

The Air Force account in Blue Book contains the following:

As the machine went by the Urie place, the trees over which it had almost directly passed (Mormon poplar) did not just bend with the wind as if a plane had gone by but in Urie's words, "spun around on top as if they were in a vacuum."

Keith Urie, eight years of age, said he first saw the machine coming down the canyon, heading from east to west and following the contours of the ground. Billy, ten, saw it almost immediately. Both watched it fly out of sight behind a tree in a matter of moments. They said they ran to their father and learned that he too had seen the machine.

Urie seemed completely sincere about the incident. He said his wife and daughter were in the house at the time and had not seen the machine. He questioned his brother, who also lives in the canyon, but his brother had been eating at the time and had seen nothing. Urie and his two boys maintained that they had never before seen one of the discs. Urie, when interviewed, appeared to be a sober, middle-aged man. John Brosman, the *Times News* reporter who originally furnished Special Agents with information about the incident, likewise stated that Urie appeared completely sincere about the machine.

No further attempt was made to locate [two other men who repeatedly had seen the object] inasmuch ———, who was with ——— at the time were fishing at Salmon Dam while ——— was supposed to have been working in Twin Falls [thus is Science robbed of evidence].

In my report to Sign I wrote:

There is clearly nothing astronomical in this incident. Apparently it must be classified with the other bona fide disc sightings. Two points stand out, however: the "sky blue" color and the fact that the trees "spun around on top as if they were in a vacuum." Could this, then, have been a rapidly traveling atmospheric eddy?

The Air Force was only too happy to accept my conjecture: "It seems logical," the Project officer wrote, "to con-

cur with Dr. Hynek's deduction, that this object was simply a rapidly moving atmospheric eddy."

The fact that I have never seen such an "eddy" (or as
far as that goes, never even seen one described in books)
and that I blithely discounted other pertinent evidence,
haunts me to this day. I wonder what would have happened had I written: "We must believe these witnesses,
especially in view of the many similar reports received
during the recent past. This was indeed a strange craft, involving technology far beyond ours. It is essential that, regardless of cost, a major scientific effort be mounted not
only to investigate each report in far greater detail than
has yet been done and to carefully study the interrelation
of these reports, but to set up observing stations at every
military and defense installation in the country to attempt
to gain vital scientific data."

The late Dr. James McDonald, Professor of Atmospheric
Physics at the University of Arizona, never forgave me for
not having made such a recommendation in this and many
other cases. He accused me of covering up data and told
me that I had been derelict in my scientific duty in not pro-
claiming the seriousness of the UFO phenomenon to the
world—a phenomenon which he considered the most
serious problem to face the human race.

What, indeed, would have happened had I done so? I
fairly well know. Sitting where I could see the Pentagon
scoreboard very clearly, I knew that my services would
very shortly have been dispensed with on the grounds that
they had no need of a "flying saucer nut." Had I been an
Einstein, a Nobel Prize winner, at least I might have been
politely listened to—but as a young professor at a Mid-
western university . . . ! I decided to wait for more and
better data.

The "perfect" report never came. A report of a craft
landing, say, at half-time at the Rose Bowl game, witnessed by thousands, and photographed by hundreds—or
close-up movies of a Close Encounter or an invited inspection of a landed UFO by a group of scientists and
newsmen. To be sure, UFO reports continued to flow in;
the UFO phenomenon did not "dry up and blow away" as
in the early days we all had predicted it would. The same
sort of anecdotal reports from persons of integrity con-

tinued to abound, but never the truly "hard data" the physical scientist demands.

Little note was taken of another report from Twin Falls just six days later, and of one from the Rapid City AFB in South Dakota at about the same time. The following is a memorandum from the Butte, Montana SAC base to the FBI. (Because this report is not in the public domain, the names of the individuals involved are fictitious.)

Mr. Busby, who is the Executive Director of the Twin Falls Housing Authority, explained that he and his wife and Mrs. Henry Swift, a neighbor, were sitting on their front porch at approximately 9:30 P.M., Aug. 19, 1947. He said that Mrs. Busby suddenly shouted and pointed to the sky and thereafter stated that she had seen an object traveling at a terrific speed in a northeasterly direction. The object was out of sight before Mr. Busby and Mrs. Swift could see anything.

Approximately ten minutes later, while they were discussing what Mrs. Busby had seen, all three saw ten similar objects proceeding rapidly in the same direction, in the form of a triangle. As the group of objects was disappearing, three of the objects on the left flank peeled off and proceeded in a more northerly direction. The remaining objects appeared to close ranks and proceeded in a northeasterly direction.

From three to five minutes later these same individuals saw another group of three objects proceeding in the same direction, and again in the shape of a triangle. From three to five minutes later all three observed another group in a triangular formation consisting of five or six objects. They were proceeding in the same direction.

A few minutes later the three persons saw a large group of objects, estimated at from thirty-five to fifty, flying in a triangular formation in the same direction. Approximately twenty or twenty-five minutes after the large group of objects was observed, similar objects were noted coming back over the city in a southwesterly direction. These objects were generally in groups of three, five, and seven, and followed each other at approximately five-minute intervals. . . .

On the night in question the sky was overcast and the objects could not be seen clearly; however, they were distinct enough so that all persons could observe what they described as a glow going through the air. They said the objects appeared to be lighted from the inside and were of a color similar to regular electric lights.

Mrs. Busby called Detective Frazier of the Twin Falls Police Dept., who was then accompanied by Officers Rauch and Semans. The three officers watched for a few minutes and observed a group of about twelve objects flying in formation over the city.

Both Detective Frazier and Mr. Busby stated that . . . they flew at a terrific speed and were visible for only a few minutes at a time. Both persons said that the objects could not have been geese or ducks and that the lights were not a reflection of the city lights on some objects. . . . None of the persons were drinking at the time. No other persons in Twin Falls reported seeing these objects; however, Mr. Busby and Mr. Frazier stated that it was purely by accident that they had seen the objects and that they would not have seen them unless they were looking for them, because of the speed at which they traveled.

And now comes the finishing touch: "No further investigation is being conducted by the Butte Office, and the case is being closed."

The Air Force evaluation of this case and the following one was: *Birds*. And maybe they were. But certainly the investigation was quite insufficient to establish this evaluation. It remains just a guess.

The report from Rapid City AFB at about the same time came from Headquarters 28th Bombardment Wing, Office of the Intelligence Officer, Rapid City Air Force Base, Weaver, South Dakota. It reads (name changed):

Major Smith stated that shortly after dark one evening between 15–20 Aug. '47, he was sitting in the parking lot near the line area when he sighted approximately 12 objects flying a tight diamond-shaped formation, stacked down from the lead. They were approaching from the northwest in a shallow descent, leveled off at approximately 5,000 feet, made a gentle, large radius turn of about 110 degrees to the right about 4 miles from the observer and started climbing to the southwest. The angle of attack was estimated to be between 30 deg. and 40 deg., and they appeared to accelerate rapidly in the climb. They appeared to be traveling between 300–400 miles per hour during the observed period. The objects were elliptical-appearing in the plan view and appeared to be about the size of a B-29 in span. No estimate was made as to the aspect ratio but they didn't seem to appear unnaturally thick or thin compared to the overall configuration. There were no aircraft being run up on the line at the time but no noise could be heard nor any exhaust trail or flame observed. No other light could be observed except that the whole object seemed to have a yellow-white luminous glow.

The following sketch accompanied the report.

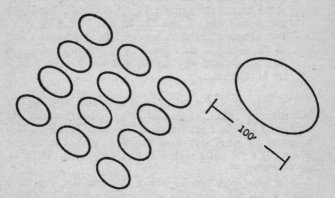

UFOs observed by Major Smith in August 1947, in Rapid City, South Dakota. A reproduction from original sketch by witness.

Now *birds* might be the appropriate evaluation if one completely discounts Major Smith's background—intelligence officer charged with the interrogation of all crews of the 28th Bomber Wing. If he, experienced in evaluating intelligence information from his crews, couldn't tell birds from 12 objects that fly in tight diamond formation, coming down from 10,000 feet and leveling off at 5,000 feet, traveling at 300–400 miles an hour, climbing and accelerating rapidly at an angle of 30–40 degrees—well, what are intelligence officers coming to?

Yet this case was not investigated further. Why investigate birds, unless you belong to the Audubon Society?

It is rather amusing that the evaluations "possible balloon," "possible aircraft," "probably astronomical," were very widely used—but never "possible UFO." Since there are no such things as *truly* unidentified flying objects (even though some 600 "Unidentifieds" are listed in the files), how could one possibly have a "possible UFO"?

A few further examples from the files are even more enlightening.

January 7, 1966. Georgetown, Ala. Single witness reported that he saw a round object about 10–12 feet in diameter, silver in color, which had a ring or hoop extending 8 to 10 inches out from its equator. It had a 5-foot hatch on the bottom. Observer's watch stopped at the time of the sighting. Object hovered 5 feet above the ground when it was just 20 feet from him. After 1–2 minutes, object disappeared in a gradual climb to the northeast after sound of engine increased, and then accelerated very rapidly and was gone in a matter of seconds.

The observer was a student, eighteen, and, to quote the interrogating officer, "appeared to be reliable, which was confirmed by a character witness. His instructions on how to get to the rural area were very accurate." The sighting was made three miles southwest of Georgetown, Alabama, on Highway 63.

Now what does one do with a case like this, especially when one is not aware that very similar reports have been made from several countries? What are the chances for misidentification at twenty feet, in broad daylight, and watching it hover five feet above the ground for one to two minutes? Aircraft won't do; neither will star or mirage. Balloon? Possibly, but with a hatch and a hoop, and the sound of an engine, and disappearing in a few seconds? No, a balloon couldn't do that. Ah, we have it! It's psychological (despite the character reference, and the ob-

server's ability to give a detailed description of the phenomenon and accurate directions to the place where it was
sighted). That the person might have seen what he said he
actually did would never even be considered—because *it
can't be!* But then neither could telephones, radio, airplanes, etc., *be* before they were invented.

Readers may think that I have included here only very
special cases. That is not so. They have been picked almost at random. To establish this point, let us very quickly
survey a number of others. We cannot stop for details, but
the survey will emphatically demonstrate that Blue Book
was definitely not a high-level scientific operation.

> *Aug. 12, 1958. 12 mi. NW of Las Vegas, Nev.*:
> Round, orange object; diffuse light in area where no
> "treetop level" lights of any type have been seen be-
> fore. Light moved down and to left to treetop
> level, then went back to original position. Repeated
> performance, then disappeared.

*Air Force evaluation: "Probably conventional light of some
sort."*

> *April 10, 1952. 6 mi. W of Pecos, Texas.*: A dia-
> mond shaped object in upright position 50 ft. wide
> and 75 ft. high was observed for 5 min. Bright and
> shiny, like aluminum in bright daylight. Had the sound
> of a jet engine as it rotated once a second. Hovered
> a few minutes, then climbed straight up about 2000
> ft. and then slowly veered off to the NW.

Air Force evaluation: "Unreliable source." [No reason
given in the files as to why the witness was considered unreliable.]

> *Jan 3, 1958. Old Westbury, L.I. Twilight*: Round
> object with appearance of cloud or round ball, white,
> traveling very fast and very high toward the east, ob-
> served for 8–10 seconds.

*Air Force evaluation: "This is no doubt a mistaken identity
of conventional object due to unusual or adverse weather*

conditions. [What conventional object, and what adverse weather conditions?]

August 29, 1957. Paso Robles, Ca.: One silver circular object was seen flying from N to W and was in sight for four minutes.

Air Force evaluation: "Unreliable report." [Why?]

April 6, 1955. Beaumont, Ca.: A 13-year-old boy observed a round silver object, approximately the size of a silver dollar held at arm's length. He observed it for an undisclosed time [why didn't the interrogator find out how long?]. The object then faded away.

Air Force evaluation: "Probably airway beacon" [because it was seen in the general direction of airway beacon].

August 16, 1956. Near the Azores: An Eastern Airlines flight en route to LaGuardia sighted a bright white light west of course. Object passed within 40 feet of aircraft coming in from above. Aircraft took evasive action.

Air Force evaluation: "Military flight, heavenly body, or free balloon possible cause of sighting." [A heavenly body passing within 40 feet of the aircraft?]

October 17, 1958. Grand Rapids, Mich.: Twenty-four round, amber-colored objects, size of dime, traveling at very high altitude. Two flights of twelve each. 25-second duration.

Air Force evaluation: "Meteors." [Now, that really should make the Guinness book of astronomical records!]

Sept. 7, 1961. Cape Canaveral, Fla.: Object moving vertically in tracking scope. During missile launch. Military source.

Air Force evaluation: "Image in scope was determined to be star Gamma Piscium." [Gamma Piscium is a relatively faint star, and quite stationary. It is absurd to think that a person professionally qualified to track missile launches would be puzzled by one particular star out of a great many.]

> *June 26, 1955. Holt, Fla.*: Several witnesses, both civilian and military. "Disc-shaped, blue-white with 10–14 blinking lights."

Air Force evaluation: "Unreliable observer." [On the basis of interviewing one witness found to be "unreliable," the case is dismissed. What about the other witnesses? Get rid of the report, no matter how!]

The final example (the list could go on and on) of the cavalier manner in which evaluations were guessed at (and which earned for Blue Book the facetious title of The Society for the Explanation of the Uninvestigated!) requires a bit more space:

[On January 5, 1963, at Nantucket Point, Long Island, NY]

> Mr. Cherrington was on the night shift . . . busy filling tanks about 3 A.M. The moon was on the way down. . . . He happened to look up from his work and hovering above him at what he estimated to be about 1000 feet was this craft, as he described it, perfectly round, in thickness like two saucers placed against one another; thicker in the middle and tapering toward the edge.
> Because of the moonglow, and the clearness of the night, the shining metal structure was clearly visible. On top of the object, in the center, was a plume of bright blue light, like an exhaust of some sort. He estimated it to be about 75 feet in diameter. Every once in awhile it would execute a series of runs, flips and maneuvers, in all directions, at times at terrific speeds close to the ground but never lower than about 500–1,000 feet. Finally after about an hour of maneuvering, an airliner or large jet of some sort was headed by; and just as the plane, flying at about 15,000 feet, arrived overhead, this craft zoomed straight up at a terrific speed, and as its shape blanked out the plane's running lights, he thought for sure that there

would be a crash, but it seemed to swerve off at the last minute. This happened around 4 A.M. Then, after skirting the plane, it took off at a low altitude toward the west. . . . As it was leaving, one of his co-workers came out of the train and he saw it leaving as a "morning bright star." Mr. Cherrington was shaken by the experience, and his only reaction was "if something like this has to happen, let it be on someone else's shift!"

Air Force evaluation: "Star and planet. Object has characteristics of astronomical object with distortion due to the atmospheric conditions present and the interpretations of the object's behavior by the witness under these unusual conditions."

Well, *what* unusual conditions? The night was clear, the moon was out (and apparently looking perfectly natural) and no atmospheric distortion can make a star blank out a plane's lights, have a star appear to skirt a plane, and then take off at a low altitude toward the west. It would have been far better to evaluate this case as a hallucination—but *stars!!*

My intention in citing the preceding examples is not to establish proof of the UFO phenomenon—but to illustrate the lackadaisical and irresponsible manner in which many of the UFO reports were treated by Blue Book. "Get rid of the report quickly, no matter how" seems to have been the operative principle—except in cases when it was obvious that an airtight case could be made for a misidentification; then such cases were given the full treatment and used extensively in Washington "briefings" to demonstrate what a good job Blue Book was doing in proving that there was absolutely nothing substantive to the UFO phenomenon. That way led to praise and promotion.

It was fairly obvious to the public that the Air Force was not taking the UFO phenomenon at all seriously; Blue Book's small and relatively low-ranking staff made this abundantly clear. There has been much discussion as to whether Blue Book's get-rid-of-them policy was purposefully contrived by the Air Force and the Pentagon as a smoke screen, while covert UFO investigations were being carried on at a much higher level. While secret manipulations behind the closed doors of the Pentagon cannot be disproved, certainly there is no clear-cut evidence that they existed. There is considerable evidence that the interaction of Blue Book with the higher echelons was far more of a foul-up than a cover-up (Chapter 12).

Despite the basic direction Air Force policy took, there were, from time to time, some shifts in secondary internal policies and procedures affecting the collection, investigation, and evaluation of UFO reports. Often it was difficult to ascertain how or why such changes occurred. It might happen that a policy or procedure would be established, or a long-standing policy reversed, by a mere internal memo from the Air Defense Command to bases under its jurisdiction. Or a colonel or even a major in Intelligence might, via teletype dispatch or even by verbal order, make such changes. There was an element of the right hand not knowing what the left hand was doing.

An illustration of this is the following Joint Messageform of October 17, 1952, from the Air Adjutant General of Air Technical Intelligence Center (ATIC), Wright-Patterson AFB, to the Commanding Officer of the Rock Island Arsenal, Rock Island, Illinois.

> Reference your TWX [teletype message] concerning the sighting made by Mrs. ——— on 11 Oct. *It is the policy* of Project Blue Book that *the reporting agency* will *use its own discretion* in determining whether the sighting is of *sufficient importance to transmit to this office.* It is the *opinion of this office* that the sighting made by Mrs. ——— falls into the unimportant category. [Italics added.]

In short, ATIC was saying, "It's entirely up to your judgment as to which reports you transmit, but you were dummies to send us this one!"

It is clear that the double-jointed policy expressed in this Messageform would tend to discourage local reporting agencies from sending UFO reports to Blue Book, or at least to persuade them only to send "safe" reports. And what would be a "safe" report? Obviously one that wouldn't cause criticism. It was also a part of the Blue Book policy —as I heard stated repeatedly over the phone and in correspondence between Blue Book and air-base officers during my visits to Blue Book—that local bases were to transmit only those reports which they could *not* solve at the "local level."

That obviously posed a serious problem for the local base officers. If they "solved" one and it turned out to be incorrect, was it worth their having taken the responsibility? Responsibility is a commodity that, especially in the military, one tries to buck up the line. In the military circles I was associated with, and I expect elsewhere, "pass the buck" is more than a phrase; it is a way of life. If the local officer responsible sent in a report that Blue Book regarded as "unimportant," how to deal with the next one? Suppose it was a report phoned in by a distraught person, who said that when driving along a lonely road late at night a glowing object landed in front of him, stopped his car, and that small creatures stepped out of the craft and accosted him? Wouldn't it be easier to say: "Let's play it safe—obviously a crackpot, so no point in sending this one over the military wires and getting criticized!"

And then what should be done about reports of bright flaming objects streaking across the sky in a matter of seconds? Or about a battery dropped from a weather balloon, or a piece of slag found lying in one's driveway? The first, obviously a meteor; the second, obviously a battery case, especially when the manufacturer's name was plainly visible; and the third—slag—well, all of these could easily be solved "at the local base level" but why take the responsibility? Send it in. Let Blue Book take the responsibility.

So this explains, in my opinion, why Blue Book files are crammed with obvious IFO (Identifiable Flying Objects) reports and relatively few truly puzzling reports (which have been, and continue to be, reported through other channels). This also undoubtedly contributed to the adoption by the Air Force of the "party line theory"— that since so many UFO reports prove to have been due to misidentification of meteors, battery cases, and slag, etc., it follows that *all* reports have a similar origin if one merely digs deeper. (And, of course, the corollary: Since this is so, why bother to dig?)

It is harder to understand why many truly puzzling UFO reports made by high-ranking civilians and military persons (which came to my attention in other ways) fail to appear officially in the Blue Book files. In my experience, the Pentagon wanted clear, crisp answers and solutions from Blue Book, not mysteries or vague answers. Therefore, Blue Book didn't investigate cases unless they were officially reported; they did not go out after cases they only heard or read about.

Thus, a UFO report filed by Astronaut Slayton in 1951, when he was a test pilot, does not appear in the Blue Book files, although, in a personal letter to me, Slayton confirmed both the event and that he had submitted an official report "through channels." And time and again, when I have been asked by UFO witnesses to look up their cases in Blue Book to see what was done about it, I have found no report of it. These missing reports may well have died at the local base level, having been labeled either too "unimportant" or too "kooky" to transmit.

Missing from Air Force files is the following case, related to me just recently by Mr. Philip Schumann of Milwaukee, Wisconsin (and sworn to before an attorney). It was reported to the Commanding Officer at Ladd Air Force Base in Fairbanks, Alaska, in 1951.

The case is an important one, practically unassailable as far as number and reliability of witnesses, instrumentation, and general circumstances are concerned. The UFO was allegedly tracked by gun-laying radars and visually sighted by twelve skilled Army observers using interlocking field telescopes capable of tracking aerial objects both horizontally and vertically. Schumann, who was a first lieutenant in antiaircraft artillery at the time of this event, personally and separately interviewed all twelve of the witnesses and took a sworn affidavit from each of them.

Schumann's comments to me (from taped interviews) are noteworthy: "I wish to God I knew what happened to those sworn affidavits. I personally presented them to the commanding officer, knowing that they'd get to the proper authorities that way. I never heard another word about them, but in the military you assume you are adding information to that which is already known by those in charge. You don't question what is done with it; you simply assume it is taken care of.

"That morning, however, changed my whole life. Before the incident, I didn't believe in UFOs. In fact, afterward I didn't 'believe' in them either . . . I *knew* there were UFOs."

Mr. Schumann is today a respected businessman in Milwaukee who can hardly be accused of perjury. So, what happened to those affidavits and the full report submitted to the commanding officer? Were they stopped at the source because the commanding officer "did not want to get involved"? He surely could not have doubted the sworn statements of twelve of his men. If he doubted the tracking radar, could he dismiss the visual observations made by tracking telescopes? Did he submit them and were they stopped "en route"? Or did they get to Blue Book where they were considered too militarily important to be placed in the general files? One doesn't know. At this late date, Mr. Schumann does not remember any of the names of the twelve men and therefore cannot determine their whereabouts.*

Quite apart from the incompleteness of the Blue Book files, I can attest to the frequent disregard of the rules of scientific procedures by some of the Blue Book staff, and to their disregard of their responsibility to the public. In their press releases, the Air Force deliberately led the public to believe that they were being "leveled with" at all times. The public had no way of knowing that information about the truly puzzling cases was withheld from the media as a matter of principle. As Capt. Ruppelt pointed out in his book (p. 22), "Very little information pertaining to UFOs was withheld from the press—*if the press knew of the occurrence of specific sightings.* [All italics added.] Our *policy* on releasing information was to *answer only direct questions from the press.* If the press didn't know about a given UFO incident, they naturally couldn't ask questions about it. Consequently *such stories were never released.* In other instances, where the particulars of a UFO sighting were released, they were *only the bare facts* about what was reported."

This is in itself an indictment of Air Force policy. If there was nothing about UFOs to be concerned about or to hide, why withhold this information? Further, the policy was reversed on occasions when, for some reason, Blue Book wanted information about a case that had been re-

*Should any reader of this book have heard of the incident, or be himself one of the twelve men, or in any way associated with one of them, it would be of scientific importance to communicate with the author, on a confidential basis if necessary.

ported to the press but not to Blue Book. They went to great lengths not to reveal that the Air Force was interested, using devious means of obtaining the information.

Even apart from Capt. Ruppelt's statement, the Blue Book files themselves contain sufficient correspondence and memoranda to support an indictment of Blue Book methodology. The "official" policy on dissemination of information about UFOs and related matters was set forth in a document known as "AFR-190-6," dated April 21, 1951, and titled, "Air Force Public Information Program." Paragraph 2b contains the key language:

> Air information consisting of the collection, correlation, analysis and dissemination to the public of unclassified information pertaining to the Air Force: This aspect of the program is based on the policy that the full record of the Air Force is available to the American people, subject only to security restrictions and the dictates of good taste.

Of course, the record shows that UFO information was not available to the American people at all. But there were two outs: "security restrictions" and "dictates of good taste."

Both "privileges" were invoked frequently. I can recall two cases in which the "good taste" rule was applied. In both cases, the witnesses asked that their names be withheld, since they would not have wanted their actions at the time of the sighting made public. In one case a man was "parking" with another man's wife in an isolated quarry; in another case, the UFO experience occurred while a group of men were in a private plane en route to Las Vegas for a weekend binge while their wives thought they were on a business trip! These were, of course, bona fide "good taste" cases; but Blue Book often used the violation-of-privacy excuse to keep puzzling UFO cases from the media.

On the other hand, Blue Book quickly and willingly released information about "solved" cases—those that were explained as misidentifications of common objects or phenomena, or which had been assigned an "explanation." An example of this is contained in the following excerpt from a "Record of Telephone Conversation" of November

16, 1954. This conversation was between a Lt. Athens, Officer in Charge of Flight 3B of the 4602nd Air Intelligence Squadron (the squadron utilized by Blue Book for investigative purposes) and Maj. C. Williams, Air Force Representative, of the Armored School, Fort Knox, Kentucky.

a. Major Williams stated he had been approached by a Mr. George Hart, a reporter on the Louisville *Courier Journal*. Mr. Hart was soliciting information regarding an observation of an Unidentified Flying Object made over the city of Louisville, Kentucky, on Friday 12 November 1954. Major Williams stated that he had informed Mr. Hart, on direct query by that individual, that the object in question had positively been identified as a high-altitude weather balloon. Further queries were made by Mr. Hart regarding the aforementioned.

b. The purpose of Major Williams' call . . . was to obtain information regarding AF policy on the release of information to news media regarding UFOs and what his action should be should similar occasions arise in the future.

Lt. Athens informed Major Williams that in those *cases where sightings have been positively identified as known objects,* as was the case in question, then it *was within Major Williams' authority to release such information to news media* which may be making inquiries. Major Williams was also informed that only in those cases where such sightings were not identified was he instructed *not to release any information but to* inform the individuals making queries that such release would come from AF sources authorized to give such information. AFR 200-2 was brought to the attention of Major Williams.

Signed for the Officer in Charge

It is clear from the above that when a case could be quickly disposed of, the Air Force was very cooperative with the media. Even officers at the base level, or assigned as representatives to a training school (as in this case) could give out information. But, of course, quite the opposite was true when the case was a puzzler.

Sometimes the Air Force went into its "stall" pattern when there was a UFO sighting it couldn't explain, particularly when the press already had the report. For example, an article entitled "Flyers Report Saucers Near Atomic Plant" was featured on the front page of the *Dayton Daily News* on Sunday, July 6, 1952. At about 10:30 that night the ATIC duty officer was contacted to see if ATIC had had any word on this sighting. The answer was no. The next day, when the United Press representative of the *Dayton Daily News* called Capt. Ruppelt and wanted to know if the Air Force had any comment to make, he was told that all that Blue Book knew about the sighting was what had appeared in the papers.

It is, however, on record in Blue Book that shortly after these calls, Colonel Bower of ATIC instructed Blue Book officers to "stall" off the press "with a no-comment answer."

My personal experience attests that the Air Force record was made available to the American people *only as the Air Force saw fit*, either when cases were "solved" or where an explanation of a sighting could be assigned with the hope that no one would question it. Sometimes this latter procedure would backfire and then the Air Force's fears of adverse publicity would reach crisis proportions, as happened in the Oxnard Air Force Base incident in California on March 23, 1957.* Note the panic expressed in the following decoded Joint Messageform dispatch from ATIC at Wright-Patterson Field to the Commander of the 4602nd Air Intelligence Service Squadron, ENT AFB, Colorado Springs, Colorado. (Headquarters for the Air Defense Command):

*The case itself was not spectacular (might even have been stars) and is mentioned here only to illustrate Blue Book methodology. It involved several independent witnesses, including policemen on duty, who reported seeing five lights, some red, the rest blue, maneuvering in the sky for better than an hour. Interceptor planes were sent aloft, with negative results, but observers on the ground stated that on the approach of the planes the objects (lights) converged and accelerated to extreme altitudes. There was no radar confirmation. The Air Force made no attempt to ascertain the amplitude and scope of those motions, and thus either confirm or rule out stars as the stimuli for the report.

PRT 1—REFERENCE OUR MESSAGE AFOIN-4E4, 3-398-E DATED 27 MARCH 57 REQUESTING INVESTIGATION OF OXNARD CALIFORNIA INCIDENT OF 23 MARCH, AS REPORTED ON TT-MSG 69-OPS-X FROM COMDR. 669 ACWRON. NO DETAILS CONCERNING THIS CASE RECEIVED AS YET: ONLY COMMENT IN YOUR UFO SUMMARY WITH STATEMENT WAS ASTRONOMICAL. THIS INCIDENT RECOGNIZED BY THIS CENTER AS POTENTIALLY DANGEROUS IN THAT IT COULD GIVE AIR FORCE UNFAVORABLE PUBLICITY, IF EXPLOITED BY FANATIC OR DIE-HARD "FLYING SAUCER" PROPONENTS. THIS NOW DEFINITE POSSIBILITY, WITH RECEIPT OF LETTER FROM NATIONAL INVESTIGATIONS COMMITTEE OF UFOS [NICAP] DEMANDING FULL DETAILS AND ANSWERS TO CERTAIN ASPECTS OF OXNARD INCIDENT NOT SUPPORTED BY INFORMATION IN FILE.

OFFICIALLY, THIS INCIDENT DOES NOT WARRANT ACTION REQUIRED, BUT ——— 'S ABILITY TO SLANT MATERIAL AND CREATE UNWARRANTED TROUBLE FOR AIR FORCE, HIS STOCK IN TRADE FOR ALMOST TEN YEARS.

Apparently, in this case, the intelligence boys at Blue Book were embarrassed by NICAP, which had come upon evidence that the Oxnard case could not possibly have been "astronomical." Thus, the frenzied tone of the message in relation to the question of "unfavorable publicity."

The fear of exposure to public scrutiny was not new in 1957, but had existed since the early days of the Air Force's UFO investigations. In fact, there was so much concern about "image" that at times the Air Force's investigations took on cloak-and-dagger proportions. This "we are interested in UFOs, but don't want anyone to know we are interested" syndrome is best illustrated in the following memorandum of July 6, 1950, from the Chief of the Air Force's General Investigations Division to the Chief of the Counter-Intelligence Division of the Department of the Air Force:

Subject: Unconventional Aircraft (Unclassified)
1. At approximately 1300 hours (1:00 P.M.) on this date Lt. Colonel O'Connell, District Commander, 5th OSI District, called the undersigned and stated that he had received a request from AMC (Ed: Air

Material Command), to make certain inquiries as indicated below. He said that General Cabell, Director of Intelligence, this headquarters, had called Colonel Watson at AMC with reference to an article which appeared in the Louisville, Kentucky, *Courier Journal* concerning an individual who had taken moving pictures of a flying disk. Headquarters AMC told Colonel O'Connell that General Cabell had requested that action be taken to obtain the moving pictures and to interview the person who had taken them; further that *inquiries in this matter should be made in such a manner as not to indicate Air Force interest* (all italics added).

2. Colonel O'Connell also stated that General Putt and Colonel Boushey, R&D (Ed: Research & Development) Headquarters USAF, had made an independent request upon Headquarters AMC similar to the request by General Cabell.

3. Colonel O'Connell stated to the undersigned that he is reluctant to have one of his agents contact representatives of the Louisville, Kentucky, *Courier Journal* and conduct the additional investigation indicated in this matter inasmuch as the identity of the agent as a representative of the Air Force must necessarily be disclosed and *this would indicate the Air Force interest in this matter.* Colonel O'Connell said that he feels *the best procedure might be for him to contact the FBI locally and request that a representative of that agency conduct the necessary investigation, thereby precluding any indication of Air Force interest.* However, Colonel O'Connell said that he would like to have the approval of the Director of Special Investigations before proceeding in this matter.

4. I discussed the above with Major Nold and he subsequently informed me that he had talked to a representative of the Office of the Director of Intelligence, this headquarters, and that his representative had stated that OSI should not directly (through the FBI) attempt to obtain the information indicated above.

5. Inasmuch as this is a matter *under the cognizance of the Counter-Intelligence Division,* it is hereby referred for further action as necessary, including furnishing telephonic advice to Colonel O'Connell, 5th

OSI District. (*For your information, I told Colonel O'Connell that in the future when he has any questions on matters in this field, he should contact the Counter-Intelligence Division.*)
Signed by
F. D. McGarrachy, Lt. Colonel, USAF,
Chief, General Investigations Division.

One may well ask, "Why Counter-Intelligence?" Well, according to the dictionary counterintelligence is an activity used in thwarting the efforts of an enemy's intelligence agents to gather information or commit sabotage.

This cloak-and-dagger approach was indeed contrary to the official "open book" policy. The public was, in effect, placed in the role of "the enemy," against whom "counterespionage" tactics must be employed. From my personal experience, I frequently felt that those in charge did indeed consider people who reported UFOs or who took a serious interest in them and wanted information about them, as enemies.

This became especially evident when Project Sign became Project Grudge. Capt. Ruppelt pointed out in his book* that while there was to be no "official" shift in policy of using standard intelligence procedures, there was nonetheless a real change from "unbiased evaluation of intelligence data" to biased evaluation. Ruppelt stated:

> But it doesn't take a great deal of study of the old UFO files to see that standard intelligence procedures were no longer being used by Project Grudge. Everything was being evaluated on the premise that UFOs couldn't exist. No matter what you see or hear, don't believe it. . . .
> With the new name and new personnel came the new objective: Get rid of UFOs. It was never specified that way in writing but it didn't take much effort to see that this was the goal of Project Grudge. This unwritten objective was reflected in every memo, report and directive.

---

*I have frequently quoted from *The Report on Unidentified Flying Objects* simply because I think so highly of it as a record of the early days of the Air Force involvement in UFOs, as seen through the eyes of the man who was most deeply involved.

Such "memos, reports and directives" did indeed solidify the official attitude toward UFOs, an attitude that kept investigation "in line." One example of such a memo, dated July 19, 1950, is from Col. Bruno W. Feiling, Chief, Technical Analysis Division, Intelligence Department, to Lt. Col. Hemstreet. The subject is: "Investigation of Flying Saucer Reports":

> Mr. ———'s memo dated 14 Jul 50 has been reviewed. Although investigation was requested in the matter, it appears that too much time was spent in the investigation. It is suggested that in future incidents we contact the individual concerned to get the story. . . . If, however, there have been no reports by other personnel on the same incident, it seems that there is no justification for contacting as many agencies as was done in this case [Is it being suggested here that a thorough investigation shouldn't be made, regardless of how credible the single witness?] It seems that if a legitimate sighting is made, it would be reported by a number of people. [There really is no justification for this statement. And, what if the witness were the Governor of Georgia, or Michigan, or even the Secretary of the Air Force?] Excessive contacts can only serve to keep our interest in these matters a subject of discussion by more people than we would like. [Now we have the real reason!]

If the public really felt that the Air Force *wasn't* interested, why did anyone even bother to report a sighting? Likewise, if they knew that the Air Force had adopted the "explain them all away" posture, once again, why did anyone bother to report? The answer is that, in fact, many *did not* file reports. Even during my days as consultant to Blue Book I received an occasional letter stating, in effect, "I am not reporting this to the Air Force because I know it won't do any good." And in one letter I remember distinctly, I was asked to keep the report to myself and *not* transmit it to Blue Book! I also received many letters (as did Blue Book) protesting a tame evaluation as "star" or "balloon" when the person was very sure it hadn't been. Often the person wrote, in effect, that the Blue Book evaluation had been an insult to their intelligence.

The reluctance of witnesses to report to Blue Book became more and more evident in the latter days of its existence. But the attitude existed early on, as the following Air Intelligence Information Report from the 7th Fighter Squadron, Presque Isle, Maine, referring to a UFO sighting of January 29, 1953, shows:

> The information contained in the enclosure was reported by TWX in accordance with AFL 200-5, dated 29 April 1952. The object was also sighted by at least two fighter aircraft from other squadons. The conversation among the pilots and the ROs [Radar Operators] was heard by A/1C Ferdinand who was on duty at the ADDC [radar site]. Not knowing which of the pilots and ROs were talking the conversation went as follows:
> Pilot said, "Do you see that thing above us?"
> Answer, "No."
> Reply, "It sticks out like a sore thumb."
> Then someone said, "If I were going to catch it I would drop the wing tanks first."
> *Another said that he would never admit what he saw.* [Italics added.]

Now, there's a smart fellow. Why report some strange, puzzling object in the sky that defies logical explanation when the Air Force "knows" it "can't exist" and "therefore doesn't"?*

One wonders just how many "good" UFO sightings went unreported because of the Air Force's debunking attitude? How many were never tallied as "unknown" or "unidentified?" because they were never reported at all, or never reached Blue Book if they were reported to some local air, army or naval base? We shall never know.

There were many times during my twenty years as a scientific consultant to Blue Book that I also wondered whether the very best reports were being kept from Blue Book. Perhaps some cases were sent only to the highest

---

*This attitude apparently still persists, despite the Air Force's present "hands off" policy. In a recent case investigation for *The International UFO Reporter*, an Air Traffic Controller confided, "Just between you and me, you never report anything really unusual. It takes only one, if you know what I mean."

authority, particularly if they involved top-secret or crypto-graphic information that was of an "eyes only" nature. There is, within military circles, some information of such a highly classified nature that it is for viewing by the "eyes only" of certain designated individuals who are specifically cleared for access. While I held Top Secret clearance, I was by no means permitted access to all Top Secret information in the Department of Defense. Such information is available only on a "need to know" basis.

My own suspicions about this were reinforced by Richard Budelman, who assisted me in the preparation of portions of this book. He served in a sensitive position with a Top Secret Navy Squadron stationed at Port Lyautey, Morocco (the Navy had only one other air squadron like it), from 1956 to 1958. He was responsible for writing all of the flight orders for this squadron's top-secret missions for more than a year. He is firm in his own belief that had a UFO been sighted by the pilot or crew of one of his squadron's aircraft—and several were rumored—the report would never have reached Project Blue Book. Why? Let him tell it:

> The nature of our operation in VQ-2 (Electronic Countermeasures Squadron TWO) were so super secret and sensitive that I cannot possibly believe a report of a UFO sighted by one of our crews would have been sent to Project Blue Book. The majority of our missions were so hush-hush that they were known only to a mere handful of people in the entire squadron. Access to information about our flights was extremely limited. Reports and materials related to them went directly to the Commander-in-Chief, Eastern Atlantic and Mediterranean (CINCNELM), and the Secretary of the Navy.

But there's another reason why I also believe Blue Book didn't have access to that kind of Top Secret information—that it was in certain respects "low man on the totem pole." The low rank of the officer in charge of Blue Book was a dead giveaway. A mere captain doesn't have much authority. Capt. Ruppelt couldn't even get the Pentagon to give him a staff car to do his investigations when the great UFO flap hit Washington, D.C. in July, 1952, and he was supposedly the key man in the investigation of a case that had captured the attention of the nation! In his own words:

"I called the transportation section at the Pentagon to get a staff car but it took me only seconds to find out that the regulations said no staff cars except for senior colonels or generals. Colonel Bower tried—same thing. General Samford and General Garland were gone, so I couldn't get them to try to pressure a staff car out of the hillbilly who was dispatching vehicles. I went down to finance office —could I rent a car and charge it as travel expense? No— city buses are available. But I didn't know the bus system and it would take me hours to get to all the places I had to visit, I pleaded. You can take a cab if you want to pay for it out of your per diem was the answer. Nine dollars a day per diem and I should pay for a hotel room, meals, and taxi fares all over the District of Columbia. Besides, the lady in finance told me, my travel orders to Washington covered only a visit to the Pentagon. In addition, she said, I was supposed to be on my way back to Dayton right now, and if I didn't go through all the red tape of getting orders amended I couldn't collect any per diem and technically I'd be AWOL. . . ."

Obviously Blue Book and its chief didn't carry much weight. Every paper in the country was carrying banner headlines about UFOs over the Capitol and the chief of the UFO project was asked to take a city bus!

Now, this was in 1956, 1957, and 1958, and the "cold war" that followed the Korean War was on. We were greatly concerned about Russia's missile capacity and our missions often took us right up to Soviet borders (and for all I know, in light of the later U-2 incident, inside the Soviet Union itself). There was simply no way possible that UFO reports out of VQ-2, had there been any, would have gone to Blue Book where someone without a "need to know" would have access to information about our secret missions. There is no doubt in my mind whatsoever that the same thing would hold true for UFOs sighted by SAC (Strategic Air Command) crews on Top Secret missions. It would be sheer folly to have that kind of information lying around.

On several occasions I had heard very sketchy conversations about UFOs sighted by our own flight crews, but I could never get anyone to discuss them, even though I had a Top Secret clearance. Needless to say, I couldn't prove today that those reports were anything but hearsay. The only proof would be in the Top Secret files of the Defense Department. I can't imagine how anyone would go about gaining free access to that kind of information—nor do I advocate that just anyone should have access.

These observations are well taken. In my years as scientific consultant to the Air Force I saw extremely few reports at Project Blue Book that were marked TOP SECRET —and not too many that were labeled SECRET—mostly they were classified as CONFIDENTIAL or RESTRICTED.

We have been discussing the question of whether or not Blue Book actually received all existing UFO reports. What is of far greater importance is the manner in which the reports they *did* get were treated. I close this chapter with reference to a report from the Blue Book files, which dramatically illustrates the principle, "It can't be, therefore it isn't."

The following sightings were made at Los Alamos, New Mexico. The first report was made by an employee of the Los Alamos Scientific Laboratory who was judged by the investigator to be a very reliable person. The witness stated:

About ten A.M. on 29 July, 1952, at Omega Site, Los Alamos Canyon, Los Alamos, New Mexico, I observed an object, white in color, that appeared to be changing perspective or going through gyrations. It had a fluttering appearance. I observed the object for a few seconds and then stopped looking at it. At the time of the sighting there were a few small scattered clouds and the wind velocity was low. Five minutes later, jets appeared from Kirtland Air Force Base.

A second witness, also a member of the Los Alamos Scientific Laboratory, stated:

At approximately ten A.M. on 29 July, 1952, at Los

Alamos Canyon, Los Alamos, New Mexico, I observed an undiscernible object, white in color, appearing larger than a jet at thirty thousand feet. The object was moving in a straight-line flight with an approximate speed of 1.8 degrees per seconds. The
brilliance of the object underwent changes as though
light reflected variably with execution of twisting or
turning motion. I viewed the object for approximately
twenty seconds before the canyon wall obstructed my
view. The object did leave a vapor trail. Weather
conditions were clear and no unusual wind in the canyon was present.

And still another:

On July 29th, I was north and west of the airport
[approximately a mile to a mile and a half]. I had
seen this thing for approximately thirty seconds. I
had been watching these jets with my little ten-year-
old boy at my residence and we were pointing them
out and two jets passed generally west to east [could
he have meant east to west?], leaving vapor trails. I
had just stepped in the door when my boy said he saw
three of them. So, I stepped back out and looked
and saw a shiny object just under the vapor trails,
traveling in the same direction as the vapor trails,
leaving no vapor trail. It seemed to be traveling
slightly faster than the jets did that left the trails. It
possibly could have been one of the jets that had
doubled around and gotten at an altitude below, but
it came into this position almost too fast for the
jets to have made a complete circle. It is possible that
it was a jet that swung around and came back. Sworn
to and subscribed to before me on the 31st day of
July, etc.

And another independent witness stated:

The length of time that I observed the object was
very short, only a couple of seconds. I haven't had
any previous experience as an observer but the oddity
of this object was that the air was filled with burnt
papers reflecting sunlight. At ground level, they had

drifted about a third of the way across the airstrip
and were slowly drifting in wind currents to the north.
Soon, they attained quite a high altitude. This object
was moving across the wind currents. It wasn't drifting to the north, it was going more from east to west.
Possibly just a little south to west. I saw it for just a
few seconds. It was a distance up in the sky. The man
I was with was using field glasses and stated that this
object made a turn. It was right into the wind current
that was blowing the papers in the opposite direction.
He followed the object which disappeared behind a
cloud which was to the west over the mountain range
behind Los Alamos. This was the only mass of a
cloud in that vicinity. As far as I could tell, this object had no vapor trails to the naked eye. As I saw
it, it was only a silver speck in the sky.

And still another witness:

At 10:57 hours, 29 July, 1952, at S Site, Security
Station 610, I observed an object appearing egg-
shaped in structure directly overhead, the distance
impossible to determine. The object was motionless
and appeared to have wings. The object had no glare
and appeared light brown in color. The object moved
very fast when movement began, in a northwesterly direction, taking about three seconds to disappear. I was
unable to determine whether the object disappeared
behind the horizon or disappeared in the distance
close to the horizon. There wasn't any apparent sound,
odor, or evidence of a vapor trail. There weren't
any clouds in the sky when the object was sighted.
My attention was attracted to the object while looking
for jets from Albuquerque which had been reported
previously over the radio from the air strip. This is
the first object of this type that I have seen.

Although there were even more witnesses, I think the
above should fully suffice to demonstrate the application
of the Air Force theorem, "It can't be, therefore it isn't."
One witness, and one witness alone, described burnt papers
flying in the wind. He carefully pointed out that the unknown object was moving *across* the direction in which the

paper was blowing and was traveling in a straight line. He deliberately contrasted the motion of the object with that of the fluttering papers. Yet, since "papers" had been mentioned, the Blue Book evaluator labeled this case as "probably papers in the wind."

I have seen this sort of thing happen time and again. If a witness mentioned, generally for comparison purposes, any likeness to a balloon, aircraft, bird, "papers," etc., this was all the encouragement the evaluator needed. The phenomenon was generally classified as that item mentioned by the witness, even though the item had been mentioned solely for comparison purposes.

Scarce wonder that the public became more and more reluctant to report UFO sightings to the Air Force. In the Blue Book "closed court," the witness was guilty of misidentification even before the case was heard. The examination of the evidence showed the lack of any responsible follow-up, and the evaluations, arrived at by a preset formula, serve as final indictment of the work of Project Blue Book.

4

VERY STRANGE LIGHTS AT NIGHT

"Having accepted to a reasonable degree the objectivity of the experience, I tried to explain it in acceptable and natural terms. That what I had seen was an aircraft of any kind or characteristic known to me was inadmissible."

—Watch Supervisor
Logan International Airport

The majority of reports submitted to Blue Book were of mysterious lights in the night sky. A great many of these were reported by military officers, men that the Air Force had trained in technical effectiveness and responsibility. Despite their extensive training, even these men were, on occasion, mistaken, fooled by bright planets, meteors, or twinkling stars. But sometimes there was no astronomical explanation for the nocturnal lights they perceived.

Since Blue Book could find no justification for discounting the testimony of such highly trained men, many of the Nocturnal Light cases were finally evaluated as "Unidentified." And unidentified they remain to this day. For some of these, however, the Air Force did try their hardest to come up with a natural explanation, as in the following interesting case:

The Case of the Puzzled Airport Tower Operator

The undersigned is employed as a watch supervisor in the Civil Aeronautics Control Tower at Logan International Airport, Boston, Mass. On the night of April 7, 1950, I was on duty in the Logan

Tower. Also present on duty in the tower were the following controllers: F.H., W.G.M., H.G.M.—all employed by the CAA and all holders of current senior airport traffic controller ratings.

The weather at 21:30 GMT was measured 16,000 overcast, visibility 15+, wind NE . . . with gusts up to 43 MPH.

At approximately 21:55, I noticed a light due west of the tower which caught my attention because of its unconventional color, a deep blue. I focused binoculars on the light to determine what aircraft would be showing such unorthodox light. Even through the glasses, the object appeared to have no clearly definable mass and seemed to consist of merely an ellipsoid pattern of light blurred at the edges and deep blue in color. It was moving in a path from southwest to northeast (wind was from the northeast), at what seemed to be a conventional rate of speed. I could not determine its altitude but it was about fifteen degrees above the horizon when I first saw it. As I continued watching, the light changed from deep blue to a sharply distinct white. At this point, I summoned the other controllers who verified what I was seeing in the glasses. By this time, the light had again gone to the deep blue color I had originally noted. As we watched, the single blue light appeared to dissolve into two blue lights which then began to revolve around one another [!] in the manner of two small searchlights at play. During this process, their trajectory took them from 15 to 45 degrees above the horizon. I was about to accept the lights as being two searchlights that someone was playing around with in spite of the absence of any beams and in spite of the ceiling height which precluded a "spot," when one of the blue lights passed from southwest to northeast on a horizontal course. I used the ceilometer light on the northwestern tower as a fixed base reference point and the object, now showing all white, passed the light in what appeared to be a conventional flight path and at a conventional rate of speed. The object was lost in the northeast. An immediate check was made with both Squantum and Bedford towers which ascertained that neither had any traffic reported in our area. The only reported traffic in the area was on a base-leg in the landing pattern at Bedford. [To the west of Logan] . . . the time encompassed between the moment when the objects first came and their final disappearance was . . . ten minutes.

In evaluating the experience, the undersigned has rigorously (and with misgiving) explored the possibility of the incident being subjective, but the fact of four of us seeing it would seem to minimize the possibility.

Having accepted to a reasonable degree the objectivity of the experience, I tried to explain it in acceptable and natural terms. [Here we once again have the very familiar "escalation of hypothesis."] That what I had seen was an aircraft of any kind or characteristic known to me was inadmissible. I learned to fly in 1936 and have been in aviation ever since that time, graduated from the Air Force Intelligence School in 1942, served in the southwest Pacific as a squadron commander, and director of air support for the Fifth Air Force for two years, graduated from the short course at the Air Command and Staff School, Air University in 1929, and am currently deputy group commander of an aircraft control and warning group in the Air National Guard at the rank of Lt. Colonel. I think that it is a not unreasonable assumption that I am familiar with aircraft types and capabilities.

In examining the possibility of searchlights being responsible, I was forced to discard that possibility because I had seen a mass. Once when the object was glowing white and passing the ceilometer, and again when it glowed cherry-red. Furthermore, the ceiling was measured at 16,000′ and any searchlight powerful enough to cast a spot on a cloud base at that height must surely show a definite beam.

The only solution that seemed acceptable to me and I still do not know whether it is tenable, is that what we saw may have been stellar corona or some other luminous hydro-meteor. [He was really trying hard; these terms are meaningless.] The strong winds on the surface and aloft, the overcast (a thin one) was moving at a tremendous rate of speed. A Pan American clipper from overseas had reported an hour earlier that he had picked up a heavy load of ice when descending through the overcast, so apparently the overcast was filled with ice crystals. Although not completely satisfactory, an answer of this theme [sic] did not eliminate the possibility that what we witnessed were meteorological phenomena of a sort with which we were not familiar. (For obvious reasons, no formal report of this incident was made to any source. With so many reports rampant developing from irresponsible or hysterical sources, one hesitates to solicit ridicule, but in view of the close similarity of what I witnessed and what is seen by others elsewhere, I feel it incumbent to submit this report in spite of this risk.)

A Nocturnal Light, varying from intense blue to white to red, under observation for some ten minutes, and moving against very high winds, splitting up into two lights which then for a moment revolve around each other, and then proceed merrily against the wind to the northeast, would indeed be a new and certainly unknown meteorological phenomenon. But this report is just one of the many from intelligent, technically trained people who often tried desperately to find a normal, natural solution to what they saw, and were very unhappy when they could not.

The official Blue Book evaluation of this case was "inversion effects—distortion of natural phenomena/lights from unknown source." An inversion? With high winds aloft, and ground gusts up to 43 MPH? Hardly a likely event!

A UFO Dogfight

Another example of Blue Book adopting a conventional explanation, even in the face of contradictory evidence, occurred on the night of November 7, 1950. In an official report, the military pilot described a "dogfight" with a single steady white light which at first was mistaken for another aircraft. The pilot got "on his tail":

In less time than it takes to tell, this light, without making any kind of reversal turn, poured down on me in a slight dive, passing directly over my canopy at an incredible speed, about one hundred to two hundred feet above. . . . I then pulled into a tight "flipper" reversal turn in order to see this light again. . . . This time I was positive that we were on his tail.

Once again the light rushed at him and passed over him. Up to this point, it could easily be dismissed as a rather slow-moving balloon (lighted) whose apparent speed was merely the reflection of the pilot's own speed. The report goes on:

In the meanwhile, after five or six passes, this object and I got into a port orbit. I frequently checked my instruments for altitude and engine limitations and flew in a sixty-degree climbing port bank, indicating 130–135 knots. This light continued to turn about me in wide, climbing turns, *making about two orbits to my one.* At eleven thousand five hundred feet, I abandoned the chase and simply orbited to keep the object in sight. . . . Having had experience with jets against conventional (aircraft) in "dogfights" I have a good idea of their speed. But this object in the encounter described previously, was making at least twice that speed or approximately eight hundred knots.

The evaluating officer from Director of Intelligence, a colonel in the USAF, concurred with the pilot. In his report he stated:

It appeared to circle his aircraft at a terrific rate of speed, even when climbing. The rate of climb was estimated to be over two thousand feet per minute; therefore, it would not be possible to class this incident as a lighted weather balloon, if the description is considered accurate.

If the description is considered accurate. Well, we certainly could not condone a UFO investigator who uncritically accepted everything a witness had to say. But to discount *everything* a witness says, especially in those cases when there are several witnesses involved, is both irresponsible and unscientific.

The Case of the Michigan Spaceship

Sometimes, when a natural explanation was simply not available, Blue Book resorted to the label "insufficient information." *Anything* but "unidentified"! I leave it to the reader to judge just how "insufficient" was the information in the following case:

> I, ———, was of the opinion that they [flying saucers] were objects of the U.S. government, but after my recent experience . . . it has changed my belief entirely.
>
> On Sunday night, April 27, [1952], my wife, two children, and myself were proceeding home. My wife and I both spotted a brilliant white object coming towards us out of the sky from the northeast. It descended so fast that by the time my wife could realize and state that it was a flying saucer, it had descended to its minimum height of a transport plane in flight. It stopped abruptly and rocked slightly, similar to a rowboat in choppy water. It then settled at an approximate thirty-degree angle and the brilliant whiteness diminished as to what appeared to be window lights. It sat in this exact position and spot for what was approximately three or four minutes, making it very easy for us to judge its size, shape, etc. We estimated it to be about two miles north of us, and three thousand feet high. The angle at which it rested made it very easy for us to estimate its thickness and diameter. It appeared to have two tiers of windows, each about ten feet high, which resembled looking into the playing section of a mouth organ. The windows were all around the entire diameter making visible the round flatness. We estimate conservatively that the diameter of the ship was at least two hundred feet.
>
> After what seemed to me that they were getting

their bearings, they started drifting northwest towards the city of Pontiac, about one hundred miles per hour but stopped two or three times during the time of observation. At no time did it make a noise.

Immediately, I realized that I should have witnesses to this phenomenon, so I speeded west on Fifteen Mile Road to a drive-in restaurant about a mile away. I ran in and asked some young men if they would come out and witness my experience. After persuasion, two of them went out and were amazed, causing others to follow. By this time it had drifted at least five miles northwest. At this point I called the Birmingham police and asked them to alarm all the airfields in this direction which they said they would do. I returned to my car and continued to follow it, driving west on Fifteen Mile Road. During the next five minutes, the lights in the saucer went off and on three times. The fourth time, the lights changed from white to a brilliant yellow-orange and by this time we had reached the Grand Trunk Railroad Station, a half mile from Birmingham. Thinking this experience would make a good newspaper story, I stopped at the railroad station and called the Detroit *Times,* telling them my story thus far.

After that, I again called the Birmingham police, and asked them if they had reported the incident as yet. They said they were thinking about it, so I became provoked and said that I would call Selfridge Field myself, which I did. If anyone ever got the "brush," I sure did. I was transferred to five different departments and finally got an officer who, I am sure, was awakened by my call, and was very peeved. I explained what was taking place and he mumbled something to another fellow and then said, "I'll report it. What's your name?" I gave him my name and explained, "If you ever want a close-up view of a flying saucer, get some planes in the sky at once," telling him the approximate location of the saucer. Then he repeated, "All I can do is report it, bud," [and] he hung up.

During my telephone conversation, my wife had convinced the station attendant and railroad express truck driver to observe the spectacle. I secured the truck driver's name and then proceeded west on Fifteen Mile Road to Birmingham and out about seven miles due west, following the saucer as it vanished from my vision over treetops in the general direction of Flint at 11:15 P.M. (one half hour).

I contacted the Detroit *Times* on Tuesday A.M. and gave them my complete story. Their reporter phoned Selfridge Field and Radar Division and they both told him that it was impossible for anything to be in the air at that time because nothing was picked up by radar, so naturally, the *Times* dropped the story. [I am reminded of Groucho Marx's famous statement, "Military intelligence is a contradiction in terms."]

What is to be believed here—the lack of a radar observation, or the eyeball testimony of many independent witnesses over a considerable geographical stretch? On what grounds should human testimony be rejected? If these persons had been witness to an automobile accident or an airplane crash, their testimony would have been taken seriously. Of course, in these cases, there would have been some wreckage strewn about. The lack of tangible physical parts or hardware from a UFO has been a standard stumbling block; but suppose such hardware doesn't exist?

The witness continued his account:

To prove my story, I started to track down my witnesses. After considerable difficulty, I found the two young men I had asked to come out of the drive-in and obtained written statements from each. [These statements are not part of the Blue Book files.] Then I contacted the truck driver and he was very willing to write a statement of his observations. I again went to the *Times* with my proof and the editor turned the story over to another reporter who again phoned Selfridge Field. This time, they contacted the Intelligence Division. They stated that they were receiving at least two letters a day from people who had also sighted a saucer at different points. This assured the reporter of my story and he later stated that he thought that the complete story would be in the Sunday, May 4th, issue. However, for some unknown reason, it never appeared.

I have no personal desire to see this story in print but I believe that it is about time the authorities, as well as the citizens, be openly informed of a systematic procedure for handling reports as important as this incident. I firmly believe that this saucer was making a reconnaissance tour of the area and that if my report had been handled efficiently, we would be in a more intelligent position to know more of their intentions.

I further state that, with due respect to the Army, someone was sleeping at the switch, or if it is being kept "hush-hush," that the public reaction will be mass hysteria when the unknown definitely attempts to make contact with us (as has been proven in the past). Experience has taught us that education toward events to come adjusts the human mind to accept phenomena and cope with them.

The Blue Book evaluation of this case: *Insufficient Information.*

It is clear that this evaluation was a copout. What information was not contained in the original letter could easily have been obtained through a proper Air Force Intelligence investigation, and through interrogation of the numerous witnesses, whose names and addresses had been furnished to the Air Force.

The Twin Dancing Lights

Let us now turn to some of the Nocturnal Lights that Blue Book actually *admitted* they could not identify. The first such case involves high-altitude lights, traveling much faster than any known aircraft, and yet distinctly *not* astronomical. They were observed from the deck of a yacht off the coast of New Jersey, from a boardwalk on the coast, and by a USAF pilot and his wife from the ground in a suburb located in the northern city limits of Philadelphia. The witnesses, separated by about seventy-five miles, were respectively a professor of chemistry at a major university in New Jersey, vice-president of ———— Inc., a former major in the U.S. Army Ordinance Corps, II, and a rated USAF pilot with ten years' experience.

Since professors at respectable institutions of learning rarely write to news desks unless profoundly motivated, let us start with the letter from the professor of chemistry to the City Desk of the Newark *Evening News*:

> Enclosed is a report of an observation of two objects (lights) seen in the sky on the night of July 19–20, 1952, over Lavalette, New Jersey. Since these lights were very similar to those reported over Washington, D.C., the same night, and since they do not resemble any aircraft known to the observers, either in appearance or in manner of motion or disappearance, I am submitting a complete description for possible correlation with other similar reports. I have purposely delayed this report since I have no intention of allowing my name to be associated in "newsprint" with the so-called "flying saucer scare." Therefore, while I am giving my name and position below, I request that they be used only for your files, or be given only to the Air Force, should you judge this report worth passing on to them.
>
> The objects described were witnessed by myself and a companion. We had carefully compared our impressions, and the description given consists of those impressions agreed upon by both.
>
> Sincerely,
> ————, Ph.D.
> Professor of Chemistry
> ———— University

DESCRIPTION OF OBJECT: Two moving lights were seen, each having the same appearance, approximately round, and orange-yellow in color with dull red alternately diffusing over much of the surface. They seemed about five times the apparent size of Venus or Jupiter, but only two or three times as bright. The "lights" were first seen towards the south, just off shore, about in the center of the Milky Way, at an approximate elevation angle of about forty

degrees. They moved northwards slowly, one behind
the other, and followed nearly the same path. They
appeared to be at least one quarter to one half mile
apart and moving at less than one hundred miles per
hour (assuming their apparent distance from the observers of five to ten miles). At the point where they
passed almost due east of the observer, they appeared
to be at last five thousand feet high, the approximate
elevation angle being forty-five degrees. The second,
or trailing light, did *not* keep constant distance or
course with the leading object. Shortly after passing
to the east of the observers, both lights gradually began to turn westward towards land, passing over the
coastline at approximately sixty degrees north of the
observer. Continuing to circle, the lights passed to the
west at approximately fifty degrees elevation, then
around to the south, crossing the shoreline at about
the same angle. During this first circling, both lights
were smaller and fainter but more yellow in color;
the trailing one grew fainter more rapidly, and appeared to drop further behind and to shift course
slightly to south of the leading one. At no time did any
sound come from the lights.

Out at sea, they continued circling, radius of turn
being much smaller, but the brighter leading object
crossed the shoreline once again just south of the
observer at about an eighty-degree elevation. Both
continued to grow much fainter, smaller, and more
silvery in color, occasionally disappearing and reap-
pearing as though passing over small, thin high
clouds. The second light completely disappeared just
over the shoreline. The first light continued westward, growing very faint like a small star. It seemed
many miles high and moving more rapidly. It finally
disappeared in the west at about a fifty-degree elevation. The total elapsed time from first sighting to the
final disappearance was about five or six minutes.
NOTE: . . . their motion gave the definite impression
of directed control, but the complete silence of the
objects and their rapid climbing to very high altitudes
did not resemble (to the observer) any known plane
or dirigible.

The testimony of the six witnesses who were aboard the cruiser was summarized by Major King, USAF, who did the interrogation:

At 12:15 A.M., 19 July, 1952, two unidentified objects were seen streaking across the sky in a southwesterly direction by six observers on a boat located at approximately 40° N 75° W. All members of the party observed two objects, and the three witnesses interviewed described the objects as follows: "The objects looked very much like stars, possibly slightly larger, and were of a yellowish-orange color. They were soundless and seemed to follow a very definite course across the sky. Both objects remained the same distance from each other, and it was this fact that made the observers decide that the objects were not stars (!). The observers followed the objects with their eyes as long as they were in sight, after their disappearance were unable to detect them again."

Since all of the on-board observers clearly stated that the objects moved relatively slowly, almost drifting, the "streaking" reference in this summary is hardly appropriate. However, if the objects were in view only two or three minutes, and crossed an appreciable portion of the sky, then they could hardly have been "drifting," either. There is little doubt, however, that these six persons out on the river were observing the same thing that the professor of chemistry reported.

The third independent report comes from the USAF pilot and his wife, from Elk Park, Pennsylvania. From the Air Intelligence Information Report:

I first observed what appeared to be a star of average size and light intensity moving steadily on a heading of approximately thirty degrees (north). While the object was in this overhead position, I judged that it was moving at such a rate that it covered ten degrees of the sky arc in about a minute. I then noticed a second and identical-appearing object following the first. It was about ten degrees behind. My initial reaction to sighting these objects was to accept them as the traveling lights of a very high-altitude, high-speed, aircraft. This impression was only momentary. In my experience, no aircraft lights at very high altitude look like these two objects, which could be most aptly described as moving stars of average size and light intensity. Since the night was dark, clear, and cloudless, it is pointed out that the stars appeared to be of more than average size and brightness. Furthermore, the movement of the object was estimated to be at least three times and no more than five times the apparent velocity of a conventional aircraft traveling at four hundred miles per hour ground speed at twenty-five thousand feet altitude. . . .

The rate of acceleration on the part of the trailing object was rapid enough to close the ten degrees of sky separation in about five seconds. After maintaining such formation only momentarily, the trailing object made a short, sharp ninety-degree turn to the left and again assumed "trail" position. [We have here the often-reported right-angle turn which has puzzled many UFOlogists over the years and has frequently led to the dismissal of the entire phenomenon on the grounds that right-angle turns are "impossible."]

The witness also noted that during the period of observation there were no other aircraft sighted in the area. He concludes his excellent report with the statement, "Upon due consideration upon all that I saw and heard during the period of observation, I can offer no conclusion as to the identity of the sighted objects other than that they (a) were at very high altitudes, (b) were not recognizable as any kind of aircraft traveling lights I know about, (c) were moving with extraordinary velocity, (d) apparently had the capability of orderly flight on a single heading, plus the capability of flying in formation."

Even Blue Book had to evaluate this case "unidentified." This was in the days before satellites and, anyway, an unpowered satellite could never perform the maneuvers described.

The Case of the Amateur Astronomers

It has often been said that astronomers, and others very

familiar with the skies, do not see UFOs. The fact of the matter is that they have and do.*

When I was in charge of the United States Optical Satellite Tracking Program during the International Geophysical Year, we received many reports from our Moonwatch stations concerning the strange lights that certainly weren't satellites. Many of these witnesses were amateur astronomers and generally well acquainted with the skies. Here is a letter, in the Blue Book files, from just such witnesses:

First, I wish to make it clear to you that we are competent observers. We have been amateur astronomers for many years and are well acquainted with all the constellations and planets. We are also able to recognize a meteor when we see one. During meteor showers we often watch the sky all night and we have seen many varieties and many spectacular meteors, and we knew them for what they were, of course. We are also very used to jet plane sightings, weather and observation balloons, helicopters, and all the other things, including inversions, that are often mistaken for UFOs. We have watched all the Sputniks and Echo.

On the evening when we saw this strange object, we were sitting watching television when ——— asked us to please come out and see if we could identify the strange thing that they were watching in the sky. So, we seized our binoculars and rushed out to see a staggering sight. It was an object a bit redder than Mars (orange-red) and was describing huge circles in the air. Then it would come to a sudden stop and hover. Through the binoculars it closely resembled a planet but it had something connected with it that a planet does not have. The best way I can describe it is to

*The Sturrock Survey of American Astronomers sets that record straight. More than 4 percent of the astronomers who responded to the questionnaire on UFOs reported that at one time or another they had seen something in the sky that they could not explain. They jumped to no conclusion as to the origin of their sightings, but since these sightings remained unidentified to scientists experienced in observing the sky, they qualify as UFOs, since the "U" in UFOs still stands for "unidentified."

say that it looked like a Fourth of July sparkler connected to the side of the object and it appeared to go in and out. Then the red-orange glow went out and the sparkler part kept on making dashes at terrific speeds. It went way down into Mexico and then circled some more and then returned to where we were viewing it (San Diego), went out over North Island and hovered some more. Kindly remember that seven people (three with binoculars) were viewing this object for a long time. Then it vanished and did not reappear.

There was no noise connected with it. And there was not a plane of any description in the air that night. That is very unusual here, especially on clear nights. I felt that I should report the sighting to someone and so I called up Mr. ———, who is the head of Project Moonwatch here and described the sighting to him. He was interested and gave me his residence phone number so we could call him if we ever saw it again. Perhaps manage to triangulate it.

None of the usual Air Force explanations could explain this sighting. We have not seen it again though we have looked every night.

We could not resolve the white light that seemed to go in and out from the red-orange light but we were able to resolve the red-orange light. It seemed to be very, very far away especially when directly overhead. The definition of the red-orange light was much smaller than we expected it to be. The sparkling white light seemed to move in and out a great distance, possibly as much as a hundred diameters (of the main body). It left the impression of a very bright light passing on a long pole that could only be seen on one side of the long pole, and every time the pole would go round, you could see the bright white light go in and out on one side of the main body only. The whole thing maneuvered so much in circles, going to and from us, that we must have viewed it from all sides.

This was the most mysterious, unexplainable and spectacular sighting that we have ever made and we would appreciate any explanation that you can make of it.

The Air Force did not attempt one of its usual natural explanations for this one and has it listed as "unidentified."

The Night of the Full Moon

Occasionally, Blue Book received reports of sightings that were several years old. This phenomenon is both disturbing and frustrating. Why the persons concerned had delayed so long in reporting can only be conjectured; perhaps it took them that long to "get their nerve up." But late reporting made any investigation virtually impossible. In addition, records were difficult to trace, and often witnesses had moved, leaving no forwarding address. Still, some of the late reports are quite spectacular and worth mentioning here.

Here is one that came in from the environs of St. Louis, Missouri. Its very artlessness seems to lend it authenticity. Blue Book may not have investigated this case at all, as there is no direct entry pertaining to it, and since the writer of the letter gave no definite date, it would have been extremely difficult to trace. An excerpt from the latter is, however, instructive:

It may be a little late in trying to say I saw, or believe I saw, what my brother-in-law and father-in-law probably seen [sic] in 1959. I am not sure it really was there, but whatever, it was. I never will forget it the longest day I live. [They were returning home from an errand, describing in detail exactly what route they took.] He states: "Now this exactly what has taken place. We had to go south onto U.S. 40, take a left turn to get upon the slab [?] to go west to Wensonville, Missouri. In so doing, as we came upon the slab [?], we made a turn, the car lights headed in the sky SE to the N and directly south of us towards Weldon Springs, Missouri, where there is a government plant, making something to do with atomic works, was a large round object, spinning directly over this plant. Now there is no other lights in that neck of the woods, or airfields, or weather balloons that would hover that low and cast that kind of light as we seen. Sirs, I am not making this story up, because the three of us were scared to say anything and we stopped and got out and look up at this object for at least twenty minutes before it took off in a south-easterly direction, and was out of sight in about ten, fifteen seconds, just leaving a vapor trail. Now there was a beautiful full moon that night and the three of us stood there with our mouths open, not saying a word until it was out of sight, then ———— spoke up and said, "Did you fellows see that thing?" I said, yes, but it was as if someone else said it for me. I was scared stiff. Nobody else said anything else until we got in front. And we never spoke about what we saw that night to no one. But the three of us watched the papers to see if anyone else saw this thing and we never read of anyone seeing it and so we just kept quiet about the matter until I read your article about such things don't exist [apparently an Air Force article, since this was directed to the Air Force]. I wonder a lot, did we really see it, or do people have the same vision of something at the same time. . . . I made a sketch or drawing of what I thought we saw but to me I am a firm believer in seeing is believing and yet I can not force myself to believe that we three really did see. Now I am sure that you understand in all this time that we are just plain people, not looking for publicity or newspaper write-up. If you do, you will have to consult with all three cause the only reason I am writing to you at this time, I still wonder about the whole thing. Was it really real or not? Now I am not asking no one to believe this, because any sane person would say it is too fantastic. I am sure that if someone came up to me with such a yarn as what we saw I would say that he was crazy as hell, or try-ing to gain something through publicity. I am sure we three are sane and brave men. We hunt a lot in places where no one else will go on account of the ghost stories, but I am not afraid of anything that is in reason. Please tell us if there is such a thing as we really saw. We have never told even our families. You know you can confide in us.

I wonder a lot, did we really see this or do people have the same vision of things (that are not there) at the same time?

Philosophers have pondered this question of the nature of reality, yet this appealing letter obviously came from plain, simple people who were honestly perplexed by their UFO experience.

The Vertical Red Dive

Let's move on now to an "Unidentified" object involving a foreign sighting of a Nocturnal Light. According to Blue Book, on June 22, 1952, the following incident took place on the Korean Front:

> Two sergeants, working in the ———— operations office reported sighting an object approximately four feet in diameter and orange in color at 10:45 P.M., 22 June 1952, just above the K-6 Airstrip in Korea.
>
> This object . . . was first spotted at the altitude of eight hundred feet above the K-6 Airstrip, coming from the north. Immediately after the sighting, the object went into a vertical dive and suddenly leveled off at a point approximately one hundred feet above the west end of the airstrip. During the dive, observers noted a trail of bright red flame extending from two to five feet in length. Without delay, it headed in a westerly direction about one quarter mile (two to three seconds elapsed during this maneuver), where it hovered briefly over the crest of some hills nearby.
>
> The object then circled in a hundred-and-eighty-degree turn to the right, spending about forty-five to sixty seconds in the turn. After the completion of the turn the object emitted a bright flash and headed in an easterly direction for a distance of about one-half mile. No trail was noted at this time. At this point, a second bright flash was noticed, followed by complete darkness. No moon was shining at this hour and during the entire sequence of maneuvers, no sound was heard from the object.

This is followed by a comment from the intelligence officer who prepared the report:

As a result of the combined and individual interrogation of the two enlisted men concerned, there is little doubt in the writer's mind that they did see some sort of flaming object in the sky at the time and place mentioned. Both men hold responsible jobs in the operations office of their squadron.

The Object Over the Air Base

Continuing on our foreign tour of nocturnal lights, a most interesting Blue Book case was observed on March 25, 1953, from Rabat, French Morocco. The Air Intelligence Information Report reads:

> On the night of 25 March 1953, I acted as pilot on a routine night training flight from Sale Airdrome, French Morocco, to return to Sale via Safi, French Morocco; Nouasseur, French Morocco; Sidi Slimane. Also aboard was [a crew of four].
>
> At approximately 9:23 P.M., I observed what appeared to be an approaching aircraft directly ahead and some two thousand to three thousand feet above. The automatic pilot was immediately turned to the off position, which is customary when passing other aircraft. There were no red or green running lights visible, but the light which was detected appeared to be of a normal size and intensity of a white aircraft running light. The rate of closure was quite rapid, and the light passed overhead and slightly to the right, still some two thousand to three thousand feet above our aircraft. There was no evidence of a trail or exhaust or of any red or green running lights. Major Rend who was acting as Instructor-pilot . . . watched the lights from the right window as they passed overhead and, shortly after, turned and remarked to me that this appeared to be a very unusual aircraft light. I immediately made a turn to the left to see if the object could be seen again. Upon completion of this turn, we were almost directly over Nouasseur Air Base, still at five thousand feet, and the light was visible at a slightly greater altitude than ours apparently several miles south of Nouasseur. It was in a turn to the left at this time. We continued to turn and observe the light which continued to turn above us.

During this time, the radius of turn was continually decreased [*see sketch*] and the speed noticeably diminished.

At one time we reversed the direction of our turn in order to keep the light in sight and eventually were in an extremely tight turn to the right.

During this period of some two or three minutes, I had contacted Casablanca Air Traffic Control and requested any information as to traffic reported over Nouasseur. Receiving a negative reply, I contacted

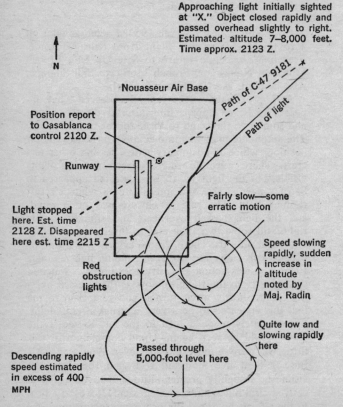

Approaching light initially sighted at "X." Object closed rapidly and passed overhead slightly to right. Estimated altitude 7–8,000 feet. Time approx. 2123 Z.

N

Nouasseur Air Base

Path of C-47 9181

Path of light

Position report to Casablanca control 2120 Z.

Runway

Fairly slow—some erratic motion

Light stopped here. Est. time 2128 Z. Disappeared here est. time 2215 Z

Speed slowing rapidly, sudden increase in altitude noted by Maj. Radin

Red obstruction lights

Quite low and slowing rapidly here

Descending rapidly speed estimated in excess of 400 MPH

Passed through 5,000-foot level here

Path of UFO as seen by captain and crew of training flight on evening of March 25, 1953, in French Morocco.

the Nouasseur tower and inquired if there were any known jet air traffic in the vicinity. Again, the reply was negative. The behavior of the light at this time was certainly very different from the movement normally associated with aircraft, and this fact was reported to Nouasseur tower. There were noticeable and abrupt changes in direction and in speed, though generally, the motion was in a smooth curve. After several three-hundred-and-sixty-degree turns which were required to keep the light in view, it moved off south of Nouasseur at a very rapid rate and in a turn of extremely large radius and began to descend rapidly. The speed at this time appeared to be a maximum and I would judge it to be well in excess of four hundred miles per hour. The light passed a one-point spread between temperature and dew point. After reporting the position of the object once again, we advised Nouasseur tower that we were proceeding on our course to Sidi Slimane. We returned to five thousand feet and advised Casablanca Control. During this entire period from the first sighting at approximately 9:23 to the grounding of the object at approximately 9:28, we were advised by Nouasseur that two other C-47 aircraft were in the area, at six thousand feet to the north and one in the traffic pattern preparing for a landing. Both of these aircraft were located visually and their positions checked continually during the period that the light was also being observed. The landing C-47 was on base-leg and almost directly below us at the time that the light approached the nearest point to the field. The landing C-47 turned almost directly over it, or what appeared to be almost directly over it, on the final approach to landing.

Outbound from Nouasseur we were again contacted by Nouasseur tower and requested to furnish our exact position. The tower operator also informed us that Nouasseur VCA was reporting four blips on their radar screen but that only three aircraft were known to be in the area. Shortly thereafter, Nouasseur requested that we return to the vicinity of Nouasseur and continue to circle in the vicinity where the object was last reported. This was done after securing the necessary clearance from Casablanca Air Traffic Control.

Upon return to Nouasseur, the light was still plainly visible on the ground and in the same location and still exhibiting the same irregular fluctuation in intensity. This was reported to Nouasseur tower and we set up a circle at four thousand feet above the position. During this time, we were advised that the airdrome officer at Nouasseur was directing a ground party to the vicinity. The circling continued for what I estimate to be some fifteen to twenty minutes. At approximately 10:15, my attention was distracted from the point on the ground momentarily; turning back, the light was no longer visible. This was also reported to Nouasseur tower. The ground fog was increasing at this time . . . however, judging from other lights in the area, the fog had not yet reached sufficient intensity to cause this disappearance.

Shortly thereafter, we were requested to fly over the area where the object was last seen and shine our landing lights directly over the spot. This was accomplished at an altitude of fifteen hundred feet. A second circle was made at an altitude of one thousand feet above the ground and we discharged a green flare to clearly identify the location. This green flare was answered with a red flare discharged from the ground party to show their location. . . . The ground fog was increasing in intensity and it became obvious that further search of the area was useless. . . . We were returning to Sale and we landed at approximately 11:15 P.M.

The lengthy report ends as follows:

To the best of my knowledge, there is no meteorological condition which could account for this sighting. At no time was there any evidence of form or shape to the object. It was particularly noticeable because the dark outline of the other two C-47 aircraft in the area could be discerned. . . . The movement of this object was observed almost entirely during the period in question by all three officers in the aircraft, including myself.

It is incredible to note Blue Book's evaluation of this sighting. Despite the minute details included in the report and the officers' concern, the evaluation is: "Aircraft/ground light." To the military mind, there could be no other possibility.

The Balloon and the F-94

Continuing our world coverage of UFO sightings, and also Blue Book's fascination with balloons (this one was evaluated as "balloon with flare"), we take you now to Chorwon, Korea:

On the morning of May 31, 1952, at about four A.M., the guard on post six called me by field telephone and called my attention to a bright object in the sky northeast of my position. At this time I was on guard duty at post four. It seemed like a falling star at first. My post was about one hundred feet above the camp which is at approximately two thousand feet above sea level in elevation. The object stopped falling at about two thousand feet and went straight back up again to about three thousand to four thousand feet. It started its fall first from about thirty-six hundred feet.

The object started to head towards the east for about one-half mile and then it stopped and reversed its course and moved back to the northeast in a smooth flight at a speed of about one hundred to one hundred fifty miles per hour. Then it reversed its heading once again in an easterly direction and started to climb at a forty-five-degree angle away from my position. As it headed away, it picked up speed in a jerking motion and then faded from sight. The facts stated in this statement are all true to the best of my knowledge.

The statement from the other guard is corroborative and adds further details:

On the morning of 31 May, 1952, I was standing guard duty when I heard a jet in the north. It had a pulsating sound like it was idling. I couldn't see anything at first but after a few seconds a small light appeared at about thirty-five hundred feet. I thought a helicopter was hovering there with a light on one side and turned that side to me. The light began dropping at a very slow rate and grew larger as it dropped. As it got larger, it took on a glow. It stopped falling at about twenty-six hundred altitude and it took the form of a disc. The center was duller in color with respect to the rim, which was much brighter.

The object started moving to the east. It seemed to me to be moving with short, jerky movements. It moved a ways and then changed direction. The change seemed instantaneous. It started moving west. It traveled west but not as far as the point from where it had first started moving to the east. Again it changed direction and then the change appeared to be instantaneous. It started heading east again. It was climbing at an angle of approximately twenty-five degrees. It traveled east for a while and started climbing to the north at an angle of approximately forty-five degrees. It kept climbing until I could no longer see it, or it had just faded out. I could still hear it. From the time when it first started climbing until it disappeared, took approximately three to four seconds. The facts stated in this statement are all true to the best of my knowledge.

But the best is yet to come. This unidentified object was observed from an F-94 sent to intercept it. A portion of the Air Intelligence Information Report follows:

A brief description of the sighted object:
SHAPE: round
SIZE: undetermined due to fact that there was no way to compare with any known object
COLOR: brilliant white
NUMBER OF OBJECTS: one
TRAIL OR EXHAUST: negative
PROPULSION SYSTEM: unknown
ESTIMATED SPEED: four hundred and fifty knots when

pulling away from the F-94 at thirty thousand feet altitude.

AERODYNAMIC FEATURES: impossible to observe at close range due to blinding light of object

ANY UNUSUAL MANEUVERS: none except that extremely capable of maneuvering

MANNER OF APPROACH: F-94 descended in left turn to intercept unidentified object six thousand feet below on a ninety-degree course at altitude of eight thousand feet. Unidentified object began a port climb at the same time to intercept with the Sunbeam F-94 and accomplished a maneuver which silhouetted the F-94 against a lighted dawn. The F-94 turned on afterburner and tried two quartering head-on passes with the unidentified object resulting in neither being able to get astern of the other. . . . Maneuvers ensued at three thousand feet where more passes were exchanged for a few minutes. The unidentified object then increased its speed to an estimated four hundred knots on a forty-five-degree heading and began pulling away from the F-94. When last seen the unidentified object had seemingly increased its speed to approximately four hundred and fifty knots whereupon the F-94 gave up pursuit at 3:55 A.M. and returned to base.

ANY OTHER PERTINENT OR UNUSUAL FEATURES: the object possessed a superior speed, superior climbing ability, and was able to turn equally well as the F-94.

MANNER OF OBSERVATION: visual

FROM AIR OR SURFACE: pilot and radar operator in the air and personnel on the ground radar station.

ANY TYPE OF OPTICAL OR ELECTRONIC EQUIPMENT USED: neither F-94 nor ground radar station could paint the unidentified object at any time.

It is of interest that the ground observers did not appear to observe the dogfight in the air. A note by the preparing officer states: "This is believed to be the same sighting on which interception was attempted by an F-94."

Now these could have been two separate reports, since the surface sighting was made at 3:50 A.M. and lasted approximately two minutes, whereas the interceptor pilot gave the time as 3:45 A.M. but stated that he had observed it for approximately nine minutes. It is nevertheless extremely puzzling that the ground observers did not see the F-94, unless the two-minute segment of the total nine minutes of pilot observation occurred at an "uninteresting" period of the interception, and the ground observers did not feel it important enough to report the presence of an F-94, to which they were fully accustomed on a daily basis. It is probably safer, however, to consider these as two separate incidents, both puzzling, both remaining "unidentified."

Let us conclude this parade of Nocturnal Lights by returning to the United States. These next three cases were "identified" by Blue book as "meteor," "conventional aircraft," and "inversion/reflections," respectively. We shall let the evidence speak for itself.

The Jet and the Meteor

This unpublicized case goes back to July 13, 1952, when the flight crew of National Airlines Flight 611, a DC-4 en route from Jacksonville to Washington, D.C., observed an unidentified flying object at about 3 A.M. EST, approximately sixty miles southwest of Washington, D.C. The Blue Book report states:

> It was dark and the crew was unable to observe any form or shape within a round ball of bluish-white light. It was hovering to the west of the aircraft when sighted, then it came up to eleven thousand feet, the aircraft altitude at the time, and hovered within two miles of the left wing of the northbound aircraft, moving along with the aircraft. The airline captain turned on all the aircraft lights (taillights, landing lights, etc.) and the object took off up and away like a star [?] with an estimated speed of departure of one thousand miles per hour. No other air traffic was reported in the general area at the time of the sighting. No activity or condition which might account for the sighting, no physical evidence, and no attempt to intercept or identify the object has been reported.

Aircraft crew submitted information to Washington National Airport Control Tower. Controller Rudick of Washington Tower advised Washington Air Traffic Control Center. Senior controller Barnes submitted information to Ohmsted Flight Service Center, 3:40 A.M., July 17, 1952.

Due to the occupation and probable experience of the reporting observers, the reliability of information is considered to be excellent.

Then why was it dismissed as a meteor? Meteors do not hover, do not move along with the aircraft, and then take off "up and away." The only way out of this one would have been for the evaluator to have claimed that *both* pilots were momentarily subject to a hallucination!

A Bright Star Getting Brighter

The following UFO report was evaluated as "conventional aircraft" despite the maneuvers described by the two witnesses, one of whom had been a technical representative for Lockheed Overseas Corporation and the Curtis-Wright Corporation in England and was also a scientific consultant to the Joint Chiefs of Staff. (He was part of the group which evaluated German aviation development after the end of World War II.) Here are excerpts from a letter sent to U.S. Air Force Headquarters by this technically qualified witness.

Gentlemen: I would like to report an unusual aerial sighting. Saturday evening, April 28 (1956), at approximately eight-thirty P.M., my wife and I were sitting on our front porch steps in semi-darkness when we were attracted by what appeared to be a bright star getting brighter. For more than ten seconds, its light increased to a white brilliance, and then it began to dim to a medium dull red.

This observance was casual until the light started to move from east to west. A transport aircraft bound for Newport was passing in the same line of sight at two thousand feet altitude and was noted to be moving at a little more than double the speed of the light.

The brightness of the light diminished after about thirty seconds' travel and it became dull red. Then its movement accelerated to what must have been enormous speed, considering its estimated high altitude. Then its light became faint as it wobbled and disappeared. Elapsed time from first noting the growing brilliance of the light did not amount to more than three minutes.

Lacking any equipment to record this phenomenon, I immediately drew a map of the southern sky as it was at the time of the occurrence. The enclosed map also details the movement of the light and other estimates which may help locate the area of the odd sighting.

He then states his credentials and continues:

Speaking from this background, I can assure you that the aerial object was not an aircraft of any revealed type, that it was not a meteor, nor a comet. I have always been skeptical about these things until now, and decided to write only after I talked with a radar man. I am sure that if what we saw was a solid body, it would have appeared on metropolitan area radar screens.

In my opinion, a man who evaluated German aviation development after the war ought to know an aircraft when he sees one! The least Blue Book could have done was to have arranged a personal interview with the man by a qualified intelligence agent.

The Two Red Bluff Policemen

Finally, we have a Nocturnal Light case which Blue Book explained away as "atmospheric inversion." This evaluation is, once again, untenable, since the physics of atmospheric inversion simply won't allow mirages to display the antics reported by these two police officers on patrol around midnight near Red Bluff, California, on August 13, 1960. Unfortunately, lack of proper investigation has deprived us of the knowledge of a great many details;

however, the case is still a fine example of the Blue Book party line: "It can't be, therefore it isn't." A letter written to the Area Commander, Red Bluff, very shortly after the sighting states:

Sir: Officer Scott and I were eastbound on Hoag Road, east of Corning, looking for a speeding motorcycle when we saw what first appeared to be a huge airliner dropping from the sky. The object was very low and directly in front of us. We stopped and leaped from the patrol car in order to get a position on what we were sure was going to be an airplane crash. From our position outside the car, the first thing we noticed was the absolute silence. Still assuming it to be an aircraft with power off, we continued to watch until the object was probably to within one hundred to two hundred feet of the ground, when it suddenly reversed completely at high speed and gained approximately five hundred feet altitude. Then the object stopped. At this time, it was clearly visible to both of us and obviously not an aircraft of any design familiar to us. It was surrounded by a glow, making the round or oblong object visible. At each end or each side of the object, there were definite red lights. At times about five white lights were visible between the red lights. As we watched, the object moved again and performed aerial feats that were actually unbelievable. At this time, we radioed to Tehama County Sheriff's Office to see if they could contact the local radar base. The radar base confirmed the UFO—completely unidentified. [There is no record in the files of this radar confirmation.] Officer Scott and myself, after our verification, continued to watch the object. On two occasions, the object came directly towards the patrol vehicle. Each time it approached, the object turned, swept the area with a huge red light. [It was never determined, even roughly, just how close the object came and over what area it appeared, at what rate the area was swept with the red light, etc.] Officer Scott turned the red light on the patrol vehicle towards the object and it immediately went away from us. We observed the object use the red beam approximately six or seven times, sweeping the sky and ground areas.

The object began moving slowly in an easterly direction and we followed. We proceeded to the Vina Plains Fire Station where we again were able to locate the object. As we watched, it was approached by a similar object from the south [the mating of mirages, no doubt]. It moved near the first object and both stopped, remaining in that position for some time, occasionally emitting the red beam. Finally, both objects disappeared below the eastern horizon. We returned to the sheriff's office and met Deputy Frye and Deputy Montgomery, who had gone to Los Molinos after contacting the radar base. Both had seen the UFO clearly and described to us what we saw. The night jailer was also able to see the object for a short time. Each described the object and its maneuvers exactly as we saw them. We first saw the object at 11:30 P.M. and observed it for approximately two hours and fifteen minutes. Each time the object neared us we experienced intense radio interference.

Nocturnal Lights may be the most numerous of all the cases in the Blue Book files. The Air Force generally disregarded them unless a positive identification could be made. Then, any case that was "identified" was held up as a shining example of the good work Blue Book was doing in solving the UFO problem.

The repetitive nature of some of these Nocturnal Light reports and the consistent lack of follow-up investigation by Blue Book remind me of a teletype message that came into the Blue Book office one day when I happened to be there. It was so representative of the offhand manner in which UFOs were being treated at that time, that I had a copy pinned to my office wall for many months. It was an impressive message, at least 95 percent of which was made up of names and addresses of people who were to receive it—a long distribution list of officers and establishments within the military and the government.

The message: JUST ANOTHER UFO.

5

FLYING DISCS IN THE DAYLIGHT

Somebody will have to show me one of these discs before I will believe it.
—*1st Lt. J.C.M., Muroc AFB*

These words were spoken in the Post Exchange at Muroc Air Force Base in California's Mojave Desert, on July 9, 1947, by the base billeting officer. It was 9:30 A.M. and the conversation had turned to reports of flying saucers—a subject which had been headlining the local newspapers for the past week.

The lieutenant's statement was soon to fall into the category of "famous last words," for just moments later, as he left the Post Exchange, he witnessed a most startling event. His signed affidavit from the Project Blue Book files tells the story:

> Upon leaving the Post Exchange, I went directly to my office and before entering heard one of our local aircraft in the traffic pattern. Looking up, as I always do, I observed two silver objects of either a spherical or disc-like shape, moving about 300 miles an hour, or perhaps less, at approximately 8,000 feet heading at about 320° (315° is NW).
>
> When I first observed these objects, I called S/Sgt. ———— and T/Sgt. ———— and Miss ———— (names on file at the Center for UFO Studies) who immediately came to where I was standing. I pointed in the direction of the objects and asked them the question, "Tell me what you see up there." Whereupon, all the three, with sundry comments, stated, "They are flying discs." To further verify my observance, I asked them to tell me in what direction the objects were traveling,

without indicating the direction myself, and again all three, in a consistent nature, stated that the objects were moving towards Mojave, California.

I had time to look away several times and renew my vision of the objects to make sure that they were not any result of eyestrain, or in any nature an optical illusion. The objects in question were not, repeat, were not, aircraft and the objects could not have been weather balloons released from this station since they were traveling against the prevailing wind and since the speed at which they were traveling and the horizontal direction in which they were traveling disqualified the fact that they were weather balloons.

After the observance of this phenomenon, hoping that I might have time to enlist further witnesses, I immediately ran into the dispensary to get personnel who are medical officers to verify, for my own curiosity, the actual observance of these objects but by the time I reached the back porch of the dispensary . . . the objects had by that time disappeared due to the speed with which they were traveling. Upon further investigation, two of us at the same time sighted another object of a silver spherical or disc-like nature at approximately 8,000 feet traveling in circles over the north end. I called the objects to the attention of [other medical personnel] and other personnel standing nearby. All of us saw the objects, with the exception of two out of seven personnel. All of us looked away from the objects several times to make sure [it was not] an optical illusion.

From my actual observance the object circled in too tight a circle and [on] too severe a plane to be any aircraft that I know of. It could not have been any type of bird because of the reflection that was created when the object reached certain altitudes. The object could not have been a local weather balloon for it is impossible that a weather balloon would stay at the same altitude as long and circle in such a consistent nature as did the above-mentioned object.

I am familiar with the results of too constant vision of the sun or any bright object and am aware that optical illusions are possible and probable. I wish to make this statement, that the above-mentioned observance was that of actual subject matter.

This statement has been given freely and voluntarily without any threat or promises under duress.

Affidavits from two other witnesses, accompanying the lieutenant's report, confirm it and add that the speed of the objects was about 400 miles per hour. One of the witnesses, who had 20/20 vision, stated, "I have been flying in and have been around all types of aircraft since 1943 and never in my life have I ever seen anything such as this."

I was impressed with this case, one of the very first that came to my attention when I became Astronomical Consultant to Project Sign. I remember wondering why the Air Force had not paid much greater attention to it and to a similar sighting that occurred at Muroc AFB (now Edwards AFB) just two hours later. The witnesses were certainly excellent, independent military men describing the most unusual sighting on a clear sunny day. What more could the Air Force want?

Capt. Ruppelt once asked: "What constitutes proof? Does a UFO have to land at the River Entrance of the Pentagon near the Joint Chiefs of Staff offices? Or is it proof when a ground radar station detects a UFO, sends a jet to intercept it, the jet pilot sees it, and locks on with his radar, only to have the UFO streak away at a phenomenal speed? Is it proof when a jet pilot fires at a UFO and sticks to his story even under the threat of court-martial? Does this constitute proof?"*

Men have undoubtedly been convicted and sent to the gallows on less evidence, but science is a strict taskmaster when it comes to proof. It is somewhat easier, of course, for science to accept newcomers like black holes in space or quasars which fit into the already established field of astronomy.

But since UFOs simply do not fit accepted patterns in science, far more evidence is demanded. The Catch-22 here is that precisely *because* UFOs don't "fit," it hasn't been considered profitable to expend sufficient time, en-

*The Report on Unidentified Flying Objects.

ergy, and resources to try to get the solid evidence that would finally constitute proof. Certainly Project Blue Book didn't make the attempt, even though I often urged this upon project officers.

Moreover, I, too, was looking for "final and positive" proof. In my own Project Sign report I had this to say about the above case:

> No astronomical explanation for this incident is possible. [As an astronomical consultant, my official responsibility ended there.] It is tempting to explain the objects as ordinary aircraft observed under un-usual light conditions, but the evidence of the "tight circle" maneuvers, if maintained, is strongly contra-dictory. This incident must be judged with reference to other similar incidents, which probably have a common explanation.

The motion and general pattern of behavior are remark-ably uniform in almost all cases of Daylight Discs. The Daylight Disc often appears metallic, and can vary in size from that of a small car to that of a commercial aircraft. The shape varies from circular to "cigar shape," but the circular or oval form predominates.

Over the years, the Daylight Disc has been consistently reported as capable of both high speed and of hovering; capable of extremely rapid takeoffs and rapid stops; and being generally noiseless. It is capable of other maneuvers (reversal of motion, turning in tight circles, non-banked curves) which even our most modern aircraft cannot dupli-cate. As for the "propulsion system" of these mysterious discs, it is as unknown to us as their origin.

If these Daylight Discs really do exist, then they must represent a technology that is foreign to our own, and one that has remained foreign since they first appeared on the modern UFO scene.

There are a far greater number of Daylight Disc re-ports in the early Air Force Intelligence files than in later years, but there is no obvious reason for the decline in re-ports.

The "First" Flying Saucer

The classic Daylight Disc case of the early years—although not the first—was the famous sighting of Kenneth Arnold near Mt. Rainier, Washington, on the afternoon of June 24, 1947. This story has so often been retold that it is almost a cliché.

Briefly, Arnold, a salesman flying his own plane, reported seeing nine crescent-shaped disclike objects (what we today would describe as Daylight Discs) flying near and around Mt. Rainier. His sighting made national headlines and the modern era of "flying saucers" was born. What most people don't realize is that Arnold's was not the first report that year; so those who ascribe much of the UFO phenomenon to the media hype surrounding Arnold's sighting are incorrect. Nevertheless, during the following months, there were so many very similar sightings that some of us were tempted to call UFOs the "Arnold Phenomenon."

Arnold's sighting was "Incident #17" of Project Sign. In my analysis, I simply stated: "There appears to be no astronomical explanation of the later flying-saucer stories. It is impossible to explain this incident away as sheer nonsense if any credence at all is given to Mr. Arnold's integrity. However, certain inconsistencies can be pointed out in the facts as found in Blue Book files.*

Although Daylight Discs are by no means the most exciting UFO reports (the Close Encounters have this honor by far), they are certainly the best reports for establishing the reality of the UFO phenomenon. They cannot be dismissed as nonsense unless one chooses to label the thousands of witnesses to these cases reported from all parts of the globe utterly bereft of their senses.

---

*Arnold stated that the objects seemed about twenty times as long as wide. Let us assume the thickness was just discernible, which means that the object was just at the limit of resolution of the eye. Now, the eye cannot resolve objects that subtend an angle of appreciably less than three minutes of arc. If, then, the distance was 25 miles, as Arnold estimated, each object must have been at least 100 feet thick, and thus, about 2,000 feet long! This is in obvious variance with his estimate of length as 45 to 50 feet. Arnold's estimates of distance and size are in obvious conflict.

The chances of all the reports being hoaxes is also minimal, for Daylight Discs have been witnessed by people from all walks of life whose collective integrity cannot be seriously questioned. Further, if these witnesses had wished merely to fashion stories for the telling, why not something more spectacular than a Daylight Disc? Why not bizarre Close Encounters: strange craft that suddenly swoop out of the skies to stop cars or disturb animals; or brilliantly illuminated UFOs that land and disgorge small beings who engage in weird activities? These kinds of reports would seem better to fit the psychology of the hoaxer and storyteller.

Because Daylight Discs are pivotal to the whole question of whether UFOs really exist, it will be very instructive to examine some of the "unknown" cases from the Blue Book files; the small sampling of cases that follows illustrate the prominent features of Daylight Discs as reported by a representative cross-section of witnesses.

UFOs Are Not for the Birds

The first to witness the Daylight Discs that "invaded" the skies of the Pacific Northwest on July 4, 1952, were a flock of pigeons in the parking lot of Precinct No. 1 of the Portland, Oregon, Police Department.

Patrolman McDowell was feeding the pigeons in the parking lot when they suddenly became excited by something in the air. Wings flapping madly, the flock quickly fluttered into the air and dispersed. What made the pigeons scatter? Here is what Patrolman McDowell described, according to Blue Book files:

> Officer McDowell stated that in looking around to see what had disturbed them [the pigeons], he saw five large discs in the air to the east of Portland, two discs flying south and three in an easterly direction. Officer McDowell . . . advised they were dipping in an up-and-down oscillating motion and were traveling at a great speed. He was unable to give an estimate of the speed or altitude of these discs as they were out of sight before any detailed observation could be made. Officer McDowell advised he notified the Police Radio

who immediately broadcast an alert. Officer McDowell advised he saw no indication of any motivating force or heard any sound coming from these discs and could give no description other than round.

The radio alert was heard by other patrolmen and the sighting of discs was confirmed almost immediately in Milwaukie, Oregon, several miles distant. According to Blue Book, patrolmen there ". . . saw three discs following each other at an undetermined altitude and at a terrific speed. No sound was made by the objects."

In the city of Portland itself, a number of other credible witnesses observed the discs. Here are reports of their statements as summarized by the Air Force and reported to intelligence agents of Blue Book.

By Patrolman Patterson, a former Air Corps pilot:

He stated that at the time the radio alert sounded, he was getting out of his car and saw one disc flying in a southwesterly direction over Portland. Patterson advised this disc was aluminum in color, left no vapor trail and was traveling at a terrific speed, faster than he has ever seen any object flying before. Patterson further advised, although not knowing the exact size of the object . . . that he estimates its altitude at 30,000 feet. He could not give any further description as its speed made observation difficult. He thought the disc was definitely some type of aircraft and thought it appeared radio controlled because the disc could change direction at a 90-degree angle without difficulty.

By Patrolmen Lissy and Ellis:

Both possess private pilot licenses. Both officers advised that upon hearing the radio alert, they saw three flat, round discs, having a white color to them. These discs were, according to these officers, flying at a terrific speed in a southerly direction away from Portland. They described them as flying in a straight line formation. Both officers estimated the altitude at 40,000 feet. Both officers stated these discs were traveling so fast that they were out of sight before

any detailed observation could be made. No sound
was heard. . . . All informants mentioned herein are
known to this agent as very dependable and trust-
worthy officers, not being afflicted with hallucinations.
The weather in the Portland area was clear with little
or no cloud formation. Ground temperature was 82
degrees.

By members of the Harbor Patrol, Portland, who
". . . stepped out when they heard the all-car alert."

Capt. Prahn, Pilot Austed and Patrolman Hoff all
saw the objects and said they appeared to be going
south high over Globe Mills at terrific speed. Capt.
Prahn said the flashes kept them from ascertaining
whether there were three or six. "The discs would
oscillate and sometimes we would see a full disc, then
a half-moon shape, then nothing at all," he reported.
"The objects looked more like a shiny chromium hubcap off a car which wobbled, disappeared and reappeared." There was not a plane in the sky at the
time, but all were emphatic that the discs were not
planes.

Another report of flying discs was made later the same
day by a Captain Smith of United Air Lines and his flight
crew. The Blue Book report states:

. . . that he and the entire crew of the westbound
UAL plane saw nine flying discs near Emmett, Idaho.
At first he saw 5 discs flying what appeared to be a
"loose formation." They called Marty Morrow, stewardess, to the cockpit to verify that they were actually
seeing the discs. She saw them, too. Then they saw
four more of them, three clustered together, and a
fourth flying by itself, way off in the distance. Capt.
Smith described them as "five somethings" which
were thin and smooth on the bottom and rough-
appearing on top. Silhouetted against the sunset
shortly after the plane took off at 8:04 P.M., "We saw
them clearly," he reported, "and followed them in a
northwesterly direction for about 45 miles. Finally
they disappeared. We were unable to tell whether

they outsped the plane or disintegrated. . . . But whatever they were, they were not other aircraft, nor were they smoke or clouds."

An interesting Blue Book notation was a "Memorandum from the Officer in Charge" referring to the sighting by Capt. Smith. The memorandum stated:

On 12 July 1947 Capt. Smith of the United Airlines was interviewed at the Boise Municipal Airport. . . . Capt. Smith reiterated the statements originally made by him to the press as to what he (and his copilot and the stewardess) had seen when eight minutes out of Boise on the route to Seattle. It is the opinion of the interviewer that due to the position Capt. Smith occupies, he would have to be very strongly convinced that he actually saw flying discs before he would open himself for the ridicule attached to a report of this type.

What was the Air Force evaluation of these sightings? Well, the discs that frightened the pigeons were described by Blue Book as "radar chaff"—bits of aluminum foil used to produce false radar targets—or flying debris. Now, this explanation is untenable because several different patrolmen, three to five miles apart, as well as other police officers and civilians, reported definite metallic discs flying at estimated supersonic speeds; some going east, others going south. Chaff flies with the wind, drops slowly, and has never been reported to startle pigeons enough to make them suddenly take to flight.

As for the objects sighted by the United Airlines crew, whether they were the same as those spotted earlier in the day near Portland is strictly conjectural. They certainly were independent observations, by entirely credible witnesses, of objects that appeared to be identical to the earlier sightings.

I personally reviewed this case for the Air Force. Unfortunately, my review was made during my "debunking" period. In my report to the Air Force, I wrote:

There is no astronomical explanation for this incident (United Airlines) nor for numerous others (cases 6, 7, 9, 12, 13, 14, 15, 16) which occurred in and near Portland on the Fourth of July, 1947.

Besides being observed in the same vicinity and most of them at the same time, the objects seen have in common a round shape, "terrific speed," abrupt tactics, and quick disappearance. Abrupt tactics certainly suggest that the objects were of a very light weight.

This investigator can offer no definite hypothesis, but in passing would like to note that these incidents occurred on the Fourth of July, and that if relatively small pieces of aluminum foil had been dropped from a plane over the area, then any one object would become visible at a relatively short distance. Even moderate wind velocities could give the illusion that fluttering, gyrating discs had gone by at great velocities. Various observers would not, of course, in this case have seen the same objects.

The above is not to be regarded as a very likely explanation but only a possibility; the occurrence of these incidents on July 4 may have been more than a coincidence. Some prankster might have tossed such objects out of an airplane as part of an Independence Day celebration. If these were aircraft of either known or unknown type, it would be difficult to explain their appearance over only one locality and at only one time, their apparent random motion, the lack of any sound or obvious propulsion method, and the lack of aerodynamic construction.

Well, I tried hard! But, in the face of flying-disc report data I've studied in the many years since, I can no longer support even the vague possibilities I offered at that time. Radar chaff? I hardly think so. But *what* then? Well, that's what the "U" in UFO means. These sightings are, in fact, *unidentified*. That, we might say, is the name of the game.

The Case of the "Negligent" Officer

Air Force Unidentified: April 24, 1949, Las Cruces, New Mexico. Time: 10:35 A.M. Since this case was described to me personally by the chief witness, Charles

Moore, in charge of a special Sky Hook balloon project at White Sands, New Mexico, my files on it are more complete, more detailed than Blue Book's. The actual story follows:

On a bright sunny New Mexico morning, a small balloon was launched to test the winds aloft preparatory to the main experiment. Such small balloons are customarily watched through a theodolite, a small telescope that pivots in two directions to give accurate sighting angles. Moore watched the balloon as it ascended higher and higher, and then, having another duty to attend to, turned the instrument over to one of the Navy men on the team, admonishing him not to lose track of the balloon. Glancing back a few minutes later, he was shocked to see the Navy observer pointing his telescope elsewhere in the sky than where Moore could see the balloon with his unaided eye. He descended upon the unsuspecting observer and dressed him down severely for having lost the balloon.

"But, I've got it right here!" the man exclaimed.

Sure enough, he did have an object in his field—an elliptical object, two and one-half times longer than wide, moving rapidly enough to require skill in following it through the telescope. Moore grabbed the telescope and confirmed the sighting. Then he called it to the attention of the rest of the crew, all of whom had no difficulty in visually spotting the object. The precious balloon was forgotten. All eyes were on the unknown object. As the crew watched, the object suddenly stopped its horizontal motion and climbed very rapidly, vertically, and was soon lost to both telescope and eyesight.

There could hardly have been better qualified observers. The desert was still that morning. There was no manmade noise. Yet, neither Moore nor his crew heard any sound from the unknown Daylight Disc!

Moore was disgusted with the Air Force's and my lack of attention to this sighting. Who can blame him? It was typical of the Air Force's practice of spending a great deal of overkill effort pinning down cases for which there seemed to be an immediate logical explanation in sight and devoting only modest follow-up to a case that was truly baffling. The Air Force, however, did finally label this case unidentified.

A Daylight Disc in Arkansas

In August 1952 (the exact date is not given in Blue Book files), two witnesses observed a disclike UFO in the vicinity of Skylight Mountain, Washington County, Arkansas. It was 3:30 P.M. The witnesses were sure the object they were looking at was real. They had a camera and tried to photograph it, but the quality of the picture turned out to be very poor. Their report was not submitted to Project Blue Book for several years; for this reason, there was no follow-up investigation by the Air Force, although in this case a follow-up would have been possible and advisable. The witnesses used a magazine reproduction of a standard Blue Book form to make their late report.

The object they reported seeing had "no protrusions, no exhaust, was about ¼ as thick as its diameter." The UFO "moved into and out of a cloud bank several times," and it looked "like two silver saucers glued together, one inverted over the other." The object was "shiny like a new tin building or even brighter!" The witnesses' description of its maneuvers were also interesting: "From a hover to a speed that took it through five-mile circles in five seconds."

The principal witness, a Navy chief petty officer and combat veteran with six years experience, had this additional comment:

> I have been in the Navy since 1946 and have observed many planes and weather balloons and have never seen anything that looked like this object. I am presently a chief radioman stationed at Naval Communications Station, Washington, D.C.

This man had flown numerous bomber missions during World War II and was familiar with all types of aircraft. He firmly believed that the object he and another witness observed was definitely not any type of known aircraft.

This report could easily have been followed up by the Air Force since the individual was still in the Navy when the report was filed with Blue Book. It would have been an important case to follow up, since the principal witness was technically competent, particularly in the matter of aircraft, and his competence was directly applicable to this sighting; he should certainly have been able to identify an aircraft! Yet the Air Force made no attempt whatsoever to gain additional information. Once again, Blue Book avoided a baffling case.

Five Witnesses and Five Discs

Blue Book Unidentified: May 1, 1952, 10:50 A.M., George AFB, California, 5 witnesses. Four witnesses in Range Control Tower, one witness on golf course four miles away.

Here we have truly independent witnesses, located four miles apart and not in communication with each other. They observed Daylight Discs for a short interval of 15–30 seconds. The discs were very maneuverable, appearing almost to collide and then break away. The statement of one of the five observers follows:

I, ———, Headquarters Squadron, 131st Air Base Group, do this date make the following statement concerning my observations on 1 May 1952:

1. The objects, five (5) in number, appeared to be round and disc-shaped. The diameter of these objects seemed to be greater than the length of an F-51 fighter plane. They were of a flat, white color and gave off no glare or reflection. They moved in formation (as per attached sketch) with the last two darting around in a circular motion. I noticed no vapor trail or exhaust. I estimated that the speed of the objects was about twice that of ordinary jet aircraft.

2. I sighted the objects at approximately 10:50 hours and they were in my sight for about 30 seconds.

3. I observed the objects from a 20-foot control tower on the small-arms range. The control tower faces north, and George Air Force Base can be seen off to the left. It was a visual observation, and I estimated the altitude of the objects to have been about 4,000 feet. Speed was approximately twice that of ordinary jet aircraft.

4. From the observations I made at the tower, I would say that they came from the southeast over Apple Valley, Ca. They headed in a northwest direction toward George Air Force Base, then veered sharply to the north and disappeared.

5. I am 23 years of age, married and have a high school education. I have spent close to six years in the Army and Air Force. . . .

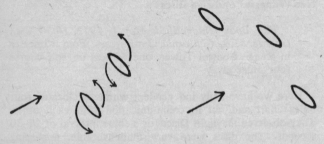

Daylight discs seen by four witnesses at George AFB, California, on May 1, 1952, at 10:50 A.M.

The brief statement of the independent observer four miles away from the range tower follows:

I, ———, Headquarters 146th Fighter-Bomber Wing, this date make the following statement concerning my observations of an unidentified flying object on 1 May 1952:

1. The shape of the object was round. I could not see if it was shaped as a ball or a disc. It was white in color, made no noise, had no visible exhaust and the speed appeared to be in excess of 1,000 miles per hour. The outline was very clear like the edge of a sheet of paper.

2. I sighted the object at approximately 10:50 hours and it was in my sight approximately 15 seconds.

3. I was standing on the golf course at Apple Valley, California . . . about four miles from George Air Force Base.

4. The object was not maneuvering in any way and

was flying in a straight east direction. I could not estimate the altitude but thought it was very high.

5. I am Wing Director of Personnel.

6. The weather was clear and there was no breeze.

The Case of the Missing Report

Blue Book Unidentified: May 1, 1952, 9:10 A.M., Davis-Monthan AFB, Tucson, Arizona.

This case is a classic. The late Dr. James McDonald made a valiant attempt to get details from original witnesses after discovering that a major report, submitted to Blue Book by the "UFO officer" (who was one of the witnesses!) at Davis-Monthan, was missing. A small part of this was apparently recovered and now appears in the Blue Book microfilms. The story is as follows:

An Air Intelligence officer (who had, as one of his regular duties, the analysis of UFO cases reported to the local air base), a B-36 crew, and an airman on the steps of the base hospital (just coming from having his knee treated) all attested to this event. Two shiny, round objects overtook a B-36, slowed down to the speed of the B-36, stayed in formation with it for about 20 seconds, then executed a sharp, no-radius 70–80-degree turn from the line of flight of the B-36, and resumed original speed and went to about one-fourth the distance to the horizon when one of the two objects made an immediate stop and hovered. There was no sound other than that of the B-36. There were no contrails from either the objects or the B-36.

Despite the detailed description (in the original report) of the maneuvers of the two shiny, silent objects, Blue Book dismissed this case as "Aircraft." The following letter from Dr. McDonald dated July 14, 1966, was sent to Major Quintanilla, Blue Book head:

Dear Major Quintanilla:

Following our second unsuccessful effort to locate in the Blue Book files any record of the B-36 incident at Davis-Monthan AFB, I have asked Maj. Pestalozzi to put down, in a letter to me, an account of such details as he can still remember with confidence (see Appendix).

Maj. Pestalozzi has told me, in previous conversations, that he was an Air Intelligence officer from about 1950 to 1960, and was stationed at Davis-Monthan during 1951–53. Field investigation of UFO sightings was one of his routine duties, not only at Davis-Monthan but also at other duty stations. The B-36 case, which he believes occurred in 1952, *was one in which he himself happened to be an observer.* Although he has now made a number of efforts to run down clues to the precise date, the latter still remains uncertain, as I indicated to you in my last visit at WPAFB on June 30.

He recalls filing a rather thick report on this B-36 case, the thickest he ever filed on a UFO. It included not only his own observations and those of the B-36 crew which he personally interrogated, but also that of an airman who was standing beside him during most of the time of his own observation. The airman (whose name he has forgotten) was coming out of the base hospital just as the major was about to enter (for treatment of an injured knee). He pointed out to me today that approximately six or seven other Air Force personnel at scattered locations around the base also reported seeing the UFOs from the ground. Because their descriptions matched closely those given by himself and the airman, he did not (at least as far as he now recalls) include them in his official report.

I have queried Maj. Pestalozzi closely about the length of time during which he had the UFOs under observation. He estimates it at something like five minutes. He actually saw the two UFOs overtake the westbound B-36, and he held them under observation as the aircraft passed overhead until the objects departed. His recollection, as of today, was that his line of sight to the B-36 at the time the UFOs moved into position was at an angle of elevation of about 50 degrees (estimated uncertainty about 5–10 degrees); and the UFOs departed when the line of sight to the aircraft was about the same angle above the western horizon. The aircraft was almost due east of the base when the objects joined it, and it lay due west when they departed. Its heading was almost due west during the entire period of observation. (In an earlier conversation, he estimated the total time of observation at perhaps 3 minutes. The latter time would be a bit more compatible with an estimated flight altitude of 20,000 ft. and the estimated angles of line of sight. But every one of these estimates is based on recollecting of an event 14 years old, so perhaps all that is now warranted is the conclusion that the UFOs paced the B-36 for "several minutes." The latter time is compatible with the fact that all of the crew, save the pilot, were able to get back to the starboard blister to see the UFO before it left.)

As he sketched the relative positions, he recalled an important detail. The UFO near the aircraft was

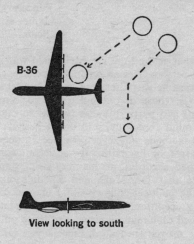

View looking to south

Estimated UFO dimensions

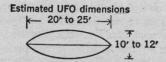

The discs sighted by crew of B-36 and observer on ground, Davis-Monthan AFB, Tucson, Arizona, May 1, 1952. Sketch shows paths of the two discs relative to the B-36.

at a level distinctly lower than the mid-section of the
fuselage (see sketch). He recalled that the crew described looking somewhat down upon it, and the
blister itself is below mid-section. This may explain
why there was no marked aerodynamic disturbance
of the aircraft's flight characteristics, one of the very
puzzling features of the incident.

The major's enclosed account does not directly
state it, but he has mentioned to me that the B-36
crew was a bit shaken by this experience. He pointed
out to me that, after the UFOs departed, the B-36
radioed Davis-Monthan control tower and demanded
permission to land immediately. It was just after they
landed that Operations called him over to interrogate
the crew. . . .

Sincerely,
James E. McDonald
Senior Physicist

I recall that at the time Dr. McDonald was regarded by
Blue Book personnel as an outstanding nuisance. This was
partly because he was interested in a scientific study of the
"true" UFOs (those that completely defied simply natural
explanation) and partly because he was so outspoken. He
spoke his mind forcefully, and didn't hesitate to criticize
Blue Book methods whenever possible. On occasion I, too,
was the target of his criticism—criticism which was entirely justified according to his very strict standards. It is
unfortunate that Dr. McDonald couldn't understand or
adjust to the political-military situation, and chose instead
to act only according to strict scientific dictates. A carefully planned diplomatic approach to these military circles
might have proved successful, especially if Dr. McDonald
had consented to work with me in a much less antagonistic
manner, as I invited him to do on several occasions. I fear,
however, that he regarded me as a lost cause and that his
temperament would hardly have permitted it.

It is due largely to the industry and perseverance of Dr.
James McDonald that this excellent case was resurrected
at all.

The Case of the Three Baffled Engineers

Blue Book Unidentified, Oct. 15, 1953, 10:10 A.M., Minneapolis, Minn. Three witnesses, all research engineers employed by General Mills Aeronautical Laboratories. A report of the Air Intelligence Service Squadron, Flight 2A, follows:

The sighting described below took place during the theodolite tracking of a 79-ft. balloon floating at approximately 80,000 feet, on Project 85021-Grab Bag. No sound was detected at any time during the observation.

The object was first observed as it passed below the sun at an elevation (solar elevation) of approximately 25 degs. heading southward in horizontal flight. It was detectable by a smoke or vapor trail which extended some distance behind it, but which did not persist, or form a cloud. The object itself was not visible even through the theodolite during the first part of the sighting. During the horizontal part of its trajectory, the object moved across the sky at a rate of 10 degrees in 9 seconds. With an estimated altitude of 40,000 ft. this represents 15 miles per minute, or 900 miles per hour. [All three men agreed that object could have been as high as 60,000 feet, which would give a speed of 1,200 miles per hour.]

After about 10 seconds of horizontal flight, the object appeared to go into a vertical dive. The possibility that the appearance of a dive was produced by the object merely receding into the distance seems unlikely since the speed normal to the line of sight was undiminished in the dive. The dive lasted for from 10 to 15 seconds, at the end of which time the object was visible two or three times as it appeared to glow or reflect the light of the sun for perhaps a second at a time. Just at this time the vapor trail ceased, and for a second or two thereafter the object, its outlines still unrecognizable, was seen through the theodolite not as a glare (reflected?) light, but as a gray mass in the act of leveling off. Its size in the theodolite field was of the same magnitude as the 79-foot balloon, which means that, since it was nearer, it would not be as large [linearly].

The observers believe that the object was most likely a jet aircraft, but several features were unusual:

1. The speed was higher than normally observed;

2. The vertical dive was a highly dangerous if not suicidal maneuver;

3. A jet aircraft in such a dive would be heard for miles, and would certainly cause a noticeable shock wave detectable in the area beneath it;

4. Vapor trails do not ordinarily occur during vertical motion though smoke trails could, of course.

It was thought that the Air Defense Command would be interested in what was seen, if,

a. They had no aircraft in the vicinity which could account for it;

b. They had an aircraft accident which might be partly explained by this report.

Well, even Blue Book evaluated this as "Unidentified." Perhaps the suicidal dive was too much for them.

More Discs over New Mexico

A sighting made at Walker AFB in New Mexico on July 29, 1952, involved four weather observers, including the base weather officer. They observed a number of flying discs through a theodolite. The apparent speed of the discs required the theodolite to be turned at maximum rate in order to track them, much faster than the rate used for conventional aircraft flying at high altitudes.

The Intelligence officer concludes his report with these words:

The scientific experience of the weather personnel making these observations is sufficient to warrant credence in their sightings and indicates an actual appearance of unidentified flying objects.

Blue Book could allow some cases to be labeled "Unidentified"; but it could never make the seemingly logical step of supporting Field Intelligence officers who, like this one, often came right out and said, ". . . indicates an actual appearance of unidentified flying objects." Somehow the evaluation "Unidentified" is not quite the same as "Unidentified Flying Object"; they are worlds apart in implication. The former suggests that some natural, everyday thing occurred but for one reason or another a positive identification was not made. The latter—well!

The official Blue Book line to the public was that *all* UFOs could be explained away as misidentifications of normal objects or events. Pray then, what was the normal, everyday object that caused the above sighting, and those many others we have examined?

The Case of the Tricky Disc

Blue Book Unidentified, Jan. 10, 1953, 3:45 P.M., Sonoma, Cal. 2 witnesses (an Air Force colonel and a security agent). The Air Intelligence Information Report on this case states:

On 10 January 1953, between 3:45 and 4:00 P.M., Col. ———— and Mr. ————, of the Federal Security Agency, San Francisco, California, observed an unidentified flying object while eight miles northwest of Sonoma, California, from a knoll in the hills northwest of the Sonoma Valley. The object was sighted at a 45° angle northwest from the location of the observers at a very high altitude, so high that the object was compared to the flat head of a pin held two feet from the eye. Speed was estimated at four times the speed of a jet aircraft with accompanying sound similar to the USAF F-86 jet at high altitude. There was no change in sound tone or volume during maneuvers. Unusual maneuvers made by the object were: (1) Three (3) 360° tight turns to the right, taking two to three seconds to complete each turn; (2) two (2) right-angle (90°) turns, first to the right, then to the left; (3) the object slowed down to almost a complete stop, then accelerated to high speed again, making this maneuver twice. The object then rose vertically and disappeared from view. Total time of observation was estimated to be between 60 and 75 seconds. There were no radar contacts with the object. No other observations of this object are known to have been made.

The object made three (3) 360° turns to the right taking two to three seconds to complete each turn. These turns were made at five-second intervals still holding on the same course. It continued on and made an abrupt right-angle (90°) turn to the right, followed five seconds later with an abrupt turn to the left which placed the object back on its original course. After this maneuver, the object slowed down to almost a stop and then accelerated to its previous speed, making this maneuver twice. The object rose vertically and disappeared from view. [The observer stated that the object could possibly have been climbing when it seemed to slow down to a stop, but that he seriously doubts it.] The 360° turns were said to be very tight turns, about one-eighth of the area required for jet aircraft.

Here, we are certainly driven to the edge of reality! Either these men deliberately made this story up or it happened much as they said. Their qualifications argue strongly against a hoax, and their technical training would indicate that when they say the object made a tight 360° turn, it made a tight 360° turn! Surely, if this had been a one-witness case (the reader will note that *all* of the Daylight Disc cases included here had multiple witnesses) one might fall back upon simple hallucination as a solution. It could be said that what they saw was actually an airborne seed, or an insect much closer to them; but in a minute and a half, they surely would have discovered this for themselves.

The Case of the Double Identity

Blue Book Unidentified, seen at Terre Haute, Indiana, and three minutes later over Paris, Illinois (15 miles apart).

One of the perennial objections raised by skeptics is

that a UFO is not seen "cross-country" and by many people. That, however, is one of the chief characteristics of the phenomenon itself, one of the "givens" in the problem. It is absolutely true that UFO events are generally isolated in space and time. They are seen in a specific locality and usually for a very short time. That's simply the way it is, like it or not.

Here, however, is one of the rare cases in which observers in separate localities saw the same UFO at almost the same time: an aircraft communicator and friends at Terre Haute and a pilot flying near Paris, Illinois. This is the original message as it came over the teletype at Wright-Patterson AFB:

ATTN ADC FOR DEPUTY FOR INTELLIGENCE. FOR YOUR INFO A UNITED PRESS NEWS RELEASE APPEARING IN THE 10 OCT NEWSPAPERS RPTD MR. ROY MESSMORE CMA EMPLOYEE CMA AT HOLMAN MUNICIPAL APRT CMA TERRE HAUTE CMA IND. SAW A "HUGE METALLIC OBJECT SPEEDING ACROSS THE FIELD" ON 9 OCT. RELEASE STATES THAT MR. MESSMORE CMA "A HARD-HEADED CAA OFFICIAL" JOINED THE RANKS OF THOSE WHO NOW BELIEVE IN FLYING SAUCERS. NO FURTHER INFO AVAILABLE AT THE TIME PAPA DO YOU DESIRE ANY INVESTIGATIVE ACTION BY THIS CMID? QUERY?

An immediate field investigation was requested by the Director of Intelligence, USAF.

A Spot Intelligence Report from the OSI, Chanute Air Force Base, came to the Director, Office of Special Investigation, Headquarters, United States Air Force, Washington D.C., dated October 25, 1951 [they lost no time]. It reads:

Synopsis: Chief Aircraft Communicator, CAA, Holman Municipal Airport, Terre Haute, Ind., reported to the Office of Special Investigations agent that on 9 Oct. 1951, at 1342 hours [1:42 P.M.], he observed an unknown unidentified aerial object directly overhead at Hulman [sic] Municipal Airport. The object was approximately the size of a half-dollar coin held at arm's length and was flying in a southeasterly direction. The day was clear and the informant's vision was unobstructed. Exact size and altitude of the object unknown. Informant advised that a pilot, one Charles Warren, sighted a similar object on the same date at approximately 1345 hours just east of Paris, Illinois, at approximately 5,000 feet. Object was last seen traveling in a northeasterly direction, south of the atomic energy plant at Newport, Ind.

The following is a short note from the Air Force Director of Intelligence referring to this second sighting by Mr. Warren:

A second sighting reported approximately 30 miles distant three (3) minutes later indicates the "objects" may have been jet aircraft observed when the reflection of the sun may have distorted the aircraft in the eyes of the observer.

It is somewhat difficult to see how the Director of Intelligence arrived at this conclusion other than by using the theorem: "It can't be, therefore it isn't." Totally neglected in this "solution" are the *reported* facts [of course, these may be wrong—but can *all* of these experienced observers be wrong?]—"size of a half-dollar coin held at arm's length," "no noise," "overhead to horizon in approximately 15 seconds," "no protruding fins or other protrusions on this aerial object" [i.e., no wings].

Flying Discs and the Taffy Apple

Our discussion of Daylight Disc Blue Book cases ends with a spectacular *non*–Blue Book case of many years ago which was communicated to me privately and which Mr. Keller, one of the principal witnesses, has given me permission to publish. An excerpt from his original letter to me follows:

Because of your interest concerning aerial phenomena and related curiosities, I thought you might like to know of an incident that occurred in late spring, 1936 or 1937, when my famly and I saw between 10 or 12 "UFOs."

It was more or less a Sunday-afternoon routine to jump into the family car for a drive in the country for a change of scenery and a stop somewhere along the way for an ice-cream treat or some other concoction. On this occasion, we stopped early because of low-hanging clouds, general overcast and what looked to be a threat of approaching inclement weather.

We parked our car at Narragansett and North Avenues where at that time existed a taffy-apple stand. After returning to our car, I, as a 13-year-old boy would do, began performing a neck-breaking act from the rear window to get a better "biting angle" by looking skyward and holding my taffy apple directly above my face. There I saw my UFOs about 5° south of my overhead view.

At this time in my life it was an exciting experience just to see and hear the approach of an airplane and to stop whatever one was doing just to admire and gaze in awe at this amazing feat. However, we really thought nothing more of this sighting of UFOs other than to say, "How curious" or, "Isn't that interesting?" and other unexciting phrases.

We watched these objects cavorting and doing their acrobatics for approximately ten minutes, when suddenly they converged, as if on signal, to one point under the clouds; stacking one above the other and climbing vertically up into the cloud bank and disappearing from sight. . . .

I say between 10 or 12 UFOs because of their constant motion and eccentric darting movements which made it virtually impossible to make an accurate count. Some were hovering absolutely still while a few would be darting haphazardly to and fro, coming to stops that were unbelievable. Their darting motions were of one constant speed with no visible evidence of acceleration or deceleration; comparable to sliding a checker piece on a checkerboard with one's index finger in quick, jerky movements. All this activity took place directly beneath the clouds within an area roughly 500 feet in diameter. They were all identical in size, shape and color. . . .

Let me assure you that this is all quite true and factual and that I have no ulterior motive in relating this episode other than wanting to share an experience of my sighting with someone interested in this type of phenomenon.

> Cordially yours for knowledge,
> Dick Keller

Thus, more than ten years before Kenneth Arnold's famous sighting, which, in a real sense, ushered in the modern era of UFOs, Daylight Discs had been seen but not reported.

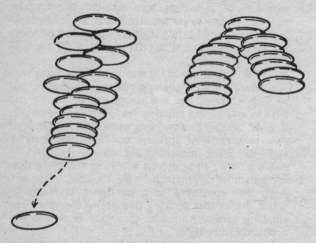

Daylight discs observed near Mexico City, December 13, 1957, for a total period of about twenty minutes.

Twenty years later, a very similar sighting was reported to Blue Book from Col Anahuac, Mexico. It was witnessed by several persons in the Mexico City area and was said to have performed in a manner similar to those discs reported by Mr. Keller.

This parade of Daylight Disc cases from the Blue Book files certainly makes the cliché attributed to Dr. Carl Sagan, that "there are no reliable reports that are interesting, and no interesting reports that are reliable" ring hollow. For these many cases of discs witnessed in broad daylight were often tracked using sophisticated instruments, and observed by persons technically competent to report and interpret. They certainly cannot be disregarded!

But whether the Daylight Discs represent a unique form of UFO, perhaps distant from and even unrelated to the Close Encounters cases and the Nocturnal Lights, cannot be determined at the present time.

6

"ANGELS," "BOGIES," AND "BLIPS": THE RADAR UFOS

*The frequency of reports of this nature has recently
increased; instructions have therefore been directed
to all radar installations within this command to report scope sightings of unusual objects.*
        —*from an Air Force report,
        classified* SECRET, *March 9, 1950*

Of all types of UFO reports, those involving radar may
be, strangely enough, the least reliable, owing to the
vagaries of radar propagation. But there are many cases
that cannot be easily dismissed. These include unusual
multiple radar confirmation cases, radar-visual sightings,
and ground-to-air radar-visual contacts. In a few cases,
even single radar contacts with unidentified targets have
proven to be extremely puzzling. The cases treated in this
chapter have confounded and bewildered the experts.

Interestingly enough, few of these cases were treated by
the Condon Committee, in its study of UFOs. Those studied by them were, almost universally, evaluated as arising
from the malfunctioning of radar equipment, false radar
echoes (angels), unidentified aircraft or other natural objects (bogies), or unusual radar returns caused by meteorological conditions.

Since Project Blue Book operated on the theory that
there couldn't be any such thing as "real" UFOs, the Air
Force searched for almost any possible reason to explain
away radar cases.

Ultimately, even the Condon Committee had to admit
that there was a "small, but significant, residue of cases
from the radar-visual files . . . that have no plausible ex-

planation as propagation phenomena and/or misinterpreted man-made objects."*

The Selfridge Sighting

According to the Condon Committee a "good radar case" must be accompanied by a simultaneous visual confirmation. In my opinion, there are *multiple* radar sightings *without* simultaneous visual confirmation that are of equal importance. One of those (not studied by the Condon Committee) was the case involving a multiple radar sighting of a UFO in the vicinity of Selfridge AFB, Michigan, on March 9, 1950—the case about which the Air Force statement at the beginning of this chapter was made.

The Selfridge sighting so impressed certain highly placed individuals in the Air Force that it led the Air Adjutant General, Headquarters Continental Air Command, Mitchel Air Force Base, New York, to send the following letter, classified SECRET, to the Director of Intelligence, Headquarters, USAF, Washington, D.C.:

> 1. Attached for your information are two narrative reports concerning radar sightings of an unidentified flying object.
> 2. The fact that the object was sighted on the scopes of two (2) radars is considered worthy of special note.
> 3. Comment of technical experts, this headquarters, was solicited and is quoted in part for your consideration.
> a. While it is relatively well known that various ionospheric conditions cause reflections at lower frequencies, it is usually considered that those layers have no effect at the frequencies used by the two radar sets mentioned except when temperature inversions or other atmospheric or tropospheric conditions cause ducting and spurious reflections. Presuming that such idealized conditions existed at the time of these observations, it is conceivable that an

*Condon Report, p. 175.

actual small change in physical lateral action in reference to the radar set could cause a seemingly greater change in relative position of the "object" as observed on the radar scope due to the varying path lengths the radar energy takes to and from the "object" as a function of the frequency-sensitive layers and angles of incidence of the propagated wave. However, the great difference in the frequencies of the L-Band CPS-5 and the S-Band CPS-4 radar sets and the *evident correlation of observations between these two sets almost rule out the possibility of anomalous propagation effects. Further, the magnitude of velocity and accelerations of the three-dimensional movements of the "objects" reported are beyond the capability of known behavior of lighter than air vehicles in controlled flight.* [Italics added.]

b. Also substantiating this unlikelihood is the fact that the "object" was reported as remaining stationary in free space for a mean period of two minutes.

c. Further validity is lent to the contention of the reports by statements that first indications, which were at high altitudes, were observed on the CPS-4 height-finder before being observed on the CPS-5 surveillance radar set. This follows logic and field experience, inasmuch as the high-altitude coverage of the CPS-5 is known to be poor and the antenna is not capable of being automatically tilted as in the case of the CPS-4 on which the controller may tilt the antenna within wide limitations to observe any high altitude or high-angle objects. It is to be noted that previous field experience with a CPS-5 surveillance radar set has indicated that targets picked up at ranges and altitudes indicated in subject report would probably have a reflection aspect ratio in the order of magnitude of a B-29 or greater.

d. In the absence of detailed vertical and horizontal coverage charts for the specific radar sites and comprehensive weather reports for the area during the period of time these observations were noted, a

capable of the incredible speeds attained by the UFO and no conventional aircraft were reported in the area. The position of the object, sighted at seventeen miles from the carrier, was also held on the radar scope at that time. The estimated altitude of the object was 52,000 feet and it faded from the radar scope at 110 miles. During the time it was in view, the coast of Korea and the island of Ullung Do were visible at a distance of twenty miles, and an escorting destroyer was visible on the scope 2,000 yards from the carrier.

The comment of the intelligence officer who prepared the report on this case was as follows:

> A thorough debriefing was made of the radar operator. Personnel stated that the operator was very intelligent, efficient and cooperative. Operator was cognizant of capabilities and limitations of the radar equipment and made careful plots, checking constantly. At time contact was closing, he queried the aircraft controller and when it was determined that it was not a friendly aircraft, the general alarm was sounded. The three minutes of careful plotting were made after the object had turned and was heading away from the station. Operator was sure of the accuracy of the plots for the three minutes, and was adamant that the speeds shown were approximately correct.

A letter classified SECRET was sent on April 8, 1952, by the Commander Naval Forces, Far East, to the Chief of Naval Operations, enclosing a track chart of the UFO in question and stating, in part: "Enclosure (1) is forwarded for information and evaluation. This is probably the first instance of a visual and radar contact on a high-speed aerial target being made simultaneously in the Far East."

The Princeton Joins the Philippine Sea

One year prior to the radar-visual UFO sighting by the aircraft carrier *Philippine Sea*, the ship was involved in a double radar UFO sighting with the carrier USS *Princeton* off the east coast of Korea. The *Princeton* had made radar

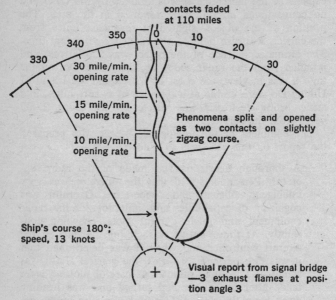

contacts faded
at 110 miles

30 mile/min.
opening rate

15 mile/min.
opening rate

10 mile/min.
opening rate

Phenomena split and opened
as two contacts on slightly
zigzag course.

Ship's course 180°;
speed, 13 knots

Visual report from signal bridge
—3 exhaust flames at position angle 3

Radarscope map of unknown object observed from the USS
Phillipine Sea.

contact with several high-speed "Unknowns" during April
and May of 1951, prior to the double contact involving
radar aboard the *Philippine Sea*. The speeds of the "Unknowns" were estimated at up to 1,200 MPH.

Excerpts from a letter to the Chief of Naval Operations
from Commander Naval Forces, Far East, dated September 11, 1951, and classified SECRET, contained this report:

The observation of rapidly moving targets on the
PPI scope of the SX radar on the USS *Princeton*
CV-37 has been reported by Lt. H.W. White, a CIC
watch officer on the staff of Commander, Carrier Division 5. The targets were observed several times
while operating with Task Force 77 during April and
May of 1951.

On one occasion the targets were observed by two
ships simultaneously. The same targets were held by

both the USS *Princeton* and USS *Philippine Sea* on their SX radars. The ships were approximately 4,000 yards apart at this time. The tracks made by the contact on the radar of the *Philippine Sea* were the same as those on the USS *Princeton*.

The targets were always 22° wide and sharply defined. The presentation was exceedingly bright in comparison with normal air and surface contacts. Appearance of the target never varied.

The SC radar was operating satisfactorily both before and after each incident. Very little sea return was observed.

Although previous observations of high-velocity targets had been reported by aircraft, this report was the first reported shipboard occurrence of this phenomena. This report is considered of particular interest in that the contacts were observed by two different radars at the same time, thereby reducing the probability that malfunctioning of the radar was the cause of the phenomena.

The Radar Case Condon Couldn't Crack

On August 13 and 14, 1956, between the hours of 9:20 P.M. and 3:30 A.M. in the vicinity of Lakenheath-Bentwaters, England, occurred one of the most baffling series of UFO radar-visual contacts ever to confront Air Force radar operators. This case was so confounding that it was eventually to cause the Condon Committee investigator who reviewed it to state all but outright that it was proof that UFOs did exist. But Project Blue Book, in its customary manner, listed it as "anomalous propagation," the all-purpose out the Air Force applied to any radar contact with a UFO that it could not explain.

An extensive analysis of this case by Gordon D. Thayer of the National Oceanic and Atmospheric Administration (and the member of the Condon Committee who conducted its review of radar cases) was examined closely by the UFO Subcommittee of the American Institute of Astronautics and Aeronautics and then published in the September 1971 issue of its magazine, *Astronautics & Aeronautics*.

Thayer's report describes the case as "the most puzzling and unusual case in the radar-visual file. The apparently rational, intelligent behavior of the UFO suggests a mechanical device of unknown origin as the most probable explanation of this sighting. . . ." He did leave open the possibility that more conventional explanations could be applied to the case due to the fallibility of human witnesses.

According to Thayer, a report by the night-watch supervisor in the Radar Air Traffic Control Center at Lakenheath submitted to the Condon Committee years after the events of the night of August 13–14, 1956, provided the most coherent account. That report was not to be found in the Blue Book file at the time of Thayer's analysis for the Condon Committee in 1967, but it *was* contained in the files released in 1976 by the Air Force. Here is the account of the night-watch supervisor as submitted to the Condon Committee:

In 1956, sometime between January and September (I can't remember the exact date or month), I was on duty as Watch Supervisor at Lakenheath RAF Station, England (a USAF base), in the Radar Air Traffic Control Center. It was the 5:00 P.M. to midnight shift. I had either four or five other controllers on my shift. I was sitting at the Supervisor's Coordinating desk and received a call on the direct line (actually, I'm not sure which line it was). Anyway, it was Sculthorpe GCA Unit calling and the radar operator asked me if we had any targets on our scopes traveling at 4,000 MPH. They said they had watched a target on their scopes proceed from a point 30 or 40 miles east of Sculthorpe to a point 40 miles west of Sculthorpe. The target passed directly over Sculthorpe, England, RAF Station (also an USAF Station). He said the tower reported seeing it go by and just appeared to be a blurry light. A C47 flying over the base at 5,000 feet altitude also reported seeing it as a blurred light that passed under his aircraft. No report as to actual distance below the aircraft. I immediately had all controllers start scanning the radar scopes. I had each scope set on a different range— from 10 miles to 200 miles radius of Lakenheath. At this time I did not contact anyone by telephone as I was rather skeptical of this report. We were using ———— on our radar, which eliminated entirely all ground returns and stationary targets. There was very little or not [sic] traffic or targets on the scopes, as I recall. However, one controller noticed a stationary target on the scopes about 20 to 25 miles southwest. This was unusual as a stationary target should have been eliminated unless it was moving at a speed of at least 40 to 45 knots. And yet we could detect no movement at all. We watched this target on all the different scopes for several minutes and I called the GCA Unit at Lakenheath to see if they had this target on their scopes also. They confirmed the target was on their scope in the same geographical location. As we watched, the stationary target started moving at a speed of 400 to 600 MPH in a north/northeast direction until it reached a point about 20 miles north/northwest of Lakenheath. There was no slow start or build-up to this speed—it was constant from the second it started to move until it stopped.

. I called and reported all the facts to this point, including Sculthorpe GCA's initial report, to the 7th Air Division Command Post at London. They in turn notified 3rd Air Force Command Post and hooked into the line. I also hooked in my local AFB Commanding Officer and my Unit (AFCS, Communications Squadron) Commander on my switchboard. And there could have been others hooked in also that I was not aware of. I repeated all the facts known to this point and continued to give a detailed report on the target's movements and location. The target made several changes in location, always in a straight line, always at about 600 MPH and always from a standing or stationary point to his next stop at constant speed—no build-up in speed, no set pattern at any time. Time spent stationary between movements also varied from 3 or 4 minutes to 5 or 6 minutes (possibly even longer as I was busy answering questions—listening to theories, guesses, etc., that the conference line people were saying). This continued for some time. After I imagine about 30 to 45 min-

utes, it was decided to scramble two RAF intercep-
tors to investigate. This was done I believe by 3rd
Air Force calling the RAF and, after hearing what
the score was, they scrambled one aircraft. (The
second got off after as I will mention later.)

The interceptor aircraft took off from an RAF station near London and approached Lakenheath from
the southwest. Radio and radar contact was established
with the RAF interceptor aircraft at a point about
30 to 35 miles southwest of Lakenheath, inbound to
Lakenheath. On initial contact we gave the interceptor pilot all the background information on the UFO,
his (the interceptor) present distance and bearing
from Lakenheath, the UFO's (which was stationary
at the time) distance and bearing from Lakenheath.
We explained we did not know the altitude of the
UFO but we could assume his altitude was above
1,500 feet and below 20,000 feet, due to the opera-
tional characteristics of the radar (CPS-5 type radar,
I believe). Also, we mentioned the report from the
C-47 over Sculthorpe that relayed the story about the
light which passed below him. His altitude was
5,000 feet.

We immediately issued heading to the interceptor
to guide him to the UFO. The UFO remained stationary throughout. This vectoring of the intercept
aircraft continued. We continually gave the intercept
aircraft his heading to the UFO and his distance from
the UFO at approximately 1-to-2-mile intervals.
Shortly after we told the intercept aircraft he was
one-half mile from the UFO and it was 12 o'clock
from his position, he said, "Roger, Lakenheath, I've
got my guns locked on him." Then he paused and
said, "Where did he go? Do you still have him?" We
replied, "Roger, it appeared he got behind you and
he's still there." There were now two targets, one behind the other, same speed, very close, but two separate distinct targets.

The first movement by the UFO was so swift
(circling behind the interceptor) I missed it entirely,
but it was seen by the other controllers. However, the
fact that this had occurred was confirmed by the pilot
of the interceptor. The pilot of the interceptor told

me he would try to shake the UFO and would try it again. He tried everything—he climbed, dived, circled, etc., but the UFO acted like it was glued right behind him, always the same distance, very close, but we always had two distinct targets. (Note: Target resolution on our radar at the range they were from the antenna [about 10 to 30 miles, all in the southerly sectors from Lakenheath] would be between 200 and 600 feet probably. Closer than that we would have got one target from both aircraft and UFO. Most specifications say 500 feet is the minimum, but I believe it varied and 200 to 600 feet is closer to the truth and, in addition the tuning of the equipment, atmospheric conditions, etc., also help determine this figure.)

The interceptor pilot continued to try and shake the UFO for about ten minutes (approximate—it seemed longer to both him and us). He continued to comment occasionally and we could tell from the tonal quality he was getting worried, excited and also pretty scared.

He finally said, "I'm returning to station, Lakenheath. Let me know if he follows me. I'm getting low on petrol." The target (UFO) followed him only a short distance, as he headed south/southwest, and the UFO stopped and remained stationary. We advised the interceptor that the UFO target had stopped following and was now stationary about 10 miles south of Lakenheath. He rogered this message and almost immediately the second interceptor called us on the same frequency. We replied and told him we would advise him when we had a radar target, so we could establish radar contact with his aircraft. (He was not on radar at this time, probably had just taken off and was too low for us to pick him up, or too far away—we had most of the scopes on short range, so we could watch the UFO closely on the smaller range.) The number-two interceptor called the number one interceptor by name (Tom, Frank—whatever his name was) and asked him, "Did you see anything?" Number one replied, "I saw something, but I'll be damned if I know what it was." Number two said, "What happened?" Number one then switched frequencies to his home-base frequency. We gave number two the location of the UFO and advised him that we still didn't have him on radar, but probably would have shortly. He delayed answering for some seconds and then finally said, "Lakenheath ———— (identification, aircraft call sign)—can't remember what call sign those aircraft were using. Returning home, my engine is malfunctioning." He then left our frequency.

Throughout this we kept all the agencies, 7th Air Division, 3rd Air Force, etc., advised on every aspect, every word that was said, everything.

We then inquired what action they wanted to take. They had no more suggestions, then finally they told us to just keep watching the target and let them know if anything else happened. The target made a couple more short moves, then left our radar coverage in a northerly direction—speed still about 600 MPH. We lost target outbound to the north at about 50 to 60 miles, which is normal if aircraft or target is at an altitude below 5,000 feet (because of the radiation loss of that type radar). We notified 7th Air Division Command Post and they said they'd tell everybody for us.

I made out a written report on all this, in detail for the officer in charge of my facility, and was told that unless I was contacted later for any further information, he would take care of it. . . . I heard no more about it. . . .

At least three separate times that same night, prior to the telephone contact with the supervisor at Lakenheath, unidentified radar echoes were tracked by the GCA unit at Bentwaters. While those incidents are quite interesting themselves, there was no visual observation involved.

UFOs with Radar?

In the fall of 1948, Project Sign received a report from Kyushu, Japan, describing the encounter of an F-61 aircraft with from two to six unidentified flying objects. Intelligence reports from Far East air forces indicated that the UFOs might have "carried radar warning equipment," because the "object seemed cognizant of the whereabouts of the F-61 at all times."

The sighting took place at about 11:05 P.M. on October 15, 1948, some 50 miles northwest of Fukuoka, off the northwest coast of Kyushu. A statement of January 28, 1949, by 2nd Lt. Barton Halter of the 68th Fighter Squadron, who was radar operator of the F-61, explains the encounter:

My present duties are Radar and Communications Maintenance Officer, and Radar Observer Night Fighter with the 68th Fighter Squadron, 347th Fighter Group (AW), APO 75. On 15 October 1948, my pilot and I started out on a routine mission off the northwest coast of Kyushu. When, at 2305 (11:05 P.M.), we were approximately 50 miles at 330° from Fukuoka, I picked up an airborne target. It showed up at a range of five miles, dead ahead and slightly below us. We increased our speed to approximately 220 MPH and obtained an advantage of 20 MPH. The target showed no evasive action at first, and we thought that it was probably one of the fighter aircraft from our home field. As we closed in, I noticed a slight change in azimuth and a rapid closure between us. Shortly thereafter, a matter of seconds, the target gave the indication of diving beneath us. We dived in an attempt to follow the target and before we could get squared away to follow, it had passed beneath us and was gone. I was notified by my pilot that we were diving at a rate of 3,500 feet a minute at 300 MPH. I had intended to ask the pilot to peel off after it split "S," but it was gone too fast.

The next, or second, interception was from the rear of the target as was the first; however, the target added a burst of speed dead ahead and outdistanced us immediately. On the third interception, my pilot called a visual at 60° portside. By the time I made the pickup it was at 45° port 3,000' and 5° below. My pilot made a rapid starboard turn in an attempt to head off the target. By the time we got astern of it, it was off again in a burst of speed and disappeared between nine (9) and ten (10) miles.

On the fourth interception, the pilot called to me that we had been passed from above from the rear by our target. I picked up the target as it went off my scope from five to ten miles dead ahead and slightly above. On the fifth and sixth interceptions, the target appeared at 9-plus miles doing approximately 200 MPH. We had an advantage of 20 MPH taking our IAS approximately 200 MPH, a safe high-speed cruise for F-61 type aircraft. We closed in to 12,000 feet, then, with a burst of speed the target pulled away to the outer limit of my set which is 10 miles for airborn targets. This took approximately 15 to 20 seconds.

In my opinion, we were shown a new type aircraft by some agency unknown to us. . . .

According to a Project Sign intelligence report, the pilot of the F-61 was able to make out a silhouette of the UFO (it was a clear moonlit night) and he described it as translucent with a very short body and stubby appearance. The object had clean-cut lines and no canopy was discernible. The entire six sightings lasted less than ten minutes with each individual sighting about a minute or so in duration. The UFO's speed varied from between 200 MPH to 1,200 MPH.

An excerpted dispatch from Headquarters, 315th Air Division, to the Commanding General of the Fifth Air Force, of February 28, 1949, relative to this case, contained these interesting comments:

2. It is believed that the object was not lost from the scope due to the normal skip "null" zones common to all radar equipment. *The pilot and observer feel that it was the high rate of speed of the object which enabled it to disappear so rapidly.* [Italics added.]

The pilot of the F-61, 1st Lt. Oliver Hemphill, Jr., had this to say:

I had an excellent silhouette of the target thrown against a very reflective undercast by a full moon. I realized at this time that it did not look like any type aircraft I was familiar with, so I immediately contacted my Ground Control Station and asked for information regarding any aircraft flying in the area.

The ground control radar reported no other aircraft and at no time could they pick up the UFO. Hemphill stated that he again caught "just a fleeting glance of the aircraft (UFO); just enough to know he had passed me," on the fourth sighting.

Project Sign reviewed the Kyushu, Japan, UFO case and ultimately classified it as "Unidentified."

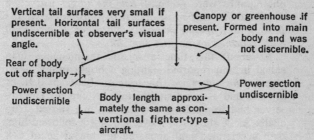

Wing size and shape undiscernible at observer's visual angle.

Vertical tail surfaces very small if present. Horizontal tail surfaces undiscernible at observer's visual angle.

Canopy or greenhouse if present. Formed into main body and was not discernible.

Rear of body cut off sharply →

Power section undiscernible

Power section undiscernible

Body length approximately the same as conventional fighter-type aircraft.

Color or markings undiscernible other than very dull or dark finish.

Silhouette of object seen by Lt. Hemphill and his co-pilot, from an F-61, against "a very reflective undercast by a full moon."

Aircraft, Plasma, Stars???

On October 28, 1956, various missile-crew personnel at Minot, North Dakota, AFB, as well as the crew of a B-52 aircraft, reported observing the erratic flight of one or more UFOs by means of ground visual, air-visual, and air-radar sightings. In addition, the B-52 aircraft that tracked the flight of the UFO took scope photos of the target. The total length of observation of the UFO by ground and airborne observers (combined) was four hours and forty-eight minutes.

Some of the more pertinent details of the sighting are

contained in the following excerpts from a Project Blue
Book Memorandum for the Record, prepared by a Blue
Book staff officer:

At about 0300 hours (3:00 A.M.) local, a B-52
that was about 30 miles northwest of Minot AFB
and making practice penetrations sighted an unidentified blip on their radars. Initially the target traveled
approximately 2½ miles in 3 sec. or at about 3,000
mi/hr. After passing from the right to the left of the
plane it assumed a position off the left wing of the
52. *The blip stayed off the left wing for approximately 20 miles* at which point it broke off. Scope
photographs were taken. *When the target was close
to the B-52 neither of the two transmitters in the
B-52 would operate properly but when it broke off
both returned to normal function.*
At about this time a missile maintenance man
called in and reported sighting a bright orangish-red
object. *The object was hovering* at about 1,000 ft, or
so, and had a sound similar to a jet engine. The observer had stopped his car, but he then started it up
again. As he started to move, the object followed him,
then accelerated and appeared to stop at about 6–8
miles away. The observer shortly afterward lost sight
of it.
In response to the maintenance man's call the
B-52, which had continued its penetration run, was
vectored toward the visual which was about 10 miles
northwest of the base. *The B-52 confirmed having
sighted a bright light of some type that appeared to
be hovering just over or on the ground.*

The Blue Book files contain the reports by fourteen
members of missile maintenance crews from five different
sights at Minot AFB who claimed to have seen a similar
object.
Lt. Quintanella sent a dispatch to Col. Pullen of the
Strategic Air Command advising him that after reviewing
preliminary information submitted by Minot AFB, it was
his belief that the object sighted by the B-52 crew on radar
and visually was "a plasma of the ball-lightning class."

How he made this determination is not explained. As for the sightings by the missile maintenance crew and security guards, he stated that some were "observing some first-magnitude celestial bodies," although he did not explain how such celestial bodies could be magnified to the degree that they would appear to be "as the sun," or give the impression of landing, as reported.

The official Blue Book record card on this case gave at least three "possibles" for the air-visual sighting by the B-52 crew. But no detailed analysis was made, and once again these explanations appear to have been straws grasped simply to close the case—quickly and quietly.

The Provincetown Baffler

Another interesting radar "Unidentified" is the case of a UFO tracked by a Massachusetts Institute of Technology radar observer while in the process of conducting a weather radar project (under a contract with the U.S. Signal Corps). The sighting took place on September 21, 1950. An extract from his letter to Major Tuttle, Staff Weather Officers, 33rd Fighter Wing, Otis Air Force Base, Massachusetts, explains the situation:

An exceedingly puzzling event occurred during the 3rd run when the planes were heading northeast at 30,000 feet. We picked up another plane (?) in the radar beam traveling about due north on a converging course toward the F-86s. It was moving very rapidly and I told the pilots about it, its range and direction from them. The echo caught up with, passed, and then crossed the course of the 86s, suddenly went into a very tight (for the speed) turn to the *right*, headed back toward Boston and passed *directly over our flight.* (Perhaps went under.) The sketch represents, as closely as we can remember, the relative positions of the two planes. Two other observers were with me at the time and we have checked over the facts rather closely. The pilots will undoubtedly recall the incident. They said they didn't see anything which is not too surprising considering the speed of the object and the fact that it may have passed several thousand feet above or below them and still looked like coincidence to the radar. Figuring *conservatively*, the speed of the object was approximately *1200* MPH, and the centrifugal force exerted on the ship during the turn amounted to something more than five *g*'s. It gave an excellent radar echo which could not be mistaken for anything else and in all respects except for the velocity seemed a normal radar target. It passed out of the beam while we continued to track our flight, but we focused on it again for a few seconds shortly after it was rapidly approaching Boston. . . ."

The letter continues with the radar observer expressing disbelief at what he has observed:

The whole thing doesn't seem to make sense as you will discover when you reflect a moment about it. It was very evidently an interception of some sort on our flight, but what? The turn was utterly fantastic, I don't think the human frame could absorb it, but if the object was radio controlled, it had no particular business flying on such courses as planes occupied on legitimate business. A few rough calculations concerning control surfaces, angles, etc., only adds to the puzzle that this object must have been entirely unconventional in many and basic respects. Perhaps the thing that bothers me the most is that it gave a very good radar echo, which implies irregular surfaces and comparatively large size, large enough so the pilots might have had a good chance to see it.

It seems highly probable that I may be poking into something that is none of my business, but on the other hand, it may be something that the Air Force would like to know about if it doesn't already. I wish you would take the matter up with your intelligence officer or C.O. and get their reactions. The whole thing has us going nuts here and we don't know whether to talk about it or keep our mouths shut. Until I hear from you we will do the latter.

Perhaps we could run another mission for the

purpose of luring it out again and this time track it, or at least get your pilots close enough for a look— they'd never catch it I'm sure. . . ."

The officer was told that someone from Otis Air Force Base would contact him concerning the sighting. However, he was never approached and no further information about the case was released.

Blue Book Boner

On the afternoon of May 21, 1949, an F-82 fighter was dispatched from Moses Lake AFB, near Hanford, Washington, to intercept a flying disc that was observed hovering in restricted air space over the Hanford Atomic Plant at an altitude of 17,000 to 20,000 feet. The silvery, disc-shaped object had been visually sighted by crew and personnel from the Hanford radar station, and confirmed on radar.

A call quickly went from the Hanford station to Moses Lake AFB, but before the F-82 was airborne, the disc suddenly took off in a southerly direction at a speed greater than that of a jet fighter! The Air Intelligence Information Report on this case states that the pilot of the F-82 was instructed to search for the object and "intercept it in hopes that it might be a disk." However, the object had sped out of the range of ground radar and the pilot of the F-82 was not able to locate it. A short time later, another aircraft was observed on radar in the restricted air space of the Hanford Atomic Plant. This one was positively "identified"—as a commercial aircraft dropping leaflets announcing a rodeo!

Yes, you guessed it, Blue Book files carry this UFO sighting under the classification of "aircraft," based on the assumption that the commercial aircraft and the UFO were one and the same object. This, despite the following comment by the investigating officer:

It is believed that two separate and distinct alert conditions existed on the afternoon of 21 May 1949. The first was caused by the sightings of Flying Saucers (noted) by Hanford using a telescope and the operations crew of the 637th ADCC. The second was caused by the dropping of leaflets by an aircraft into the Hanford area. It is believed that there is no connection between the two events.

UFOs at Oak Ridge

I have saved for last what I consider to be one of the most interesting radar and visual cases (although the radar and the visual were reported from different locations) in the Blue Book files. It is interesting not only for the sightings themselves, but because of the location—the Atomic Energy Commission's plant at Oak Ridge, Tennessee, the qualifications of the witnesses, and the comments contained in the report, classified SECRET, from the FBI Field Office, Knoxville, Tennessee, to the Commanding General of the Third Army, and the Atomic Energy Commission's Security Division at Oak Ridge.

In typical fashion, Project Grudge wrote off the radar contacts in a rather casual manner, calling them probable "weather anomalies," even though detailed weather reports were never obtained. As for the visual sighting—a very good one, as we shall see—the Grudge report had this to say:

> While it is impossible to definitely explain the phenomenon observed visually by people in the area, many of the details reported follow the pattern of reports on other incidents on which conclusions were drawn to the effect that people saw weather balloons, peculiar clouds or smoke formations, aircraft through an overcast, etc. Evidence to the effect that such sightings were made by numerous people usually breaks down since, in most cases, a would-be object is first reported by one individual and the number of subsequent reports is usually determined by the publicity surrounding the incident.

There is no doubt that a number of incidents *had* occurred at Oak Ridge, Tennessee, beginning in June of 1947, when a photograph of a UFO was taken by a civilian. The source of this information is a chronological

FBI summary of the reported events between June 1947 and October 16, 1950, in Blue Book files. But, was the Project Grudge investigating officer's analysis correct when he said that, based on prior experience, the witnesses to this event were probably just seeing things that had a natural explanation? Perhaps one should read the report of the FBI field agent about these cases before arriving at a final conclusion. Here is the kernel of that report:

> . . . The most reliable sources available were utilized in the compilation of this report. The employment records and the Federal Bureau of Investigation reports concerning the witnesses were inspected to ascertain their reliability, integrity, and loyalty to the United States Government.
>
> The opinions of the officials of the Security Division, AED, Oak Ridge; Security Branch, NEPA Division, Oak Ridge; AEC Security Patrol, Oak Ridge; FBI, Knoxville; Air Force Radar and Fighter Squadrons, Knoxville; and the OSI, Knoxville, Tennessee, fail to evolve an adequate explanation for SUBJECT; however the possibilities of practical jokers, mass hysteria, balloons of any description, flights of birds (with or without cobwebs or other objects attached), falling kites, objects thrown from the ground, windblown objects, insanity, and many other natural happenings have been rejected because of the detailed, similar descriptions of the objects seen by different persons; and because of impossibility.

In my many years with Project Blue Book, I observed similar dismissals of radar cases. Indeed, in the Congressional Hearings of April 5, 1966,* Major Quintanilla, then head of Blue Book, stated (but not under oath) in answer to a question by Congressman Schweiker, that all radar cases had been solved.

Mr. Schweiker: "No, the first question he asked you was, have any of the unexplained objects been sighted on

*From the Hearing by Committee on Armed Services of the House of Representatives, 89th Congress, April 5, 1966, p. 6073.

radar. I thought you said 'No' to that just a couple of minutes ago."

Major Quintanilla: "That is correct. We have no radar cases which are unexplained."

7

UFOs CLOSE UP: CLOSE ENCOUNTERS OF THE FIRST KIND

"I can assure you, once anyone has seen an object such as this so closely and for a period of even one minute, it would be etched in their memory for all time."

—from a June 1955 UFO report

The above statement well characterizes the Close Encounter of the First Kind, a sighting that is close up but which "does" little more than firmly impress itself into the memory of the witness. It is often a frightening experience, and always an awesome one, but when it is over there are no visible marks or other evidence of it. The event is so unusual, so traumatic generally, that even when a camera has been available (and many witnesses have confessed that they did have a camera in an automobile glove compartment or otherwise close at hand) we have no record of its having been used.

Close Encounters of all types are hard to dismiss as misidentifications of familiar objects; it is hard to label a large object reportedly sighted just a few hundred feet away as Venus or a helicopter. Venus is obviously too small-appearing, and a helicopter at a few hundred feet could hardly fail to be recognized for what it was. Project Blue Book, operating as always on the hypothesis that such strange phenomena *must* have a simple, natural explanation, was obviously hard pressed to find such, and therefore resorted to considering reports of this kind to be hoaxes or the results of fevered imaginations. Failing that, they reached for even the most remotely possible, though improbable, natural explanation. Occasionally they capitulated and called these sightings "Unidentified."

The Case of the Vigorous Weather Balloon

Take the case of the "weather balloon" that on May 19, 1960, in Dillingham, Alaska, reportedly picked up two empty five-gallon cans, swirled them in the air, and carried them for many yards. It also swirled dead grass into the air.

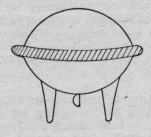

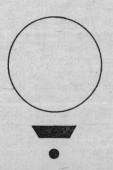

The sighting at Dillingham, Alaska, of May 19, 1960. Drawings by the witnesses taken directly from the Blue Book files.

The original teletype message that came into Wright-Patterson Air Force Base, and also went to the Secretary of the Air Force, to Headquarters, USAF, and to several other receiving points, read as follows:

(1) CIRCULAR IN PLAN, ROUGHLY FOOTBALL SHAPED CROSS SECTION.
(2) TWENTY TO TWENTY-FIVE FEET IN DIAMETER, TEN TO TWELVE FEET IN THICKNESS.
(3) METALLIC, SILVERY WHITE, COMPARED TO ALUMINUM.
(4) ONE OBJECT
(5) N/A
(6) TWO FLEXIBLE TUBES OR FLAPS APPROXIMATELY FOUR TO FIVE FEET LONG/DEPENDING/FROM EDGE. A SEMICIRCULAR, WHIRLING DEVICE IN CENTER OF BOTTOM.
(7) THE SOUND WAS DESCRIBED AS A WHIRRING WITH A SUCKING SOUND WHEN FINALLY ASCENDING. THE OBSERVERS DID NOT SEE ANY WINDOW.

The local investigator added:

The natives who observed the object stated that it came within two hundred feet of them. Several of the observers drew sketches that were very similar. When the object rose into the air, a sucking noise was heard and grass was sucked up from the ground. . . . In the past, natives have often proved to be accurate and reliable observers of unusual occurrences in the Alaskan area. No reasonable explanation of the object is readily apparent. Request your opinion whether on-the-spot investigation and interrogation of the observers by this office is warranted.

Is further investigation "warranted" indeed! One would think that natural curiosity alone, never mind national security or scientific considerations, would have made such a question academic. And in fact, a further investigation of sorts was made. Following is the report to Blue Book by the chief of intelligence division of the local base in Alaska, who interviewed the witnesses:

Mr. ——— saw the object at close range. He is a deaf-mute native and communicated his sighting to his brother, Ed. The following account was given by Ed, speaking for his brother. "Jim was in the yard of the ——— house when he saw the object flying along the ridge. He noticed that it created considerable suction, in fact, enough to pick up two empty five-gallon cans and swirl them in the air below the object. He was alarmed because some very small children were playing in the area and he was afraid that they would be sucked up. The object passed about fifty to one hundred feet from him and just cleared electric wires, estimated to be about twelve feet from the ground. Apparently, the cans were carried from one side of the ridge on which the houses stand to the other, a distance of possibly one hundred yards. The object passed between the houses, dipped slightly into the ravine and ascended at an extremely high rate of speed. As it ascended, it whirled dead grass from the meadow high into the air after it." ——— drew a picture of the object and described it as follows: it was quite round with a projection on the ends at the center line. Whether this was "fore and aft" or a flange all the way around could not be determined. There was a red band around the object between the projections. On the bottom were two appendages which moved in an undulating motion (the motion was described with arm movements). Also, in the center bottom was a half-moon object which whirled at varying speeds. Apparently, when the object descended rapidly, it whirled very fast. According to ———'s account, the angle of incidence to the object of these appendages and the half-moon object changed, but because of language difficulties, it was impossible to determine what relationship this had with the movement of the object except that it possibly occurred when it turned. The object was about as big as an automobile and was silver in color. Ed felt certain that it was not a balloon and it was metallic. It was impossible to determine the three-dimensional shape of the object. It is difficult to assess the reliability of these persons but it is probably at least average. Conversa-

tion with ——— indicated no reason to doubt the
veracity of either him or his brother. There was some
language difficulty in communication with ———.

Blue Book files further indicate that at the time of the
sightings, the weather was clear, that a breeze about fifteen miles per hour was blowing, and that the object was
headed pretty much *into* the wind.

Comments of the Preparing Officer were as follows:

"There still appears to be no logical explanation of the
sighting. It is quite obvious that an object was sighted.
Whether all of the details of the sighting are correct can
not be ascertained; however, there is no reason to doubt
their essential accuracy. At any rate, it does not appear
that a commonplace object such as an airplane or a balloon was responsible for the sighting."

Once again we have Blue Book grasping at a bit of irrelevant information undocumented, incidentally—the
statement on the UFO analysis that "there was a WX
balloon with a radar reflector which crossed the area at
the time of the sighting."

Where the information about the weather balloon came
from is not stated, nor is launch time given. But Blue
Book accepted the weather-balloon statement and completely disregarded the witnesses' reports that they saw
the object within a range of two hundred feet. Furthermore, they disregarded the sucking noise, the swirling
grass, and the reported movement of the empty five-gallon
cans. And, finally, they disregarded the statement of the
local intelligence officer. One can almost imagine the Blue
Book train of thought: "There was a weather balloon
around about that time; so, it has got to be that!"

The Incredible Flying Carpet

Here is one straight out of Grimm's *Fairy Tales* or *The
Arabian Nights*—a flying-carpet-type UFO (infant-sized),
observed by some ten employees of the McDonnell Aircraft Corporation in St. Louis, Missouri! It is informative
to read the Naval Speed Letter submitted by the Bureau
of Aeronautics representative of the McDonnell Aircraft
Corporation:

Subject: Unidentified flying object; reporting of FLYOBRPT. In accordance with Ninth Naval District Instruction 3820.1 of 28 July 1954, the following is submitted for information:

1. Shape—irregular rectangle; size—18″ x 18″ x 8″; color—pale milky white; number—one; aerodynamic features—none; trail or exhaust—none; propulsion system—none observed; speed—3–8 MPH; sound—none; maneuvers—approach from East, descending from 30 feet to ground, stopped on ground, elevated to 4 feet, right-angle turn to North, advanced approximately 75 feet to 8-foot cyclone fence, rose over fence to disappear in overcast. Appeared opaque and consistency of cotton candy or spun glass.

2. Sighted approximately 0750 CDT on 14 July 1954 for approximately 3–5 minutes.

3. Visual observation only from ground and automobiles.

4. Location of observers—in driveway and parking lot of Propulsion Laboratory, McDonnell Aircraft Corporation, St. Louis, Missouri. Location of object with respect to observers—4–200 feet. Object observed from ground, and from passing automobile affording downward view.

5. Estimated 10 observers, 5 reporting. All McDonnell employees with aeronautical experience.

6. Weather and winds—overcast, Southeast light and variable, 2–6 MPH.

7. No activity or condition which might account for sighting.

8. No photographs taken. Search revealed no fragments.

9. Object followed by one observer at approximately 5-foot distance. No attempt made to contact.

All observers believed completely reliable. Observers could not identify as any known material. Proximity lends credence to experience.

Lateness of report due to this activity having been only recently advised of sighting.

C. H. S. Murphy

DISTRIBUTION LIST

Director of Intelligence
Headquarters, USAF
Washington 25, D.C.

Air Technical Intelligence Center (ATIAA-2C)
Wright-Patterson Air Force Base, Ohio

Commander, Air Defense Command
Ent Air Force Base
Colorado Springs, Colorado

Commander, Eastern Air Defense Force
Stewart Air Force Base
Newburgh, New York

This report went to the Director of Intelligence of the
United States Air Force, Blue Book, the Air Defense
Command in Colorado Springs, and the Commander of
the Eastern Air Defense Force, and *all* of them let Blue
Book get away with the evaluation "*debris in wind.*" The
wind, you will remember, was southeast light and variable,
two to six miles per hour. This gentle wind allowed the
object to descend from thirty feet to the ground, stop on
the ground, elevate it to four feet, make a right-angle turn
to the north and advance approximately seventy-five feet
to an eight-foot cyclone fence, rise over the fence and disappear upward into the overcast! Apparently, very little
attention was paid to the contents of the report itself.

The Case of the Dogs and the Derby Hat

On March 13, 1957, the owner of a shooting preserve
wrote the USAF Filter Center in Trenton the following
letter:

> I have learned (belatedly) that your office is the
> proper place to report the sighting of an unidentified
> flying object described in the enclosed affidavit by my
> wife. . . . We would be most interested to know if
> my wife's experience tallies in any respect with any

sightings by anyone else in this area on or about
March 6.

We wish absolutely no publicity for ourselves in
this connection.

The affidavit signed and sworn to by Mrs. ———— reads
as follows:

Even at the risk of being called hysterical, hallucinated or worse, I feel I must make record, on my
oath as a woman, an American and a member of the
human race, of the following:

That I saw an airborne object which bore no re-
semblance to any airplane, helicopter or balloon ever
made and flown by man, so far as I know.

That I was in full possession of my senses and my
sanity at the time, and all during the time, of my
seeing this object, which lasted for at least one minute.

That I saw the object at a distance of not more
than 150 yards at about 2 P.M. on Wednesday,
March 6, 1957, first from a rear window and then
from out in the back yard of our home on the road
from Great Meadows to Hope, New Jersey.

That the weather was clear under a low overcast,
and the position of the object hovering in the air
over the slope below our house was such that I could
see it—and hear it—with absolute certainty and with
concentrated effort to observe and remember every
detail.

That my attention was first drawn to the *object's
presence by our dogs barking in their pens* behind the
house, and by their looking upward at the object, as
they and I continued to do so easily until the object
departed.

That the shape of the object closely resembled that
of a huge derby hat with a rounded domelike crown
30 to 40 feet high, and at least 50 feet in horizontal
diameter above a slightly curled-up "brim" that extended outward for 12 or 15 feet from the bottom of
the crown. This brim or bottom surface of the object
appeared to be sealed over smoothly and completely
in a gentle curve, with no holes or ports or windows

An admitted hoax. A hubcap was tossed out and photographed "for fun" but the fun got out of hand, and the hoax was admitted. The obvious similarity to Daylight Disc photographs (believed to be authentic) demonstrates the need for great care in analysis.

Donnybrook, N.D., Aug. 19, 1966. One of the indentations allegedly left by a 30 x 15 foot dome-topped craft, reported by a Border Patrol officer who stated that the object first hovered 20–30 feet over a reservoir. The officer, in the process of taking a prisoner to Canada, stated that he wished no publicity and would deny any knowledge of this event if his name was used. His first instinct, he stated, was to pull a revolver and empty it into the craft, but fear of the unknown restrained him. The officer is personally known to the author, and is at present an investigator with the Treasury Department.

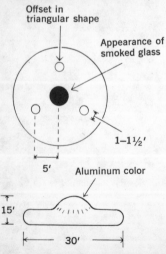

Offset in triangular shape

Appearance of smoked glass

1–1½′

5′

Aluminum color

15′

30′

Drawing of object sighted by Border Patrol officer at Donnybrook, N.D., Aug. 19, 1966.

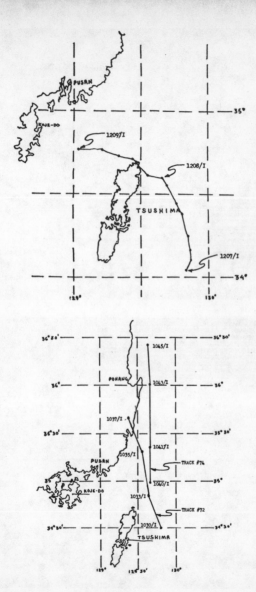

Examples of radar plots made in the Korean War Zone during 1952. Note the continuous tracks and the distances covered in successive minutes. No satisfactory explanation exists for these observations.

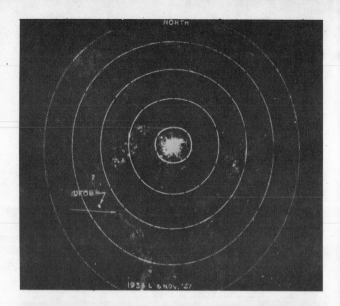

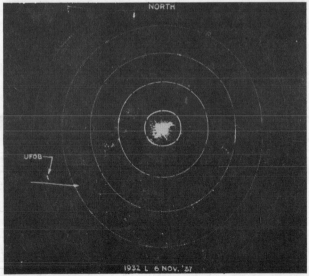

Examples of radarscope photos from Blue Book files showing appearance and motion of unidentified object during successive radar sweeps.

Officer Zamora (right), the principal witness to the Socorro landing case. Sgt. Chavez (left), who arrived minutes after Zamora said the craft had departed, verified the smoldering bushes and the ''landing marks'' on the ground.

A ''UFO'' photograph submitted to Blue Book from Japan. Photographic experts hold this to be merely a photographic defect.

The controversial Barra de Tijuca photograph—one of five taken by two photographers from *O Cruzeiro* magazine, Rio de Janeiro, on an expedition to the Ilha des Amores for the purpose of photographing amorous couples. They returned with these photographs instead, claiming them to be absolutely authentic and asking $25,000 for the five negatives. They found no takers. Taken on May 7, 1952.

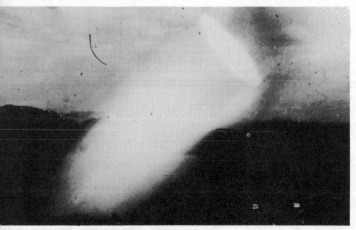

Norway, July 24, 1957. The photographer, an unsuspecting tourist, was photographing the Norwegian scenery and found to her surprise that a "UFO" appeared when the film was developed. The author interviewed the photographer and found that the photographs on the same roll taken just before and after the one shown were normal. No explanation for this "UFO" has been found.

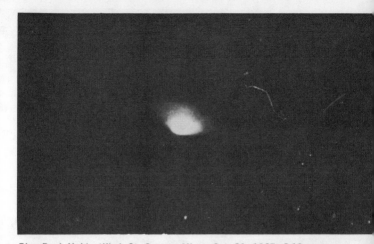

Blue Book Unidentified: St. George, Minn., Oct. 21, 1965, 6:10 P.M.
The dark sky was cloudless as five witnesses observed this pulsating light hover for five minutes and then shoot off "at a tremendous speed overhead." Color photo taken with 804 Instamatic camera.

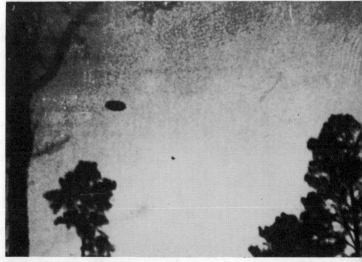

Photo taken by a 15-year-old boy in Hampton, Va., on Jan. 25, 1967. Object was stated to be the size of a Piper Cub airplane at 1000 feet altitude. Capt. Cauley, the Air Force investigator, stated: "In my opinion the photo is authentic. Mr. ———— seems quite intelligent for his age and I am including his description of this sighting as he presented it to his science teacher. The teacher instructed him to report it to the Air Force."

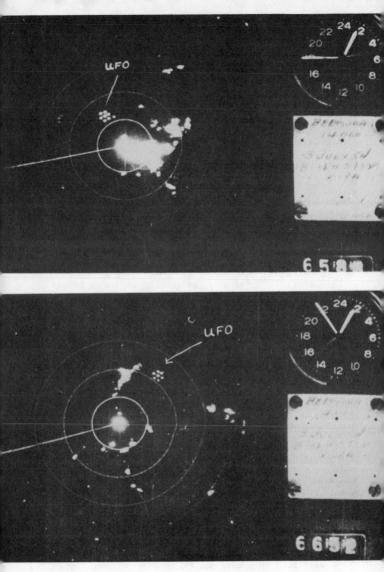

Official radarscope photos of UFOs off Bermuda, taken on July 3, 1954. Blue Book identified these as a battleship and six accompanying destroyers but the experienced radar operator stated that the radar returns were definitely unidentified and unlike any ship returns he had ever seen.

The now famous Trent photographs taken at McMinnville, Ore., May 1950. Two independent detailed photometric studies argue that these photographs are of a relatively distant object, and hence are not fakes.

Two of the photographs of the Trindade, Brazil, Daylight Disc.

Daylight Disc at Bear Mountain State Park, Dec. 18, 1966.

The much publicized Salem, Mass., UFO photograph taken by a Coast Guard photographer. This has almost conclusively been shown to be a photograph of interior lights reflected from the windowpane.

Actual airport radar room and professional air traffic controllers. Although this is a scene from the motion picture *Close Encounters of the Third Kind*, it illustrates the manner in which an unidentified object would actually be observed on radar.

Landing site at Socorro, N.M. (April 24, 1964), showing "landing pod" marks and greasewood bushes, some of which were charred.

Close-up of one of the four "landing pod" marks. (Stones were placed around these marks within a few hours of the event to protect and mark the evidence.)

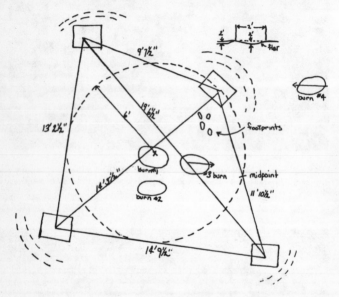

Map by W. T. Powers of the dimensions and relationship of the various features at the reported Socorro landing site.

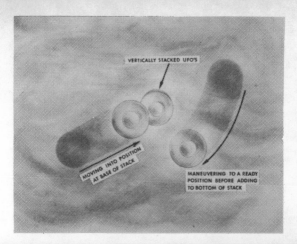

VERTICALLY STACKED UFO'S

MOVING INTO POSITION AT BASE OF STACK

MANEUVERING TO A READY POSITION BEFORE ADDING TO BOTTOM OF STACK

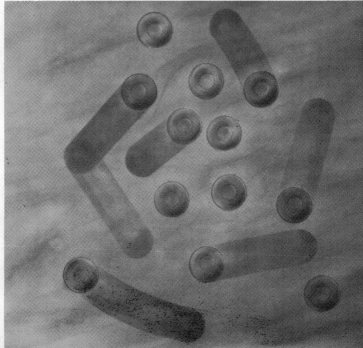

The Flying Discs of 1936, as drawn from memory by the witness, Mr. Richard Keller, now a professional commercial artist.

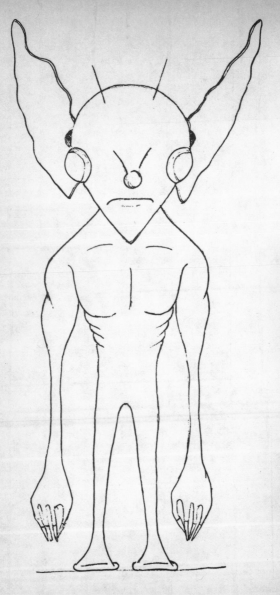

Artist's reproduction of the Kelly-Hopkinsville creatures, as seen by one male witness the day after the event. Drawing by Mr. Bud Ledwith, an associate of the author's for several years.

or vents of any kind, of which I could see none anywhere else on the entire object.

That, in the absence of any openings into it, I could
see no beings, human or otherwise, inside the object
who might be operating and riding in it, and no crew
or passengers were visible on the object's exterior
during its visit.

That the color of the object, all over, was a uniform white, dull but clean, with no spots, stripes or
other markings whatsoever. Its texture was apparently non-metallic but reminded me strongly of pipe
clay.

That a moderate breeze, from the northeast I think,
was blowing in which the object hovered quite stationary except for a gentle rocking motion, *like a
boat at anchor on water*. As the object rocked and in
the same cadence it made a low growling or rumbling
sound that rose and fell irregularly.

That beneath the object, extending vertically toward the ground, I seemed to see, and then not see,
and then see again, a lot of streamers or lines of
some material (or force) that twinkled like the frag-
ile strands of tinsel with which one decorates a
Christmas tree.

That without any marked change of sound except
a soft rush of air, sucking away and not blowing toward me, the object abruptly ascended almost vertically, slightly northeasterly at immense speed into the
thick cloud cover (maybe 300? feet up) and was
instantly gone from sight and hearing.

Within an hour of my experience my husband
telephoned me from New York City. I told him
what I had seen, and told him again in fuller detail
when I joined him at 7:20 that evening in the city.
At his insistence I later that evening repeated my account and answered many questions while my memory was still fresh at the home and in the presence
of Mr. and Mrs. ———, 35th Street, N.Y.C. I told
my story reluctantly again to several other friends in
the next three days (March 7, 8 and 9), *but made no
formal report to any authorities, fearing ridicule.*

The Air Force got around this one by labeling it "insufficient information." Their summary card merely states:

> Huge white UFO shaped like a derby hat hovering low over field with shimmering rays below. Had a rocking motion, undulating rumbling sound. Finally, shot skyward to northeast. Dogs barked.

The Air Force made no attempt to gain further information.

The "Incident at Exeter"

"Incident" is hardly the term for this classic Close Encounter case which is known to virtually all who have followed the UFO phenomenon. This encounter at Exeter, New Hampshire, gained national prominence, and caused both the original witnesses and the Air Force considerable embarrassment. Not only is this a fine example of a Close Encounter of the First Kind, but it is a showcase illustration of Blue Book negligence, put-down of witnesses, attempts to explain away the testimony of responsible witnesses with a parade of "official" explanations, and of capitulation on the part of the Pentagon which, months later, had to admit that the case should have been carried as "Unidentified." The file folders in Blue Book, however, still have the original evaluation of "Astro-Stars/ Planets" and "Aircraft from Operation Big Blast." (The astronomical evaluation is completely untenable and Operation Big Blast terminated more than an hour before the incident at Exeter began. according to official records.)

The story of this case is well documented in John Fuller's book *The Incident at Exeter*, and in an excellent report by Raymond Fowler and his associates, who did a far better job investigating the case than did Blue Book. I am indebted to Mr. Fowler for the excerpts from his report that follow. Blue Book files on this case are fairly extensive in themselves although they draw heavily on the report by Mr. Fowler.

Blue Book's first mention of the incident at Exeter is dated October 15, 1965, and comes in the form of a request from the Headquarters of the 817th Air Division

(SAC) at Pease AFB, New Hampshire. Written by their Director of Information, for the Commander, and addressed to the Information Officer at Wright-Patterson AFB, it reads:

There have been an unusually high number of reported sightings of unidentified flying objects in the Pease AFB, New Hampshire, area which have been the subject of much discussion and numerous newspaper, radio, and television reports. Many of these sightings have been reported to this base and your records will show that we have performed thorough investigations of them. . . . Several members of this command have actually been called to view UFOs by sincere and sober citizens but as yet, we have always been too late or "unlucky." The most interesting sighting, in the nearby town of Exeter, aroused special interest as two policemen saw the object at very close range. . . .

This office has, of course, not commented on sightings reported to the Air Force other than to say that they have been or are being investigated, that the reports will be sent to your organization, that further releases will be made from the Public Information Office of the Secretary of the Air Force, etc. The fact that we cannot comment on the investigations has led to somewhat alarming suspicion of Air Force motives and interest in this area, the most popular belief being that ". . . the Air Force won't release the truth because if the truth were known, everyone would be panicked." I have attempted to counter this by explaining the USAF's interest in this matter every time I speak to the press or private citizens about this matter. . . . Still, however, an alarming number of people remain unconvinced [!].

Many members of the two nearby Military Affairs committees and key citizens from surrounding towns and cities have inquired concerning the possibility of an Air Force speaker on this subject. Do you operate a speaker's bureau or would you be able to suggest where I might be able to obtain knowledge of an Air Force spokesman who could explain the Air Force

UFO program and what happens to reports sent to your organization? If speakers from your organization are available, it might be possible for us to arrange transportation via Pease Base C-47. Billeting poses no problem.

Your assistance is greatly appreciated.

For the Commander
A.B.B., 1st Lt. USAF
Director of Information

The initial report which came in from Pease AFB on September 15, 1965, was the soul of brevity.

The following report of an unidentified object is hereby submitted in accordance with AFR-200-2.

A) Description of Object
    1) round
    2) baseball
    3) bright red
    4) five red lights in a row
    5) lights were close together and moved as one object
    6) none
    7) none
    8) none
    9) extremely bright red

B) Description of Course of Object
    1) visual sighting
    2) object was at an altitude of approximately 100 feet and moved in an arc of 135 degrees
    3) object disappeared at an altitude of approximately one hundred feet on a magnetic heading of approximately 160 degrees
    4) the object was erratic in movement and would disappear behind houses and buildings in the area. It would then appear at a position other than where it disappeared. When in view, it would act as a floating leaf.
    5) object departed on a heading of 160 de-

grees and was observed until it disappeared in the distance

6) one hour

C) Manner of Observation
   1) ground-visual
   2) none
   3) N/A

D) Time and Date of Sighting
   1) 3/9/0600 Z
   2) night

E) Location of Observer
   1) 3 nautical miles SW of Exeter in New Hampshire

F) Identifying Information of Observer
   1) civilian, Norman J. Muscarello, age 18 . . . appears to be reliable
   2) civilian, Eugene F. Bertrand, Jr., age 30, Exeter Police Department, Exeter, New Hampshire, patrolman, reliable
   3) civilian, David R. Hunt, age 28, Exeter Police Department, Exeter, New Hampshire, patrolman, reliable

G) Weather and Winds
   1) weather was clear with no known weather phenomena. There was a five-degree inversion from surface to 5,000'.
   2) winds at Pease AFB (the winds were uniformly from the west, low velocity near the surface to quite high above 10,000')
   3) clear (unlimited)
   4) 30 nautical miles
   5) none
   6) none

H) None

I) None

J) None

K) Major David H. Griffin, Base Disaster Control Officer, Command pilot
   1) at this time I have been unable to arrive at a probable cause of this sighting. The three observers seem to be stable, reliable persons, especially the two patrolmen. I viewed the area of the sighting and found

nothing in the area that could be the probable cause. Pease AFB had five B-47 aircraft flying in the area during this period but I do not believe that they had any connection with this sighting.

The report in Blue Book continues with the statements of the three witnesses involved. The first, from Norman Muscarello, follows:

I, Norman J. Muscarello, was hitchhiking on Rt. 150, three miles south of Exeter, New Hampshire, at 0200 hours on the 3rd of September. A group of five bright red lights appeared over a house about a hundred feet from where I was standing. The lights were in a line at about a sixty-degree angle. They were so bright, they lighted up the area. The lights then moved out over a large field and acted at times like a floating leaf. They would go down behind the trees, behind a house and then reappear. They always moved in the same sixty-degree angle. Only one light would be on at a time. They were pulsating: one, two, three, four, five, four, three, two, one. They were so bright I could not distinguish a form to the object. I watched these lights for about fifteen minutes and they finally disappeared behind some trees and seemed to go into a field. At one time while I was watching them, they seemed to come so close I jumped into a ditch to keep from being hit. After the lights went into a field, I caught a ride to the Exeter Police Station and reported what I had seen.

Signed,
Norman J. Muscarello

The statement from the first patrolman, who after being called to the scene also witnessed the UFO:

I, Eugene F. Bertrand, Jr., was cruising on the morning of the 3rd of September at 0100 on Rt. 108 bypass near Exeter, New Hampshire. I noticed an automobile parked on the side of the road and stopped to investigate. I found a woman in the car who stated she was too upset to drive. She stated that a light had been following her car and had stopped over her car. I stayed with her about fifteen minutes but was unable to see anything. I departed and reported back to Exeter Police Station where I found Norman Muscarello. He related his story of seeing some bright red lights in the field. After talking with him a while, I decided to take him back to where he stated that he had seen the lights. When we had gone about fifty feet, a group of five bright red lights came from behind a group of trees near us. They were extremely bright and flashed on one at a time. The lights started to move around over the field. At one time, they came so close I fell to the ground and started to draw my gun. The lights were so bright, I was unable to make out any form. There was no sound or vibration but the farm animals were upset in the area and were making a lot of noise. When the lights started coming near us again, Mr. Muscarello and I ran to the car. I radioed Patrolman David Hunt who arrived in a few minutes. He also observed the lights which were still over the field but not as close as before. The lights moved out across the field at an estimated altitude of one hundred feet, and finally disappeared in the distance at the same altitude. The lights were always in line at about a sixty-degree angle. When the object moved, the lower lights were always forward of the others.

Signed,
Eugene F. Bertrand, Patrolman

From the third witness:

I, David R. Hunt, at about 0255 on the morning of the 3rd of September, received a call from Patrolman Bertrand to report to an area about three miles southwest of Exeter, New Hampshire. Upon arriving at the scene, I observed a group of bright red lights flashing in sequence. They appeared to be about one half mile over a field to the southeast. After observing the lights for a short period of time, they moved off in a southeasterly direction and dis-

appeared in the distance. The lights appeared to remain at the same altitude which I estimate to be
about one hundred feet.

Signed,
David R. Hunt, Patrolman

Blue Book's way of dealing with these witnesses' reports was to make every effort to locate some type of aircraft operation in the area in question; none was successful.

A news clip from the Amesbury *News*, Massachusetts,
stated that the UFO was identified as an "ad gimmick";
but Ray Fowler checked with the Skylight Aerial Advertising Company and was advised that their aircraft was
not flying on the night of September 3. He was also
informed that the company aircraft rarely flew into
southern New Hampshire, and when it did, it was usually in the Salem and Manchester areas, miles away from
Exeter. Furthermore, he learned that the "Skylight" aircraft does not carry red flashing lights; it carries a rectangular sign with white flashing lights. Yet the manager
of the advertising company had stated to the Amesbury
News that "perhaps some UFOs reported in the New
Hampshire area could have been their aircraft." Unfortunately, the press anxiously latched on to this bit of irrelevant information to "explain" the Exeter case.

The two simultaneous investigations of this case are an
interesting study in contrasts. The Air Force records are
at best sketchy, and focus essentially on attempts at lo-
cating existing aircraft in the area; as usual, Blue Book
started out its investigation with a negative premise. On
the other hand, Raymond Fowler and his associates made
an exhaustive examination of the case, keeping their
minds open at all times. Their final reports were duly
submitted to Blue Book.

The following is excerpted from Fowler's report, which
supplements Muscarello's statement to the Air Force investigator:

Muscarello reported the incident to Desk Officer
Reginald Towland at about 1:45 A.M. EDT. Side view
and angle view seen. He was hit with fear and hardly

able to talk. A radio call was made to Officer Bertrand asking him to return to the station, pick up Muscarello, and investigate at the scene of the sighting which he did. Upon arriving at the Carl Dining field, the object was nowhere to be seen. After waiting and looking from the cruiser for several minutes, Bertrand radioed headquarters that there was nothing there and that the boy must have been imagining things. It was then suggested that he examine the field before returning, so Bertrand and Muscarello advanced into the field. As the police officer played his flashlight beam back and forth over the field, Muscarello sighted the object rising slowly from behind some nearby trees and shouted. Bertrand swung around and saw a large dark object carrying a straight row of four extraordinarily bright, red, pulsating lights coming into the field at treetop level. It swung around toward them and just clearing a sixty- to seventy-foot tree and seemingly only one hundred feet away from them. Instinctively, Officer Bertrand drew his service revolver (he stated that Muscarello shouted, "Shoot it!"), but thinking this unwise, replaced it and yelled to Muscarello to take cover in the cruiser. He told me (Fowler) that he was afraid that they both would be burnt by the blinding lights closing in on them. They ran to the cruiser where Bertrand immediately put in a radio call to headquarters for assistance. Officer Hunt arrived within minutes, and the trio observed the object move away over and below the tree line.

Now let us return to the Blue Book coverage for a look at an interesting exchange of letters between the then Major Quintanilla and the police officers involved. Quintanilla states:

Our investigations and evaluation of the sighting indicates a possible association with the Air Force operation "Big Blast." In addition to aircraft from this operation, there were five (5) B-47 aircraft flying in the area during this period. Before final evaluation of your sighting can be made, it is essential for us to know if either of you witnessed any aircraft in the area during this time period, either independently or in connection with the observed object. Since there were many aircraft in the area, at the time, and there were no reports of unidentified objects from personnel engaged in this air operation, we might then assume that the objects observed between midnight and two A.M. might be associated with this military air operation. If, however, these aircraft were noted by either of you, this would tend to eliminate this air operation as a possible explanation for the objects observed.

> Signed,
> Hector Quintanilla, Jr.
> Major, USAF, Chief,
> Project Blue Book

It is interesting to note that Maj. Quintanilla had used the term "before a final evaluation of your sighting can be made," whereas the Pentagon had in fact already issued its evaluation (attributing the sighting to Operation Big Blast) some time before Quintanilla wrote his letter.

Maj. Quintanilla received a prompt reply from Officers Bertrand and Hunt. Their letter of December 2, 1965, reads:

Dear Sir:

We were very glad to get your letter during the third week in November, because as you might imagine, we have been the subject of considerable ridicule since the Pentagon released its "final evaluation" of our sighting of September 3, 1965. In other words, both Patrolman Hunt and myself saw this object at close range, checked it out with each other, confirmed and reconfirmed the fact that this was not any kind of conventional aircraft, that it was at an altitude of not more than a couple of hundred feet and went to considerable trouble to confirm that the weather was clear, there was no wind, no chance of weather inversion, and that what we were seeing was in no way a military or civilian craft. We entered this in a complete official police report as a supplement to the blotter of the morning of September 3rd (not September 2 as your letter indicates).

Since our job depends on accuracy and the ability to tell the difference between fact and fiction, we were naturally disturbed by the Pentagon report issued which attributed the sighting to "multiple high-altitude objects in area" and "weather inversion." What is a little difficult to understand is the fact that your letter arrived considerably after the Pentagon release. Since your letter says that you are still in the process of making a final evaluation, it seems that there is an inconsistency here. Ordinarily, this would not be too important except for the fact that in a situation like this, we are naturally very reluctant to be considered irresponsible in our official report to the police station. One of us (Patrolman Bertrand) was in the Air Force for four years, engaged in refueling operations, with all kinds of military aircraft; it was impossible to mistake what we saw for any kind of military operation, regardless of altitude. It was also definitely not a helicopter or balloon. Immediately after the object disappeared, we did see what probably was a B-47 at high altitudes, but it bore no relation to the object that we saw.

Another fact is that the time of our observation was nearly an hour after two A.M. which would eliminate the Air Force Operation Big Blast since as you say, this took place between midnight and 2 A.M. Norman Muscarello, who first reported this object before we went to the site, saw it somewhere in the vicinity of 2 A.M. but nearly an hour had passed before he got to the police station and we went out to the location with him.

We would both appreciate it very much if you would help us eliminate the possible conclusion that some people have made in that we might have: (a) made up the story, (b) were incompetent observers. Anything that you could do along this line would be very much appreciated, and I am sure that you can understand the position we are in.

We appreciate the problem that the Air Force must have with the number of irresponsible reports on this subject, and don't want to cause you unnecessary trouble. On the other hand, we think that you prob-

ably understand our position. Thanks very much for
your interest.

Sincerely,
Patrolman Eugene Bertrand
and Patrolman David Hunt

They received no reply to this letter. They wrote again
on December 29:

Dear Sir:

Since we have not heard from you since our letter
of December 2, we are writing this to request some
kind of an answer since we are still upset about
what happened after the Pentagon released its news
that we had just seen stars or planets, or high-altitude
air exercises.

As we mentioned in our last letter to you, it could
not have been the Operation Big Blast you mentioned
since the time of our sighting was an hour after that
exercise and it may not have even been the same
date since you refer to our sighting as September 2.
Our sighting was on September 3. In addition, as we
mentioned, we are both familiar with all the B-47's
and B-52's and helicopters and jet fighters which are
going over this place all the time. On top of this,
Patrolman Bertrand had four years of refueling experience in the Air Force and knows regular aircraft
of all kinds. It is important to remember that this
craft that we saw was not more than one hundred feet
in the air and it was absolutely silent with no rush
of air from jets or chopper blades whatever. And it
did not have any wings or tail. It lit up the entire
field, and two nearby houses turned completely red.
It stopped, hovered, and turned on a dime.

What bothers us most is that many people are
thinking that we were either lying or not intelligent
enough to tell the difference between what we saw
and something ordinary. Three other people saw this
same thing on September 3 and two of them appear
to be in shock from it. This was absolutely not a case
of mistaken identity.

We both feel that it is very important for our jobs

and our reputations to get some kind of letter from you to say that story put out by the Pentagon was not true; it could not possibly be because we were the people who saw this, not the Pentagon.

Can you please let us hear from you as soon as possible?

Signed,
Patrolmen Eugene Bertrand
and David Hunt

More than a month later, the patrolmen received the following response from the Office of the Secretary of the Air Force:

Gentlemen:

Based on additional information submitted to our UFO Investigation Officer, Wright-Patterson AFB, Ohio, we have been unable to identify the object that you observed on September 3, 1965. In nineteen years of investigating over ten thousand reports of unidentified flying objects, the evidence has proved almost conclusively that reported aerial phenomena have been either objects created or set aloft by men, generated by atmospheric conditions, or caused by celestial bodies or the residue of meteoric activity.

Thank you for reporting your observation to the Air Force, and for your subsequent co-operation concerning the report. I regret any inconvenience you may have suffered as a result.

Sincerely,
John P. Spaulding
Lt. Col., USAF

Whether this letter satisfied the patrolmen, I do not know. Between the lines, it still says "It can't be, therefore it isn't" and that therefore their sighting must undoubtedly have some natural explanation. At least, however, the patrolmen had the satisfaction of the final admission from the Pentagon that they had been unable to identify their sighting.

So we close Blue Book's file on the Close Encounters

of the First Kind—cases so extraordinary that they are real only to the person who has experienced one, just as snow is real to an inhabitant of the tropics only after he has experienced it by traveling to northern latitudes. The major difference, of course, is that snow is accepted by science; UFOs are not. But in failing to deal with the evidence, the scientific establishment, like the Pentagon, is actually admitting that it has no explanation.

8

THE UFO LEAVES ITS MARK: CLOSE ENCOUNTERS OF THE SECOND KIND

Lt. —— desired this incident reported to the Air Force but did not want the story to get to the newspapers for fear that he may be the object of the ridicule that he has heretofore bestowed upon others relating similar occurrences.
—from a letter written by Lt. Col. Smith to the Commanding General, Robbins AFB, Georgia

The Case of the Whimpering Dogs

Among the 587 Air Force "Unidentifieds," there are 33 Close Encounters of the Second Kind (CE-IIs), those cases in which associated physical effects were reported. There were also CE-IIs among the cases which the Air Force evaluated as "Identified," though in many such cases "Identified" meant either "Psychological" or "Unreliable Report."

Here is one example of a case the Air Force declared "psychological" even though it involved two witnesses who observed the object for several minutes. It occurred on the evening of February 24, 1959, in Victorville, California. The intelligence officer described the principal witness as "an average young man of average intelligence ... liked by his schoolmates and teachers." His CE-II is summarized below:

The young man's attention was first captured by a bright light shining into the interior of his darkened bedroom. It was a bright, white steady light which was reflected against the wall opposite his bedroom window. He realized that it was much too intense to be the headlights of a car. As his parents were at night school and he was in charge of the house and his younger brother, he got out of bed, dressed, and went out on the front porch of the house to see where the light was coming from. Also, the family's pet dogs had by this time commenced to howl and run around as if terrified, and he wanted to let them into the house.

He first sighted the object in a due westerly direction, at an elevation of about twenty degrees, but at an undetermined distance. It resembled an elongated egg (see sketch), about 156 feet in length [derived from the boy's statement that the object was slightly larger, top to bottom, than his hand spread (7.5 inches) at arm's length (27 inches) when at a distance of about 80 feet]. The object was about twice as long as it was thick.

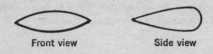

Front view   Side view

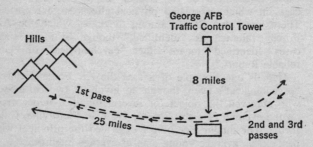

George AFB
Traffic Control Tower

Hills

1st pass

8 miles

25 miles

2nd and 3rd
passes

The Victorville, California, UFO as observed by two witnesses and reported to Blue Book. Sighting occurred on February 24, 1959. Sketch shows (a) the shape of the large object and (b) the path of object (three passes) as viewed from the witness's home.

Despite its brightness, the object had a dull red color with purple waves coursing through its extremities. It emitted a sound which was described as similar to the hum of a large transformer, but higher in pitch; or similar to, but vastly greater in volume from, a whip swishing through the air.

The object came toward him, its first approach lasting about ten seconds. It flew directly toward his house, on a steadily declining altitude of approach, and passed over his front yard at an altitude of about eight to ten feet. It then veered gradually to the northeast. Oddly enough, he could hear the object only while he could see it. Even odder, the boy was puzzled at his inability to see the object from the rear, when this should have been possible.

He went back into the house to calm his younger brother and the dogs. When he went outside again, after five minutes, he observed the object due west of the house and once again approaching him. It appeared that this time the object would pass closer to the house; by now truly frightened, he went back into the house to get a gun. But as the object sped past the house he lost his opportunity to use it. It was at this point that his younger brother saw the object through the front living-room window, which was covered by a split bamboo blind. About five minutes later the boy went outside again and once more observed the object to the west of his position, but this time approaching at a high speed. He re-entered the house as the object sped past. Twice more the object passed directly over the house, the last time some fifteen minutes after the first pass. By the last approach, the vibration of the object could be felt throughout the house.

In addition to the disturbance of the animals, it was reported that the radio, which had had very clear reception until then, was completely blocked by intense static. The static on the radio was not evident before 10:00 P.M. nor after 10:15 P.M., which seems to indicate that some electrical or magnetic disturbance was present in the immediate area during that time. The witness further stated that each time the object passed overhead he could hear a very sharp cracking noise which he compared with the spark gap of an automobile spark plug, but of greater volume and intensity. He was emphatic that this noise was not that of a sonic boom, which he had heard many times previously. When his parents arrived home at approximately 11:00 P.M. the incident was over; but the family pets were still whimpering and shaking and hiding under the furniture.

Two neighbors living in the area were questioned separately and admitted that at "about that time," they also experienced severe radio and television interference. They would not, however, give any details nor did they give the reporting officer permission to use their names.

The interrogating intelligence officer stated that the witness "was sincere, did not change his story although questioned several times on different points and seemed generally convinced that what he saw actually exists."

The parents testified to the strange behavior of the animals; and there was no evidence from either parents, neighbors, or friends that the boy was unstable. Nevertheless, Blue Book chose to label this case "psychological."

The Case of the Terrified Bull

We turn now to some of Blue Book's "Unidentifieds," and this next interesting case. The original report came from the State Police—Chautauqua County Police Barracks—and was followed up by an investigating officer and technicians from the Niagara Falls Municipal Airport. The incident took place in Cherry Creek, New York, on August 19, 1965. The Blue Book summary reads:

> The witness was working in a barn (a few minutes after sunset) when he noticed unusual AM radio interference plus a beeping sound. When he went outside he saw an object which he described as being saucer-shaped like two plates lip to lip. The object was described as fifty feet long and twenty feet thick and its color was shiny silver with red glowing streamers projecting downward from the entire perimeter plus a trail from red to yellow color. The object appeared to land near the farm and when the observer sighted it, the object rapidly ascended into the clouds. The clouds then turned green (color of tree leaves) and an odor like burning gasoline from the object was also noted.
>
> Forty-five minutes later the object reappeared (this time observed by a second witness) descending

slowly from the clouds towards a wooded area and then almost immediately rose again into the clouds leaving a dim red trail. The clouds again turned green near the object. The object reappeared at nine P.M. (half an hour later) descending towards the surface. It then rose to a height below the clouds and moved away SSW all the while emitting yellow trail. The object was reported to have caused reduction in the milk from the farmer's cow from two and a half cans to one can, disturbed a bull in a field, and caused a dog to bark.

The original report from the State Police gave more details:

The saucer-shaped object is reported to look like two dinner plates held face to face, silvery and very shiny, fifty feet long and twenty feet thick. It was reported that a bull tethered near the barn became so frightened that it bent the iron bar in the ground to which it was tethered. After the parents of the boy were questioned as well as the neighbors, regarding the character and reliability of the boys, the investigating officer and three technicians were convinced that the sighting was not a hoax or fabrication. The fourth technician remained unconvinced.

A follow-up report stated:

The observers maintained their story exactly as reported in the initial report under polite but vigorous questioning.

I remember when this case came into Blue Book. From the evidence at hand, it appeared that a total of three or four youths (farmboys) had seen the strange object descend from the clouds and ascend again, coloring the clouds green—a maneuver that was repeated several times originally and then again a half-hour later. Physical effects apparently included static and beeping on the radio, the reaction of the dog, the reaction of the tethered bull, and the reduced milk production on the part of the cow.

There was a strong impulse at Blue Book to regard this case as a hoax, but the evidence pointed in the opposite direction. In addition, the witnesses concerned were from a rural family and there seemed nothing to be gained from fabricating such a story. As a consequence, Blue Book reluctantly carried this case as "Unidentified."

The Squad Car and the Glowing Sphere

When NBC was preparing a documentary on UFOs, I was asked to participate in the re-interrogation, for TV purposes, of the witnesses involved in a most interesting case that was some nine years old by that time. It concerned two policemen and a fireman who had been cruising in a patrol car in the Chicago suburb of Elmwood Park, Illinois. After nine years, the two policemen were still employed on the force and all three were available for re-interrogation in the presence of NBC crewmen. The following is a letter that I wrote to Maj. Quintanilla on June 1, 1965, summarizing the NBC-inspired re-interrogation:

Dear Major:

This is a report on the very old sighting of November 4, 1957, made by two police officers and a fireman riding in one patrol car at shortly after 3:00 A.M., in Elmwood Park, Illinois.

I monitored the making of this part of the NBC documentary on UFOs, as I did on the previous night at Elk Grove Village, on the evening of May 27, 1965. Fortunately, all three witnesses are still holding down the same jobs, but only two were available for interview on this evening. The names of the witnesses were Officer ———, Officer ——— and Fireman ———.

All men stated that the incident had been reported to ——— but that ——— had merely said that they had nothing on their screens. Here's another case where ——— failed to follow through and report a sighting.

Officer ——— was ill on the night of the filming for the documentary, but I did talk at length with

Officer ———— and with the fireman ————. Both
are ———— in ————. Before passing any final judgment, I would like to talk with Officer ———— if I
ever get the chance. If there had been only one witness of the caliber of either of the two I interviewed,
I would tend to dismiss the incident as the product
of an overwrought imagination. However, with three
witnesses, with the two officers being on active duty,
I feel that something was definitely sighted. Furthermore, the sighting occurred the day after the Levelland, Texas, cases, and the description is quite similar. However, it was determined that these men had
no knowledge of the Levelland sighting of the previous day. They stated that after they came back to
the station house at dawn, the morning *Tribune* had
just been delivered, and in thumbing through the
pages, they then came across an account of the
Levelland sighting. They made a definite point of
the surprise with which they met the Texas account.

I re-enacted the entire incident with them, riding
in the car with the fireman, while the NBC people
were in the squad car ahead. The officer and fireman's
story agreed in the basic account, although they dis-
agreed somewhat on sizes and on the height at which
the object was observed.

At about 3:00 A.M., a squad car was patrolling
the alleyway behind a row of stores on Belmont St.
They had proceeded about two blocks down the
alley (the total length of which was nearly a mile),
when they perceived an open window in the back of
one of the stores. They stopped to examine it with
their spotlight, but just then the spotlight and their
headlights dimmed very much, so much so that the
officer said that a match would have been brighter.
This being the case, they took a flashlight from the
car and went out to examine the window and to look
under the hood. At this time, they said they noticed a
bright spherical object above and ahead of them. I
questioned them very long on the size and appearance and the best I could get was that it was like an
iridescent orange beach ball except much larger. The
fireman said that whenever after that he bounced a
beach ball, it always brought back this incident to

him. As the object moved down the alley, but above the alley, the car lights came back on. The engine, however, never had stalled but kept going the whole time. They trailed the object and whenever they turned their lights off, the object seemed to hover and, so to speak, watch them. As soon as they turned their lights on, the object moved off.

The men trailed down the alley for fully a half-mile to the end of the alley where it met a cemetery. They paused at the end and turned their lights off. The object slowly descended and hovered just a few feet off the ground. Here Officer ———— kicked on the "brights" and the object ascended very rapidly "fifty or sixty miles an hour." It also took off westward. The officers now jogged right for a quarter of a block to join Belmont Street and pursued the object down Belmont Street. Here Officer ———— said that it cavorted from curb to curb back and forth as though "playing games with them." The fireman maintained that the object was higher up.

The color or brightness never changed throughout the entire episode, which lasted some ten or fifteen minutes. There is a stand of trees in the cemetery and alongside Belmont on both sides. The object periodically became lost behind the trees. After about a mile and a half, they made a U-turn and came back east on Belmont, having lost sight of the object. As they got back into Elmwood Park, the object approached them from the left from a stand of trees, passed over them and to the rear. They made another U-turn and pursued the object again westward. Very soon after this, they said the object ascended to a great height.

Officer ———— said to about five thousand (5,000) feet, but this may or may not be the case since I do not particularly rate his judgment about dimension, or facts for that matter, very high. But both the fireman and the officer agreed that the object disappeared as though a person pulled a black shade up from the bottom, or as though one were filling the spherical object with a black ink. After it disappeared, high in the air in this manner, it did not reappear. Apparently, the only other witness to the incident was a dog which was disturbed and barked at the object somewhere along the route.

The story does not hang together very well. The men are ———— but they certainly stand to gain nothing from having perpetrated a hoax and, in fact, it could cost them promotions.

The object was described as bright but not hard on the eyes, and very beautiful. After considerable coaxing and trying to get the idea of simulation across, they agreed that if I brought in a balloon painted bright orange and of a size of about an ordinary moon, and held it in the sky, that it would look very much like the object they remembered. It must be remembered that this sighting happened some eight years ago, and memories over that length of time have probably deteriorated considerably.

According to the men, the moon was out that night, but to the east, whereas the object at that same time was toward the west. The sky was basically clear, although there was a fog in the cemetery.

One primary incident occurred when the squad car had stopped at the end of the first long alley just before they jogged on into Belmont Street. The lights were out and the object was descending. At this time, it lost its circular shape and took on a cigar shape surrounded by a fogginess which seemed to emanate from the object itself. There was disagreement as to how much fog, if any, there was in the cemetery that night. The crucial time of the incident seems to have been when the officer kicked on the lights as the object was descending and had assumed a cigar shape. As soon as the lights came on, the object rose up rapidly, resumed its circular shape, and sucked up the fogginess around it.

One other high spot occurred apparently just before the second U-turn when the squad car was going east on Belmont. The object came at them from the woods to the left, and according to Officer ———— came so close to the car that he could have reached out and touched it. The fireman did not agree, feeling that the object had always maintained a respectable distance.

The similarity to the Levelland case is striking and

if we can believe (I think we can) that they were unaware of the Levelland sighting at the time they made theirs, it becomes all the more interesting. The object definitely passed in front of objects from time to time and the object could not be seen through the light. The object, or the illumination, was not transparent.

No sound or noise was ever associated with the object. It seemed to glow and its color was compared by both men to the color of a setting sun, but not as bright.

It is unfortunate that the incident did not occur to witnesses better trained as observers, and more articulate ones.

Other small items: ——— said that his "hair stood on end" when he saw the object, and the other officer said that ——— wanted to shoot at it, but was cautioned by Officer ——— not to shoot until he knew more about it.

Meteorological conditions for this night should be checked to be compared with similar data from Levelland. Likewise, comparisons should be made with the Lock Raven Dam case and the Swiss equivalent of the Lock Raven Dam case which occurred just two or three days before the Lock Raven Dam case.

I would recommend that all cases of luminous globes of light which apparently do not appear to be attached to a tangible object be collected and be examined for similarities of behavior and ambient conditions. We may have here, and I say just possibly may, have an indication of something new in atmospheric physics. Cases should be limited, however, to more than one-witness cases.

This case should not be closed until I have a chance to talk with ———. I have a feeling that he may provide something which will either strongly corroborate the above or throw it out of court.

Sincerely,
(signed) Allen
J. Allen Hynek

The Case of the Baffled Businessman

And now, another "incredible tale told by a credible witness." A businessman in the Williamsburg, Virginia, area, who was very anxious to have his name withheld from the press because of his professional status, made a report to the Williamsburg City Police Department. This report was subsequently released to the press by the police department and, in turn, prompted many other reports, mainly from the Richmond area. Most of these other reports were passed on to the press and radio stations and not to the Air Force.

At 8:30 A.M. on January 23, 1965, twenty minutes before the observer reported his sighting, he was driving near the intersection of U.S. Highway 60 and State Route 614, when his car (a late-model Cadillac) suddenly stalled. At about the same time, he spotted an object, hovering over a nearby field, only four feet off the ground. The object was shaped like a mushroom or light bulb, about seventy-five to eighty feet in height, twenty-five feet in diameter at the top, and ten feet in diameter at the bottom. It was of metallic gray, with a red-orange glow on the side closest to the observer and a blue glow on the farthest side. While the object was hovering, there was a sound similar to that of a vacuum cleaner.

From his stalled car he continued to watch the object which, after hovering for a short while, performed a "rapid vanishing maneuver" by moving horizontally to the west. After it disappeared, the observer got out of his car and, noting that the car behind him also appeared to be stalled, walked over to it and asked the driver if he had also seen the object. Indeed, he had.

Blue Book carried this case as "Unidentified" simply because they could find no natural explanation. And that was not for lack of trying. They investigated the possibility of an ascending weather balloon, a low-altitude temperature inversion, a reflection of the sun, and possible isolated low clouds combining to form a mirage,* though

*The last explanation was based on a deputy sheriff's statement that low clouds had briefly moved in from the east at about the time of the sighting.

it must have seemed unlikely that any of these could behave in such a way as the object sighted—or have caused
cars to stall.

It is difficult to imagine a reputable businessman fabricating a story like this one and reporting it to the police.
One might wonder why there weren't more witnesses to
the event; but, as we have already noted, one of the chief
characteristics of UFO sightings seems to be their isola-
tion in time and space. This is, of course, a highly puzzling feature and has contributed greatly to attempts to
discredit the phenomenon.

The Case of the Leisurely Boomerang

In all my years with Project Blue Book, I never ceased
to be impressed with the phenomenon of mature adults
with respectable positions in their communities reporting
to the authorities (generally out of a sense of duty) the
most incredible tales. In most of these cases there was
no discernible motive for a deliberate hoax. Why then
the report? Hallucination immediately suggests itself, but
the witnesses generally have no previous record whatsoever of such an aberration. Furthermore, how can one
exactly ascribe the same hallucination to two or more
witnesses?

This next case, which occurred during Capt. Hardin's
term as Director of Project Blue Book, is outlined in a
letter written by Mr. Jack W——— and Mr. Ernest
A———:

At about 11:00 A.M. on Sept. 22, 1954, myself,
Jack W———, and Ernest A———, both being
employees of Webster Gas Company of Marshfield,
Missouri, were returning from Bracken, Missouri,
where we had completed a delivery. Approximately
3 miles east of Marshfield, Missouri, on what is
known as the Scout Camp Road, we observed far to
the west three clouds, or formations of silver objects. They were far enough away or so small that
they appeared as no more than a silver dot to our
eyes; there were, as a rough guess, many thousands of

these objects. [Could have been birds.] I stopped the truck to watch these objects and after about 2 minutes my partner noticed another object at what we guessed to be 600 feet high and about 200 yards SW. This object was somewhat like a boomerang in shape with the exception that one side or wing was very short and the other side or wing much longer. If the object was as close as we thought I would guess the entire width to be about 6 or 7 feet. This object was very thin in the wing section and the body as well. This object was silent. It appeared to be covered or made of some sort of plastic or very thin material. It revolved very slowly, the entire object revolved, not just the one wing. As it revolved and the wing came around near the sun it seemed to shine through or nearly through because of the changing in color; it would seem to be much lighter in color when the sun was behind it. The color was of a dark tan with 2 black stripes near the end of the wing or rotor. After we watched the object for a few minutes it started to climb without changing its flight characteristics or without gaining any RPM of its wing. After rising to what we thought to be about 1,500 feet it then started to come down much slower than it had climbed as the climb took only about 20 seconds; after coming down to what we thought about 500 feet it changed its revolving action in that it started tumbling but not any faster than it had revolved. After falling a short distance in this position it emitted a puff of white smoke or vapor. This was not in a trailing form but just one big puff of smoke or vapor; [neither] at this time or any other time did we ever hear any noise, [and] after emitting this smoke or vapor it stopped all motion and fell straight into a small patch of timber; we did not actually see this object hit the ground because of the rough terrain but we did see it go behind the timber line. We then left our truck and went into the woods to see if we could find any other trace of this object. After some minutes we found two places in the earth completely pulverized but didn't show any sign of an animal track; this might or might not [have] had anything to do with it but it did seem strange in such soft dirt that if an animal or human had made it that it did not leave any track.

When we first noticed this object it seemed to hover at about the 600-foot level. The wing or rotor was slightly curved upward at the tip and near the two dark stripes. When this object stopped its rotating and started to fall the wing or rotor was pointed up indicating the base of this wing which would be the body—the heaviest part. At no time was there much speed involved in any fashion. While falling it did not flutter or turn at all but fell straight down past the timber line. Before falling past the timber line we watched this object for about 15 minutes. After the two of us searched the area very thoroughly we returned to Marshfield, Missouri, and I called the Fordland Air Base and talked with CWO A.R. Justman about this object; he sent four men to Marshfield, Missouri, where they picked the two of us up and we returned to the area and made a more thorough search and of a much wider area but without finding any more traces of this object than we had found before. At about 6:00 P.M. CWO A.R. Justman and myself returned to the area and made a third try at finding the object but still failed to find anything at all other than the two places in the earth that [were] torn up.

After leaving the truck in the beginning to start the first search Mr. A——— and myself did not see the silver object again that first attracted our attention. The two of us had time to study the object and it is just as I have described it.

/s/ JACK ———
Marshfield, Mo.
/s/ ERNEST A———

The Air Force investigator's report included the following:

I dispatched several airmen to object site who combed the wooded area and found a patch of ground which appeared to be literally pulverized, dirt was agitated on surface, and rocks, small in size,

were disturbed in this spot. I examined area later in
the day and observed that area had no prints of any
animal, yet appeared to be beaten up by something.
Nearby foliage was undisturbed with no signs of
burning, scorching, etc.

A rotating, boomerang-like propeller, maneuvering by
itself in the daytime air does not fit the general UFO pattern. One gets the feeling that the UFO phenomenon,
whatever it may be, is indeed "playing games with us"
and leading us a merry chase.

The Case of the Blue Egg

Blue Book did not call the next two cases "Unidentified" but "Unreliable Report" and "Psychological," respectively. In both cases there appears to be no evidential
justification for these evaluations.

The first of these occurred two evenings after the famous Levelland, Texas cases.* Blue Book attempted to
dismiss the Levelland sightings as "ball lightning" but
oddly enough did not dismiss these strikingly similar ones
in like manner.

In the first case, occurring in El Paso, Texas, a thirty-
five-year-old border inspector observed approaching his
car an egg-shaped object with a bluish glow and with a
whirring sound similar to an artillery shell. He did not see
this object, however, until he got out of his car to investigate why it had stalled and why all his lights had dimmed
and gone out. It was then that he noticed the "blue egg"
approaching him from the southwest at a thirty-degree
elevation. It passed over his car at an altitude of one
hundred feet and moved off on a westerly heading, while
changing in altitude at irregular intervals. After it reached
the Franklin Mountains, the object lifted vertically. The
observer was at this time three miles southeast of the International Airport at El Paso and the time was 7:30 P.M.

Once again, Blue Book conducted no further investigation and labeled the case "Unreliable Report." "Insufficient Information" would have been more appropriate.

---

*These Blue Book cases have been fully described in the author's
The UFO Experience, pp. 141-7.

The Case of the "Hypnotized" Lieutenant

This next case is a good example of Blue Book's application of the label "Psychological." Somewhat more attention than usual was given this one by the Blue Book staff because the primary witness was an Air Force first lieutenant who had just completed advanced survival training, and was on his way home to Delaware from Stead Air Force Base in Nevada when the incident occurred.

III. SOURCE'S DESCRIPTION OF THE SIGHTing: Source was returning to Newcastle County Airport, Delaware, after completion of USAF Advanced Survival School, Stead AFB on 23 Nov 1957 in his automobile. At about 0610, he was approximately thirty miles west of Tonopah, Nevada, traveling towards Las Vegas at about eighty MPH when the engine of his car suddenly stopped. Attempts to restart the engine were unsuccessful and Source got out of his car to investigate the trouble. Outside the car he heard a steady high-pitched whining noise which drew his attention to four disc-shaped objects that were sitting on the ground about three hundred to four hundred yards to the right of the highway. These objects were totally unlike anything he had ever seen, and he attempted to get closer for a better look at them. He walked for several minutes until he was within approximately fifty feet from the nearest object [road hypnosis is a momentary thing; the apparition does not last for several minutes!] The objects were identical and about fifty feet in diameter. They were disc-shaped, emitting their own source of light causing them to glow brightly. They were equipped with a transparent dome in the center of the top which was obviously not of the same material as the rest of the craft. The entire body of the objects emitted the light. They did not appear to be dark on the underside. They were equipped with three landing gears, each that appeared hemispherical in shape about two feet in diameter and of some dark material. The source estimated the height of the objects from the ground level to the top of the dome to be about ten to fifteen feet. The objects were equipped with a ring around the outside which was darker than the rest of the craft and was apparently rotating. When the Source got to within fifty feet of the nearest object, the hum which had been steady in the air ever since he had first observed the objects, increased in pitch to a degree where it almost hurt his ears, and the objects lifted off the ground. The protruding gears were retracted almost instantly after takeoff; the objects rose about fifty feet into the air and proceeded slowly (about ten MPH) to the north across the highway, contoured over some small hills about a half mile away and disappeared behind those hills. As the objects passed directly over the Source, he observed no evidence of any smoke, exhaust, trail, heat, disturbance to the ground, or terrain or any visible outline of landing gear doors or any other outlines or openings in the bottom. The total time of sighting lasted about twenty minutes. After the objects disappeared, Source examined the place where he had first seen them. [Imagine a victim of road hypnosis calmly examining the place of landing some twenty minutes later.] There was no evidence that any heat had been present or that the ground had been disturbed in any other way than several very small impressions in the sand where the landing gear had obviously rested. Impressions were very shallow and bowl-shaped, triangular in pattern (an equally sided triangle). Source did not measure the distance between the impressions but estimated it to be about eight to ten feet. After his investigation of the impressions, Source returned to his car and the engine started immediately and ran perfectly. [This is a typical reported experience after a UFO has stopped a car. After the disappearance of the UFO, the car is fully operable.] The car Source was driving was a 1956 Chevrolet [thus a year or two old] and he did not experience trouble of similar nature before or after the incident. At the time of sighting, Source had driven from Reno, Nevada, to point of sighting during the night and had slept for about two hours in his car between 2400 and 0200 that same day [psychologist maintains that witness was exhausted despite the witness's own statement that he was feeling fine at the time]. Source had had no intoxicants or sleep-retarding drugs. He described his physical condition at the time of sighting as excellent. After the sighting, Source proceeded to Indian Springs AFB, Nevada, where he reported the sighting to the base Security Officer. [It is most unlikely that a victim of road hypnosis would later, upon calm consideration, report such an experience to an Air Force base!]

The times of day referred to above are given in Pacific Standard Time. At the time of the sighting, it was daylight although the sun was still behind the mountains. The sun was about to rise in front of the Source. (Source was traveling SSE and the sun at that season would rise well to the south of east.) There were no stars or moonlight. There was no overcast. The weather was dry and rather cold and there was no wind. There were no other witnesses to the observation to the best of Source's knowledge. [Captain Gregory made much of the fact that the Nevada Highway Department indicated at that time that there might be some twenty-five to thirty cars passing along that road. In my opinion, there could have been five hundred cars passing whose drivers would pay little attention to some activity on the desert some several hundred feet off the road.]

The witness provides the following sketches of the objects.

A memo in the Blue Book files points up the primary reason why the Air Force put as much effort into investigating this case as it did:

The damage and embarrassment to the Air Force would be incalculable if this officer allied himself with the host of "flying saucer" writers, experts, and others who provide the Air Force with countless charges and accusations. In this instance, as matters now stand, the Air Force would have no effective rebuttal, or evidence to disprove any unfounded charges.

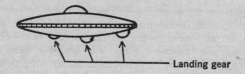

Landing gear

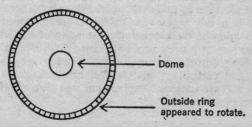

Dome

Outside ring
appeared to rotate.

The Tonopah, Nevada, object, sighted November 23, 1957, as described and sketched in original Blue Book files.

The records show a several weeks' attempt to obtain the services of a nearby university psychologist to examine the evidence, an effort that was finally successful. The psychologist had this to say:

> This is indeed an unusual report. With one important exception, it has many of the characteristics of a deliberate hoax and reports of psychopathological cases. This exception was that it was made by an Air Force officer, a pilot who presumably should be a most competent observer. On the basis of the evidence, I can only offer conjectures on the nature of this incident. These conjectures may be helpful, however, in the collection of official evidence.
>
> First, there is the possibility of deliberate hoax, even in an Air Force officer. In order to check this possibility, I would recommend a discreet investigation that is conducted before granting a security clearance. Specifically, do friends, neighbors, etc., know of any evidence in the officer's background that would suggest a hoax? . . . It was possible that the officer was suffering from a temporary condition such as has been sometimes called "road hypnosis"

brought on by excessive fatigue and loss of sleep. There are well-documented cases of truck drivers, for example, who have driven off the road to avoid (entirely imagined) houses, buses, etc., ahead of them on the road. This is most likely to occur on long desert roads, especially at night.

Thus, the psychologist, on very little evidence, dismissed the case as probable "road hypnosis." There is no record as to how he arrived at this conclusion. Nor is there any mention of the psychological stability of the witness. Did he have a history of mental instability? Did he have a medical record? What is so frustrating in these kinds of cases, and particularly in this one, is the readiness with which a "Psychological" explanation was grasped without adequate justification.

The Case of the Flying Tadpole

Blue Book also classified this next case which took place in Nederland, Texas, as "Psychological." Quoting directly from the Blue Book investigator's report:

On Sunday morning 6 Feb 1966 at approximately 0545, Mr. ———'s eleven-year-old son came to their bedroom on the way to the bathroom and turned the light on in the bathroom, and in doing so, awakened his parents. While the boy was in the bathroom, the lights went out causing Mr. ——— to get out of bed and look out of the window to see if the streetlights were also out, which appeared to be the case. While looking out of the window, Mr. ——— was amazed to find that the lawn in front of his house and the surrounding area was engulfed in a reddish glow which appeared to be pulsating similar to a red flashing light on a police car. However, he did not see any police cars in the area. A few moments later, he noticed some peculiar yellowish type and reddish lights coming from an object approximately five hundred feet off the ground. The lights seemed to be moving back and forth in a horizontal direction and appeared to be similar to neon light tubes which he estimated to be eight in number.

There was no apparent sound; however, both Mr. —————— and his wife claimed that their ears were bothered by what appeared to be a very high frequency pitch. There was a high overcast with no stars or moon that night. Therefore, it was quite dark and Mr. —————— was unable to determine size and shape of the object at this time. However, the object traveled approximately a mile and a half to the west towards the Jefferson County Airport. About this same time an aircraft took off from the airport and turned in the direction of the unknown object. As the aircraft approached, the lights on the object went out. The landing lights on the aircraft remained on and reflected off the UFO, giving Mr. —————— an opportunity to see what it looked like. He stated that the best way to describe the shape of the object was that it looked like a tadpole. He estimated that the object was about eight feet in diameter with a tail about six feet in length and two feet wide. There appeared to be cone-shaped bulges on the top and in the middle of the object. The previously mentioned lights seemed to be coming from the tail of the object. After the aircraft had flown over the object, its lights came on again and he noticed what appeared to be three separate times when these lights were energized. Each time the object appeared to move up and about five degrees to the left. It disappeared at about twenty to twenty-five degree angle above the horizon, traveling in a westerly direction and in a slow rate of climb. Mr. —————— observed all this with the naked eye and was unable to get any pictures.

Although Mr. —————— was very fearful of ridicule from the local populace, he nevertheless had the opportunity to discuss the power failure with a man from the power company and determined that the reason for the power outage was . . . the failure of a transformer. He further found out that this transformer was located very near to his house and that the failure occurred at almost the same time as the sighting of the UFO.

Mr. —————— found it very difficult to describe the UFO and admitted that he was not very good at drawing pictures, but if the Air Force thought it was necessary, he could probably describe it well enough to an artist so that a fairly representative picture could be drawn.

Mr. ———— was unaware of any other residents who had seen the UFO but attributed this to the fact that he was very hesitant in mentioning it to anyone since he definitely does not want any publicity on the sighting. However, after the sighting, he did call the control tower at the Jefferson County Airport to determine if they had seen it also but found that they had not seen anything and laughed at his explanation and request.

CONCLUSION: preliminary investigation did not disclose any reasonable explanation for Mr. ————'s sighting. A more detailed investigation and a personal visit will be accomplished if requested from your headquarters.

Readers will no doubt recognize here a number of features commonly reported in UFO sightings: First, the reddish glow which "appeared to be pulsating similar to a red flashing light on a police car" (in other reports the identical comment has been made—"at first we thought it was a red flasher beacon on a police car"); second, the object turning off its lights when approached by an aircraft; and finally, the power outage, ascribable to a burned-out transformer. In this and many other cases, transformer damage or damage to electrical appliances very similar to that which occurs under ordinary circumstances or during a lightning storm seems to be coincident with the appearance of a UFO. This was true in the Cuernavaca, Mexico, case which I personally investigated. And during the granddaddy of all "power outages," the great Eastern states blackout of 1965, very definite UFO activity was reported near the geographical center of the blackout!

It is clear to any serious UFO investigator that "coincidence" is strained beyond all reasonable limits in these occurrences, and labeling them "psychological," attributing them to reports by "unreliable witnesses," or calling them "Unidentified" does not represent a step in the solution of the problem. Perhaps at this time it would be well to quote Carlos Casto-Cavero, a general in the Spanish Air Force who, commenting on the dilemma of governments who have to deal with UFO reports, made the following statement:

> I believe in the existence of UFOs. The position is that it is as difficult for official quarters to admit that something exists as it is for the Church to affirm that this or that is a miracle.*

Casto-Cavero went on to assert that the fact that governments do not publicly recognize the reality of the phenomenon is due to their reluctance to venture an opinion in the face of what they consider to be intangible evidence.

The general stated it well. The United States Air Force, as well as the military in other countries, does not appear to be guilty of some sinister cover-up; rather, they appear to be honestly baffled. Since the UFO phenomenon cannot be solved easily—but neither can it be ignored—the military, in their bewilderment, does its very best to wave it away.

The Willful Car

Here is an interesting case which Major Quintanilla passed on to me for evaluation late in 1968—just about the same time as the Condon Committee was to make public its report dismissing the entire UFO phenomenon as having no substance. I investigated the case; but Blue Book records contain only the following brief statement of my findings.

> The sighting was investigated and evaluated by Dr. J. Allen Hynek, Air Force Scientific Consultant on UFOs. The following represents a brief summary of his analysis and conclusions regarding this sighting [the analysis has apparently disappeared].
>
> Witness saw a brilliant light directly above the road about two hundred feet ahead of him and fifty

to seventy-five feet off the ground, as he rounded a bend in the road in his 1967 Ford. [The date of the sighting is November 23, 1968.] The area was sparsely settled. There was no definite object, just light. The car radio faded into static. The light itself emitted a beam downward that illuminated the nearby trees.

Light was then retracted as if the beam were a ladder; it was five to six feet wide and well defined. The main light was fuzzy on the edges. Now the engine cut out as did the radio. Main light appeared scintillating with a subtended arc of several degrees. Light then disappeared after a few seconds, going straight up. Engine started by itself and the car had been left in "drive" gear. Conclusion: Unidentified.

Another case of car-stopping—and this time, car-starting—all by itself! Any physical scientist would say this was preposterous; yet it has been reported many times. The handwritten witness form contained the following statements:

I observed what appeared to be a self-luminous oval-shaped object between forty and fifty yards in diameter which glowed with a yellowish-white light. It seemed to me to be non-transparent but I have no idea as to how solid it may have been. It was much brighter than any other light present. There were no distinct edges but rather a fuzzy outline with a general oval shape.

. . . 67—Ford Custom—(paved gravel road)—all windows were closed with the heater on. No other traffic on the road.

As to the apparent size, I can only estimate that if I were to hold my entire thumb at arm's length, no more than one-tenth of the object would have been covered.

As to how his attention was first called to the phenomenon:

I topped a small hill and started into a curve coming up onto where this object was located. The brightness, size, etc., immediately caught my attention. As I approached the light, a beam of light came down to my car causing the engine to stop and all electrical components to malfunction.

As to the final disappearance of the object:

The object changed colors from a yellowish-white to a brighter reddish-orange and moved straight up at a very high rate of speed. It was completely out of sight in less than fifteen seconds.

Although this is a single-witness case, one gathers from the handwritten comments of this witness, and from his manner of expression, that he was a reasonably articulate young man. Since this case has much in common with other CE-IIs, including the beam of light being retracted "like a ladder," it is hard to believe it could have been an out-and-out hoax, unless the witness was very familiar with UFO literature. My recollection of the investigation is simply that I was unable to find any logical, natural explanation. Having no evidence to support a "Hoax" or "Psychological" evaluation, I simply had to classify the sighting as "Unidentified."

The Lieutenant's Blimp

Over the years, it has been my experience that some of the best reports come from previously militant skeptics who, after having had a UFO experience of their own, suddenly find themselves the butt of the type of ridicule that they had previously heaped upon others. Following is a letter from the Blue Book files from Lt. Col. Charles Smith, Jr., Commanding, 9325th Squadron, Gainesville, Georgia, to the Commanding General of Robbins AFB, Georgia, to the attention of the Chief, Intelligence Section:

On the evening of Oct 31 at 7:40 P.M., while traveling north on Highway 85, toward Atlanta, some four miles from Fayetteville, a strange object was seen flying overhead.

This strange object appeared to be flying at treetop level as I approached it. It was of orange color and very similar to an air blimp. I was traveling at a speed of 60–70 MPH as I approached this object. It was coming down directly over the road some two hundred yards ahead. So, I immediately thought of falling aircraft and tried to stop before traveling beneath it. However, as I went under, the object was moving very slowly across the road. As I passed under it, the radio on the car was silent as if traveling under a bridge or underpass. There was no static, just silence until the object passed.

As I quickly got out of the car, the object seemed directly overhead at an estimated five hundred feet. The length was estimated as four times the height and width (80′ by 20′ by 20′). A clear bottom view, sideview and angle-view was seen. After lingering for about twenty seconds overhead, the nose seemed to point in a forty-five-degree-angle climb, steadily increasing its speed and angle climb until it disappeared slightly to the left of the moon and in an easterly direction. The speed was tremendous and the object completely disappeared in approximately thirty to forty seconds.

There were no sparks nor was there any sound. The night was very clear and the stars and moon very bright. There were no light beams visible and I looked all around.

This object was very dull orange near the center line and was brighter near the outer edges.

As the object passed between the view of the moon and my location on the upper climb, the color seemed to blend in with that of the moon but it was still visible.

Signed,
Lt. Col. Charles Smith, Jr.

Cases reported by Air Force officers and Air Force pilots were particularly trying for Blue Book. Here were some of their own highly trained men reporting incidents which the Air Force itself was ascribing to misidentification of natural objects or to hallucination. It wasn't easy for them to call one of their own officers a "psychological" case, nor did they wish to demean a military officer's intelligence; how different the attitude when it's one of your own!

The Case of the Bawling Cattle

I personally investigated this next CE-II in the latter days of Blue Book. It was a single-witness case, if one does not count the cattle as "witnesses." The sighting took place near Groveton, Missouri, on February 9, 1968, at 3:20 A.M. The story begins with a letter:

February 9, 1968

To the Hon. Robert McNamara
Secretary of Defense
Department of Defense
The Pentagon
Washington, D.C. 20301

Dear Sir:

I reside on a farm approximately thirty miles north of Kansas City, Missouri. The residence is approximately one quarter of a mile back from the highway with a pasture in front of the dwelling. I am employed in town and operate a cow herd and allgrass farm. If there is a disturbance among the cattle, I arise to their bawling as would a mother to her crying child.

Last night I heard several cows bawl as if frightened or scared. I immediately jumped out of bed and ran to the picture window in my living room. It was a dark night but there was a distinct glow giving off considerable light immediately in front of the house (approximately three hundred to three hundred and fifty feet away). It made sufficient light for me to maneuver around the card table left in the middle of the room and to see the cattle in the pasture in a rough semicircle to the left of the light glow.

As my vision adjusted from darkness to this moderate light, I was able to see parts of what appeared to be a tremendous circular object, reproduced as best I can on the attached sketch.

The light was a yellowish-green and came from the concave side of the craft. I could not tell whether it came from the translucent surface or was reflected from the base of the craft against a shiny surface and then back to the ground. In any event, there was sufficient light to see the major limbs on some of the walnut trees, a stump, the cows, the fence in the foreground, and other details.

The object appeared to be at least one hundred feet in diameter, and to be hovering twenty to twenty-five feet above the ground . . . although I could not say that it was not on the ground or possibly higher in the air. There were definitely seven openings or portholes in the approximate center of the concave side. Their spacing would indicate that if the craft were in fact round, there were probably sixteen of these equally spaced around the craft. I could not see distinctly enough to see if they were square, rectangular, oval, or round. It was difficult to arrive at a perspective to judge their size, but I would guess that they were two feet to approximately thirty inches in diameter. I saw no door or distinct opening. I saw no living thing enter or depart the craft. I have no idea whether I watched half a minute or five minutes, I was so entranced by the sight.

I have been losing a cow or two now and then, undoubtedly stolen without a trace. My first reaction on hearing the cows was that someone was among them. On seeing the craft, I remember thinking, "No wonder I have found no evidence! They are being hauled off by air!" At that point I had no idea of what I saw as being a possible UFO, but rather as some monstrous helicopter or other craft.

Some of the cows were staring at the object from perhaps one or two hundred feet away. Cows with younger calves were bawling and some of the calves were answering. Finally, one cow whirled and ran with tail high towards the barn. The others followed and in only a few seconds, there were no cattle in sight. The craft remained some little time after the cows departed, but I have no idea whether this was half a minute or considerably longer. It was during this time that I concentrated on the object in an attempt to make out all the details that I could.

All during this time there had been a distinct noise that I had difficulty in describing. It sounded something like the swish of a piece of wire which one might whirl around above his head at a high speed and yet it had a pulsating rhythm of some kind. [Note earlier case which described the sound as similar to that of a "whip swishing through the air."] When the craft departed, this noise became two or three times louder and the sound of pulsations were more rapid. The craft moved away rapidly to the southwest, arising at about a forty-five-degree angle without the craft being tilted in any way from the horizontal position it had maintained at or above ground level. . . .

Maj. Quintanilla asked me to look into this case via telephone and after doing so, I reported to him: "Mr. ————'s manner of speech was careful, and he made no attempt to embellish his story or to do anything other than stick to the facts. He did not desire publicity and has not mentioned the incident to anyone other than in his letter. He feels no good could come of talking about it. I would have to give Mr. ———— a very good rating as to stability and unexcitability. He is, however, nearsighted and although he tells me that he can drive without glasses, he rarely does. Had he had his glasses on, he feels that he could have observed more details than he did."

Blue Book did not, of course, consider it worthwhile to expend time and money for me to visit this witness to get a face-to-face account. A visit to the actual point of sighting is immensely helpful, for it enables the investigator to ask more relevant questions, questions that might not otherwise come to mind. But alas, in this case, such a visit never took place. Blue Book simply stuck on a label, [unidentified] and considered the case closed.

The Case of the Armed Witness

Finally, we have a two-witness Blue Book case that stretches beyond all the boundaries of common sense. Was the witness fabricating such a bizarre story? You be the judge. The following Blue Book excerpt is from the records of the FBI field office in Baltimore:

Mr. ———— was interviewed at his residence, ————, May 10, 1952, and with reference to the incident in this case, he related in substance as follows: ————, accompanied by his friend ————, [was] returning to Baltimore from Glen Burnie, Maryland, via the Richey Highway, on 29 March 1952. They were in a 1949 Anglia Vampire, an English car, and were proceeding in a northerly direction, having just left a Howard Johnson's restaurant adjacent to the intersection of Richey Highway and U.S. Highway 301. While approximately opposite a harness track, about three hundred yards north of the above-named intersection, ———— related: "We observed a strange-looking craft appearing on the horizon ahead of his automobile. ———— described the aircraft as being a flat disc with a cupola or dome in the center of one side. He described the dome as having what appeared to be a small porthole on one side and a shadowy outline of what appeared to be a "hatch" similar to those appearing on a ship. He stated that this craft approached his vehicle from a northeasterly direction and hovered above his automobile.

He further described the object as being of a luminous silver color and emitting bright light around the edges, similar to neon tubing of high brilliancy. He stated that at the time that the incident occurred he had in the rear seat of his vehicle a Thomson submachine gun with which weapon he left the automobile and walked around the car several times, debating as to whether or not he should fire on the aircraft. He advised that his companion ———— remained in the automobile and pleaded with him not to discharge the weapon for fear of retaliation from the aircraft. Mr. —————— declined to comment as to the origin, present whereabouts, or owner of the above-named weapon. —————— stated that when the aircraft came to rest above his automobile, it appeared to be at least fifty feet in diameter and wavered slightly. While in sight, the aircraft gave off a sound similar to that of a vacuum cleaner. —————— averred that the aircraft maintained its position above the automobile for approximately three minutes and then turned on its edge, thereby presenting its flat surface to his vision, and appeared to roll across the sky at a rate of speed greater than that of a jet aircraft. —————— estimated the horizon to the southwest of his vision towards which the object was traveling was approximately three and one half miles from his position and that the object as it disappeared across the horizon was approximately the dimensions of a five-inch disc held at arm's length. He advised that when the object first appeared, it appeared to be at an angle to the horizon of sixty degrees, and as he was proceeding north, it appeared on the northwest horizon on the crest of a hill. He also advised that during the period that the object was within his vision, he noticed no sign of activity within it and discerned no odor from it.

—————— advised that during the time of the above observation of the aircraft, there was only one other automobile in the immediate vicinity. He described this to be a 1948 Pontiac convertible, yellow, with a 1952 Maryland license plate, the first three digits of which were "600." He realized that the car was apparently occupied by a man and a woman and that the man had dismounted the automobile, looking at the aircraft but upon being hailed by ——————, had returned to the automobile and driven off rapidly. It was Mr. ——————'s opinion that he did so on seeing the aforementioned Thomson sub-machine gun. Mr. —————— informed the writer that he was not addicted to or a casual indulger in any form of alcoholic beverages and was not under such influence at the time of the sighting. He further advised that he wore glasses only for the purpose of reading and that the only obstruction to his observation of the above-described aircraft was the windshield of his automobile when first sighted; however, when he emerged from the automobile, he was able to observe the aircraft without any trouble.

———— contended that the above incident had a singular effect on his automobile in that it killed the motor and, apparently, magnetized his wiring. It also resulted in the paint on his car cracking.

AGENT'S NOTE: An inspection of ————'s automobile revealed that it had been recently painted.

Blue Book once again labeled this "Unidentified."

We have presented here only a small sampling of the fascinating Close Encounters of the Second Kind. These cases seem to describe a UFO that is capable of leaving physical traces on its surroundings, but whose behavior does not correspond with our present technology and certainly not with the technology of 1947 or 1948. Since we are always inclined to believe in physical evidence—what we can see with our own eyes—CE-IIs tend to offer more convincing evidence than any other type of UFO sighting that the UFO phenomenon is "real."

9

APPROACHING THE EDGE OF REALITY: CLOSE ENCOUNTERS OF THE THIRD KIND

"As we watched, men came out . . . on what seemed to be a deck on top of the huge disc. One figure seemed to be looking down at us. I stretched my arm above my head and waved. To our surprise the figure did the same. . . . All the mission boys made audible gasps."

—*Rev. William Gill*
Boianai, Papua, New Guinea

If Project Blue Book officers refused to take seriously the "incredible tales from credible persons" that concerned strange lights in the night, flying discs, and the Close Encounters thus far described, it is scarce wonder that they dismissed with alacrity the Close Encounters of the Third Kind, those in which "beings" were reported in association with the UFO sighting.

Why should it be more difficult for us to accept encounters with "creatures" than with "craft"? Probably because once we dare to admit that beings alien to ourselves exist, we are forced to face our deepest fear of the unknown, along with our more basic and specific fears of competition and hostility. But, as in the other types of UFO experiences, we cannot ignore the reports which *do* exist, for they are made by seemingly credible persons and are widespread.

Reports of Close Encounters of the Third Kind, whether they be single- or multiple-witness cases, are characterized by a high degree of strangeness and by the complete bewilderment of the witnesses. There is generally a great reluctance to report, and once the report is made, there is a strong desire to avoid further publicity. Since the majority of these sightings last for several minutes, and the witnesses are generally able to recall specific details, it seems highly unlikely that the witnesses are hallucinating; hallucinations are usually transitory in nature, and the "victim" is not generally able to describe things in detail.

The circumstances under which Close Encounters of the Third Kind occur do not seem to differ at all from those surrounding other types of sightings. Like the others, they happen spontaneously and without warning to the witnesses, who generally find themselves engaged in perfectly ordinary tasks just prior to the sighting—driving the car to work, putting the car in the garage, taking out the garbage, or resting on the porch or lawn.

Close Encounters of the Third Kind have been described so well in UFO literature that I will confine myself to relatively few cases in the Blue Book files, including three classic cases, the Father Gill case in New Guinea, the Socorro, New Mexico, case, and the famous Kelly-Hopkinsville, Kentucky, case.

The Radio Man on the Highway

Let us begin, however, with one for which virtually all information comes from the Blue Book files. This case occurred on the morning of August 25, 1952, in Pittsburgh, Kansas. The lone witness was doing what he had been doing routinely at that time of day for five or six years—driving from the farm where he lived to the radio station where he worked. On this date he left his farm at 5:30 A.M. CST and was driving a 1952 Jeep station wagon on a rough gravel road. He was just about a quarter of a mile from U.S. Highway 60, when he noted an object off the right side of the road at a horizontal angle of about 40° and at a distance of about 250 yards. The object was approximately 70 feet long and 12 feet high. A number of windows were observed and the witness stated he distinctly saw a "man" inside who seemed to control the "object." The Blue Book report states:

> He immediately started slowing down his car and continued to view the object through the right-hand side of the windshield. When he came to a point

where the object was visible through the right door
glass and about ninety degrees to the right of his vehicle, he stopped and slid his body over to the right-
hand door of the vehicle, opened the door and
stepped out onto the road. At all times, he attempted
to keep the object in view. After he had stepped out
to the side of the road nearest the object, it began a
rapid vertical ascent. He estimated that he viewed the
object for about one-half minute. At this time, he
estimated that he was about one hundred yards from
the object. When the object reached the height of
about how high an airplane flies, the object then increased acceleration at a tremendous rate and rapidly
disappeared from view, straight up into the broken
clouds. Clouds did not obscure the view of the disappearing object at any time. He described the object as platter-shaped; by this he [meant to say] that
it looked like two platters or bowls had been put
together by reversing one platter and placing it over
the first one. He estimated that it was almost seventy-
five feet long and forty feet wide and about fifteen
feet through the midsection, measuring vertically in
the center of the object. Object was about ten feet
off the ground when first seen and remained in this
position until starting its rapid ascent after he
stepped to the side of the road. The object was hovering or moving slightly up and down and to the
side, or rocking slightly as it hovered about ten feet
off the ground. Mr. ———— then went on with a
more detailed description of the object: it was of a
dull aluminum color; smooth surface; one window
in front section and the head and shoulders of a man
sitting motionless [were] visible, facing forward to
the edge of the object; clear glass, light in forward
section, and medium blue continuous light. In the
midsection of the object were several windows extending from top to rear of object; midsection of ship
had a blue light which gradually changed to different
shades. There was a lot of activity or movement in
the midsection which could not be identified as being
human as it did not have a regular pattern of movement. There were no windows, portholes, doors,
vents, seams, etc., seen by the observer in the rear

section of the object or under the object (viewed at time of ascent). Another identifiable feature was that along the edges of the object . . . there were a series of propellers about six inches to seven inches in diameter spaced closely together; these propellers were mounted on a bracket so that they revolved in a horizontal plane on the edge of the object. The propellers were rotating at a high rate.

The Air Force Investigator in this instance did a good job in obtaining character references (e.g., "prominent local businessman connected with the witness's radio station advises that he has known the source for ten years and holds him in the highest regard. He considers him completely reliable"). There were also physical effects associated with the sighting.

The object was reported as hovering over an open two-acre field used for cattle grazing. The general area is heavily wooded. In the field over which the object hovered, the grass was pressed down forming a circle of sixty-foot diameter impression with the grass in a recognizable concentric pattern. Loose grass lay over the top of the impression as if drawn in by suction when the object ascended vertically at high speed. Vegetation and grass are approximately four to five feet high. Matted grass was verified by several witnesses. Samples of soil and grass were sent to Dayton and analyzed by the Technical Analysis Division with the results that the samples show no evidence of any radioactivity, burning, or stress of any kind.

The Blue Book report adds that:

After stopping his car, Mr. ———— turned off his ignition and after stepping out of his car, he heard a deep throbbing sound coming from the object. As the object started its ascent, it made a sound like a large covey of quail starting to fly at the same time. There was no visible exhaust or color detectable by the viewer. There was only one object seen. Mr. ———— described the weather as being warm, and the sky dotted by clouds. He does not recall a wind at the time of the sighting. Mr. ——— said that the sun was just rising as he was going to work that morning, and it was light enough to see all objects in the area. The viewer cannot recall any aircraft, trains, or vehicles in the area at the time of the sighting. He stated that to his knowledge, he was the only person to view the object. He wanted to go into the area over which the object had hovered; however, he did not since the terrain was rough (ditch, fence, tall weeds, and he has an artificial leg which prevents normal movement). Mr. ——— said that the grass was moving under the object as it was hovering. Mr. ——— was at a total loss in attempting to explain the viewed object as being a "vision" [or] "optical illusion," or some other explainable phenomenon. When pressed, he stated that he thought it was probably a new device of the government.

I remember puzzling long and hard over this case, one of the very early ones received by Blue Book. My skepticism was so great at that time that I was quite willing to dismiss it as a hallucination. In view of the great wealth of data that I have accumulated since then, I find that I can no longer take refuge in this hypothesis.

I admit that I am still puzzled as to what level of "reality" should be attributed to these "events"; but I no longer entertain any doubt whatsoever that the witness in this case and the ones that follow all sincerely believed that what they had had was a true, tangible experience.

The Case of the Former Mayor

One of the more interesting but isolated Air Force "Unidentifieds" came to Blue Book in the form of a (then) secret CIA document:

Information from Foreign Documents or Radio Broadcasts.
Country of origin: Germany
Subject: military, scientific
How published: daily newspaper

Where published: Athens
Date published: 9 Jul 1952
Language: Greek
Source: I. Kathimerini

BERLIN—Furnished with sworn testimony of an
eyewitness, Oscar Linke, a forty-eight-year-old German, and former mayor of Gleimershausen, West
Berlin, intelligence officers have begun investigating
a most unusual "flying saucer" story. According to
this story, an object "resembling a huge flying pan"
and having a diameter of about fifteen meters landed
in a forest clearing in the Soviet zone of Germany.

Linke recently escaped from the Soviet zone along
with his wife and six children.

Linke and his eleven-year-old daughter Gabriella
made the following sworn statement last week before a judge:

"While I was returning to my home with Gabriella,
the tire of my motorcycle blew out near the town of
Hasselbacht. While we were walking along towards
Hasselbacht, Gabriella pointed out something that
lay at a distance of about a hundred and forty meters
away from us. Since it was twilight, I thought that
she was pointing at a young deer.

"I left my motorcycle near a tree and walked towards the spot which Gabriella had pointed out.
When, however, I reached a spot about fifty-five meters from the object, I realized that my first impression had been wrong. What I had seen were two men
who were not more than forty meters away from me.
They seemed dressed in some shiny metallic clothing.
They were stooped over and were looking at something lying on the ground.

"I approached until I was only about ten meters
from them. I looked over a small fence and then I
noticed a large object whose diameter I estimate to
be within thirteen to fifteen meters. It looked like a
huge frying pan. There were two rolls of holes along
the periphery, about thirty centimeters in circum-
ference. The space between the two holes was about
0.45 m. On top of this metal object was a black
conical tower about three meters high. At that mo-

ment, my daughter, who had remained a short distance behind me, called me. The two men must have heard my daughter's voice because they immediately jumped on the conical tower and disappeared inside. I had previously noted that one of the men had a lamp on the front part of his body which lit up at regular intervals. Now, the side of the object on which the holes had opened began to glitter. Its color seemed green but later turned to red. At the same time, I began to hear a slight hum. When the brightness and the hum increased, the conical tower began to slide down into the center of the object. The whole object then began to rise slowly from the ground and rotate like a top.

"It seemed to me as if it were supported by the cylindrical plant which had gone down from the top of the object through the center and had now appeared on the bottom of the object. The object, surrounded by a ring of flames, was now a certain number of feet above the ground.

"I then noted that the whole object had risen slowly off the ground. The cylinder on which it was supported had now disappeared within its center and had reappeared on the top of the object. The rate of climb had now become greater. At the same time, my daughter and I heard a whistling sound similar to that heard when a bomb falls.

"The object rose to a horizonal position, turned towards a neighboring town, and then, gaining altitude, it disappeared over the heights and forests in the direction of Stockholm."

Many other persons who live in the same area as Linke related that they saw an object which they thought to be a comet (meteor). A shepherd stated that he thought he was looking at a comet moving away at low altitude from the height on which Linke stood.

After submitting his testimony to the judge, Linke made the following statement: "I would have thought that both my daughter and I were dreaming if it were not for the following elements involved: when the object had disappeared, I went to the place where it had been. I found a circular opening in the

ground and it was quite evident that it was freshly
dug. It was exactly the same shape as the conical
tower. I was then convinced that I was not dreaming."
Linke continued: "I had never heard of the term
flying saucers before I escaped the Soviet zone into
western Berlin. When I saw this object, I immediately thought that it was a new Soviet military machine. I confess that I was seized with fright because
the Soviets do not want anyone to know about their
work. Many persons have been restricted in their
movements for many years in East Germany because
they knew too much!"

The Radio Announcer's Surprise

I include this next Blue Book case because it contains several elements that have recurred in many CE-IIIs.
On October 23, 1965, a radio announcer, of good reputation, was driving toward Long Prairie, a community west
of Minneapolis. When he was just four miles from town,
in rolling hill country, he rounded a curve and there, just
before him in the road, was a rocket-shaped object, silver
in color.

It would almost appear that one's chances of seeing a
UFO are greater if one is driving a car than if one is
merely out in the open. In case after case, reports contain the phrase "after rounding a bend in the road." While
these objects are not *always* standing in the road, they
seem to do so often enough. When there is open country-
side on either side of the road, one can't help but wonder
why.

What happened to the radio announcer next will be recognized by the experienced reader as a second common
feature: his car engine stopped and his car lights went
off. He remained in his car, transfixed by the object which
was standing on fins and was thirty to forty feet tall, about
ten feet thick, and had light shining from its bottom. This
young man's own narrative account states:

I was driving west on Minnesota Highway 27 when
I went around a bend in the road and my car engine stopped running and my lights went off. I looked

up and saw this object standing in the middle of the road. It was around 7:15 P.M. . . . I had just checked my watch a minute before, so I know what time it was. I finally coasted to a stop about twenty feet from it. . . . I tried to start my car but it would not start. I did not get any response to my starter. I then got out of my car with the idea to go up to it and try to rock the center of gravity and topple it over so that I would have the evidence right there in black and white. I got to the front end of my car and stopped with no further interest in going further because three little "creatures" came from around behind and stood in front of the object. I think that they were looking at me. I cannot be sure because I did not see eyes of any sort. I know that I was looking at them and I was quite fascinated with what I saw. You might ask why, since I was willing to go up to them before, I did not go up to them now. I used what I hope was common sense. I felt that if they could stop my car, they could surely do something worse to me and I wanted to live to tell the story so that the people of the United States would know that there were things of this nature. I can safely say that we "looked" at each other for about three minutes. Then they turned and went under the object and a few seconds later, the object started to rise slowly. After it was about one quarter mile high (this is only a guess), the light went out and my car engine started to run again (I did not have to touch the starter), and my headlights came on. I looked at the area that it had been sitting on over and could see no evidence that it had been on the ground. I then drove to the Todd County Sheriff's Office and reported what I had seen to the sheriff. He went back out to the spot and could not find anything on the road that would show they were on the ground. That is what happened. I know that this is quite a wild story but if you do not believe me, well, ———, that's your tough luck.

Signed,
J.F.T.

I personally investigated this case via telephone. In talking with the local sheriff, I learned that, according to reports, several coon hunters had also seen the object. And there were also corroborating witnesses (four of them) to its takeoff. The sheriff told me that Mr. T——— had a good reputation, and that when he came in he was "really scared." There were streaks of oil and water on the road which were reported to have been found at the object's landing site. It was determined that radar had not picked up the object but that it had reportedly been seen in many other towns. The sheriff in nearby Anoka stated that he had seen it.

There is another feature here, common to CE-IIIs: The reported "creatures" generally climb aboard and take off without seeming to desire communication. One would think that if all these cases were hoaxes, imaginative and detailed descriptions of the "creatures" would be even more bizarre than Mr. T———'s statement that "the creatures were brown or black, cylindrical in shape, had very thin 'arms' and walked on two 'fins.'"

In any event, Blue Book closed this case with no official investigation. I conducted my personal investigation of it and did not submit an official report to the Air Force.

The Mysterious Baseball Cap

Here is another Close Encounter of the Third Kind account, this time by a civilian instructor at Sheppard AFB, Wichita Falls, Texas. According to Blue Book, he was driving his car along the highway when he spotted a strange-looking object parked so that it blocked the outer portion of a road curve sign (i.e., just *before* a bend in the road). The object had the appearance of a conventional aircraft but without wings or motors. There was a Plexiglas-like bubble on top, similar to a B-26 canopy. As the observer approached, he noticed a man wearing a baseball cap (!) enter the object by steps from the back. After the man had entered, the object began to rise from the pavement and headed in a southeasterly direction at approximately 700 MPH. The object had forward and aft lights which were very bright. As it rose from the ground, a high-speed-drill-type sound was heard plus a sound like that of a welding rod when an arc is struck. The object was reported to be seventy-five feet long, nearly eight feet from top to bottom, and about twelve feet wide. There were some kind of supports on its underside.

After the object had disappeared from view, the witness got back into his car and drove for several miles on the highway. Then he stopped his car to talk with another individual who was parked on the side of the road. The second man was watching some lights along Red River, approximately five or six miles to the southeast.

An Associated Press report appeared in the Dallas *Times-Herald* on March 27, 1966. Its statements are not at variance with the Air Force's, but it presents the sighting from a slightly different angle:

Acquaintances and friends call Eddie Laxson, 56, a "calm, solid sort." And that's what the former newspaperman wants to stay in the eyes of his associates.

So when Laxson saw what might be described as a flying saucer-fish shape, he decided not to say anything about it. But then he talked to C. W. Anderson, a truck driver, and decided to tell his story. Anderson said that he also saw the strange craft.

"It takes more courage to report a thing like this than it does to forget it," he told newsmen this week. "I know that people will say that Laxson is durned crazy. But that's what I saw."

Laxson said that he was driving west on U.S. 70 in southern Oklahoma about five A.M. Wednesday morning when "I saw what I first believed to be a huge van or a house being moved, stalled on the highway," he related. "I got this impression because the red lights had flashed on and off." [We have here a familiar example of the escalation of hypothesis— an attempt to explain something first in natural terms.] "Since I couldn't get by it, I parked my car about one hundred yards away and walked towards the object, thinking that I might lend it some assistance. As I got closer, I saw that the vehicle was in the shape of a perch-fish, seen from the side. I noticed also a plastic bubble on the front. On the side I made out the [letters] 'TLA' with the last two figures '38.' " He said that the figure between the four and the three was either a seven or a one but could not be sure.

"When a man wearing what appeared to be a mechanic's hat with the brim rolled up, climbed a ladder into the object, I thought about the camera that I carried in my car and turned to get it. But just then, the object rose from the ground with the sound of hissing geese or welding torch and took off towards Red River to the south.

"The episode made the hair stand up on my head," Laxson smiled. "I then examined the spot where the vehicle had been parked and saw no sign of scorching."

Laxson had made up his mind not to tell the story, he said, but about a mile down the road he came upon Anderson, standing beside the truck which the Snyder, Oklahoman drives for Magnum Oil and Gas Company.

Anderson said he, too, had watched the strange flying object and that he believed that it had been following him. He said that he watched it in his rearview mirror for several miles. . . .

Laxson, pressed by newsmen about the craft, was asked if it could have been a helicopter.

He said that he got as close as fifty feet to the reported craft, was familiar with military aircraft, and that the strange vehicle "definitely was not a helicopter."

The Hunter in the Tree

This next case took place on the night of September 5, 1964, near Cisco Grove, California. Mr. S———, a young man, out on a hunting trip, became separated from his two companions and, as dusk was approaching, decided to take shelter in a tree. He strapped himself to a branch with his belt to keep from falling off in his sleep.

While seeking shelter, Mr. S——— witnessed three flying objects, each equipped with a protruding and rotating light that emitted cooing noises. Upon first noticing the lights, he figured them to be helicopters out

looking for him (once again the escalation of hypothesis
or seeking of a natural explanation first). Mr. S———
left his tree-nest and lighted signal fires on the ridge over-
looking Granite Creek Valley. The lights then appeared
to be three silvery objects that were circling his position.
Two unknown objects were dropped by them in their
descent. Within a few minutes, he heard a loud crashing
in the underbrush below and, frightened, he took sanctu-
ary in the lower branches of a tall pine tree. He there-
upon witnessed two humanlike individuals approaching
his signal fires. They were garbed in silvery collarless
suits, had unusual, protruding eyes, and communicated
to one another via an unintelligible cooing noise. According to Mr. S———, they were trying to dislodge
him from his tree position when a third "alien," described by Mr. S——— as a "robot," appeared on the
scene. Mr. S——— fired some arrows at the "robot" but
failed to distract or divert any of the strange individuals.
Then he tried lighting parts of his clothing on fire and
throwing it at them to frighten them away. The individuals had violent reactions, and at the time their craft began to ascend upwards, emitting a vapor which caused
him to black out. The only thing that prevented his falling was his bow wedged into a crotch of the living tree.
    Regaining consciousness in the early dawn, Mr.
S——— discovered that the UFO and its occupants had
disappeared. He rejoined his hunting companions and
told them his incredible tale. They remarked that it probably had something to do with the meteorite that the
government was looking for. Later on, he related the
story to his father-in-law, who persuaded him to get in
touch with the authorities. Mr. S——— contacted a local
astronomy instructor who subsequently notified Mather
AFB officials.
    According to Air Force reports, Mr. S——— was ap-
proximately twenty-seven years of age, married, and employed at a local missile production plant. He appeared
stable and consistent in telling his story and believed that
the incident occurred exactly as described. The actual tape
recording of his narration of the encounter were retained
by the Air Force, as well as the arrows he fired at the
aliens. Blue Book labeled this one "Psychological," but
to the best of my knowledge, never studied the tapes.

The story of a bow-and-arrow hunter, held at bay high in a tree, setting flame to parts of his clothing and tossing them down onto the heads of his assailants until he was half-naked, passing out because of strange fumes emitted by "aliens," is certainly hard to believe, unless one considers it within the framework of the whole parade of stories similar to it. Apparently, however, the local astronomy instructor believed Mr. S——— sufficiently to report his story. Would he have done so if the witness was obviously unstable? Yet Blue Book persisted in calling the case "Psychological" for the record.

In the next three cases, Blue Book did not do much better; but independent of Blue Book a number of dedicated civilian investigators pursued them and did the best they could with limited time and funds.

Since these cases are classic and much has been written about them, the reader will do well to examine other sources for a lengthier analysis of each. It is very significant that the more detailed independent investigations of these three cases failed to turn up evidence which would discredit them: on the contrary, closer scrutiny increased the "reality" of these events. Let us consider these cases chronologically.

The Kelly-Hopkinsville Sighting

This case, which occurred on August 21, 1965, on a farm in Kelly, Kentucky, is often termed the Kelly-Hopkinsville case since Kelly is just a local cluster of houses seven miles from Hopkinsville.

Although the Air Force never officially investigated the case, Maj. John E. Albert "formally" looked into it. According to his statement from the Blue Book files:

> On or about August 22nd, 1965, at about eight A.M., I heard a news broadcast concerning an incident at Kelly Station, approximately six miles north of Hopkinsville. At the time I heard this news broadcast, I was at Gracey, Kentucky, on my way to Campbell AFB, where I am assigned for reserve training. I called the air base and asked if they had heard anything about an alleged flying saucer report.

They said they had not and suggested that as long as I was in the area, I should determine if there was anything to this report. I immediately drove to the scene and located the home belonging to a Mrs. Lenny Langford.

Then appear in Blue Book the following series of statements which later investigators showed to be untrue: that Mrs. Langford belonged to the Holy Roller Church (she belonged to the Trinity Pentecostal, which holds conventional-type services); that on the night of the occurrence she had gone to a religious meeting; that her sons, their wives, and some friends had become worked up into a frenzy, becoming very "emotionally unbalanced." All of these statements are completely unsubstantiated. They were apparently obtained from Deputy Sheriff Patts, an avowed skeptic, and not from any of the witnesses.*

Most of Blue Book's information on this case comes from local air-base officials who took a peripheral interest in it. One of the captains from Campbell Air Force Base wrote a letter which closes with the following statement.

> . . . I would like to point out that out of all the cases I investigated for the commander and out of all the incidents that happened around Campbell during my three and a half years there, this incident impressed me the least and furthermore, I was never even remotely connected with it. It follows then, that my memory concerning this incident is rather faulty, and I am not even sure when it took place. Therefore, I am afraid that I have not been of much help and for this I apologize.

Even though he wasn't even "remotely" connected with it, the case impressed him very little!

*The Center for UFO Studies is shortly to publish a detailed account of this case by Isabel Davis, incorporating much of the investigation of the incident performed by Bud Ledwith and therefore made before Mrs. Langford and her family had grown thoroughly disgusted with curiosity-seekers. Ms. Davis took up the trail a year later after things had completely quieted down, and obtaining the cooperation of the primary witnesses, reviewed the entire incident from this remove in time.

My synopsis of the case is based on material obtained directly from Bud Ledwith, who at that time was engineer-announcer at radio station WHOP in Hopkinsville, and who on the morning after the event interviewed all seven adult members of the group. What follows are a number of relevant passages from the notarized account of the investigation he made on the morning following the sighting:

Seven adults were interviewed in three groups: the three women at noon the following morning, the one man who had been in the field working since about eight A.M. the same morning, and the other three men after they had returned from an all-day trip to Evansville, Indiana, about eight P.M. that evening. The following was a correlation between those three separate reports. None of the involved groups had an opportunity to talk to each other about the event since around eight A.M. that morning.

All groups agreed that the height of the creatures was from two and a half to three and a half feet. They all agreed that the head was bald, the same color as the body; the head was rather oblong like an egg. Mr. Ledwith recorded the following comments from various of the witnesses: 'many bullets were fired and a twelve-gauge shotgun was used. . . . Whenever it was hit, it would float or fall over and scurry for cover. . . . The shots when striking the object would sound as though they were hitting a bucket. The objects made no sound . . . while jumping or walking or falling. The undergrowth would rustle as the objects went through it. . . . There was no sound of walking. The objects were seemingly weightless as they would float down from trees more than fall from them.

When they approached the house in all cases, the arms were raised in a "stick 'em up" fashion, and they would approach very slowly on their hind feet. When struck with bullets or a flashlight, they would drop to hands position and run. Since the talon curls much in the same fashion as a hawk's and the hands were raised above the head, it apparently looked rather like an attack position. However, it may have been a friendly gesture to indicate that they had no weapons. They would move slowly when in this position towards the houses and made no attempt to enter. They just stood and stared until they were frightened away. On several occasions, all lights were turned out back and front and then they would approach from any angle. My personal observations of the people involved are this: the three women know exactly what they saw and accepted drawing number one as the objects involved. I had them describe, to the best of their ability, each individual detail that is in the picture. I attempted not to lead them . . . but rather tried to follow their lead in drawing it part by part but the whole operation took about an hour and a half before the final drawing was made. As for the three men: I had laid the drawing on the table before the men came in . . . and one of them picked up the drawing and exclaimed, "That's it!" We sat down to make changes in accordance with what they saw. . . . The two main differences were the shape of the face . . . and the husky upper body.

The story quite naturally met with complete disbelief on the part of most persons, except those who knew the family well. There is no question that Mr. Ledwith, who made the only serious investigation following the event, firmly believed the witnesses. He could find no motive whatever for a hoax—the simple folk were not seeking publicity, and indeed suffered horribly from curiosity-seekers, reporters, and sensation-mongers. It is also highly unlikely that a hoax would involve that many persons and a midnight dash to a police station miles away.

Although I had no official connection with the case, I did make an attempt to find out whether there had been any traveling circuses in the area from which some monkeys could have escaped. The monkey hypothesis fails, however, if the basic testimony of the witnesses can be accepted. Under a barrage of gunfire from Kentuckians,

over a somewhat extended period, it is unthinkable that
at least one cadaver would not have been found. Furthermore, monkeys do not float down from trees: they
either jump or fall. And anyway, I was unable to find
any trace of a traveling circus!

If, then, one assumes that the event did take place as
reported, and if the creatures had a physical reality, why
was not one of them killed under fire? Why did they
flip over when hit?

Bizarre? Yes. But Close Encounters of the Third Kind
are *by no means infrequent.* Long after the end of
Project Blue Book, during the months of September and
October 1973, some *seventy* Close Encounters of the
Third Kind were reported in the United States alone.*
But even during the Blue Book period there were many
more CE III events reported in the press and to private
investigators than were officially recognized by Blue
Book. In UFOCAT, the computerized data bank of UFO
cases maintained by the Center for UFO Studies, there
appear about twenty times as many CE-III cases as appear
in the Blue Book files for the same period.

A Strange New Device of You Americans

The classic account of Father William Melchior Gill, an
Anglican priest stationed at the mission of Boianai in Papua, New Guinea, has been published in several places.
However, the most extensive account, by the Reverend
R.G. Crutwell, has unfortunately not had the wide circula-
tion that it deserves. In various forms, it was privately circulated and then published in *Flying Saucer Review,* Special Issue No. 4, August 1971. More recently, A.H.
Lawson, professor of English at California State University at Long Beach, has published a fifty-page treatise
on the Father Gill case, reprinting the study by Reverend
Crutwell.**

*See *1973: The Year of the Humanoids,* by David Webb, published by the Center for UFO Studies, 924 Chicago Ave., Evanston,
Il. 60202.

**This and other publications in connection with Professor Law-
son's studies are available through the CSU library or through the
Center for UFO Studies.

The Blue Book material on the case is almost entirely from the Air Attaché in Australia, and does contain much of the same material appearing in Rev. Crutwell's treatise. What is different is Blue Book's "attitude" toward the case, which they dismiss as "misinterpretation of astronomical bodies" despite the fact that many of the observations were made under an overcast sky. The Australian Air Force evaluation was no more satisfying: "RAAF could come to no definite conclusion on the report, and inquiries within the United Kingdom and the United States had no clues or answers. As a result, these sightings have been classified as aerial phenomena [sic] but most probably they were reflections off a cloud of a major light source of unknown origin."

This case has always intrigued me and I was therefore grateful when the opportunity presented itself to visit Boianai with Rev. Crutwell. We located six of the original witnesses and even though the sighting was by then fifteen years old (it took place in the latter part of June 1959), the event was rendered in great detail. Rev. Crutwell was to act as my interpreter with the natives. At first, many of them felt that I represented a government authority, and would not open up; but after a while the information flowed freely. How *accurately*, I have, of course, no way of knowing. But from the facial expressions and gestures of the natives, I sensed that the event had been real as far as they were concerned.

The reader should bear in mind that in addition to the Father Gill sighting, there were sixty-one others that year in the same general area. The following table shows that the distribution of the majority according to locality:

Boianai	18 objects
Baniai	13 "
Ruabapain	7 "
Dagura	6 "
Dabora	5 "
Giwa	4 "

The rest of the sightings were fairly well distributed around the eastern tip of Papua.

When the famous sightings occurred at Boianai on June 26 and 27, 1959, Rev. Crutwell was away on a walking tour of the mountain stations in the Dago Country. While he was away, Father Gill wrote the following letter to his old friend and confidant, the Reverend D. Durry at St. Aidan's in Dagura:

Dear David:

Life is strange, isn't it? Yesterday, I wrote you a letter (which I still intend to send you) expressing opinions on UFOs. [Although this letter is not on file, it apparently expressed grave doubts about UFOs because, in conversations with Crutwell, he told me of his great reluctance to believe in such matters. Visitations of that sort are not entirely acceptable in Anglican theology, or so I am told.] Not less than twenty-four hours later I had changed my views somewhat. Last night, we at Boianai experienced about four hours of UFO activity, and there is no doubt whatever that they are handled by beings of some kind. At times it was absolutely breathtaking. . . .

There have been many references to Father Gill's careful note-taking while the event was in progress. This in itself is *most* unusual, especially when a flashlight was needed to record most of his observations. But I know Father Gill as a painstaking, methodical, and unexcitable person—just the sort to stand calmly by and take notes at the height of the exciting action. The Blue Book files contain these notes, since they were officially reported to the project by the Air Attaché in Australia. Just a few will suffice to highlight the action:

6:45 P.M.—Patches of low clouds. Sighted bright white light from front door.

6:50 —Clear over Dagura and Menape. Call Stephen and Eric Langford.

6:52 —Stephen arrives. Confirms not a star. Five hundred feet? Orange?

6:55 —Sent Eric to call the people. One object on top moves—man? Now three men, moving, glowing, doing something on deck. Gone.

7:00 —Men one and two again.

7:04 —Gone again.

7:10 —Cloud ceiling covered sky; ceiling 2,000 feet [and thus, no stars or planets]. Men three, four, two [appeared in that order]. Thin electric blue spotlight. Men gone. Spotlight still there.

7:12 —Men one and two appear again. Blue light.

7:20 —UFO goes through clouds.

8:28 —Clear sky here, heavy cloud over Dagura. UFO seen by me overhead. Called station people.

8:50 —Clouds forming again. Big one stationary and larger—the original? Others coming and going through the clouds. As they descend through clouds, light reflected like a large halo on the cloud—no more than 2,000 feet, probably less (height of clouds is judged by height of nearby mountain).

9:46 —Overhead UFO reappears; is hovering.

10:50 —No sign of UFO.

11:04 —Heavy rain.

Gill had drawings made and obtained the signatures of witnesses. There were thirty-eight in all, of whom twenty-five signed the report (the children were excluded). Apart from Gill, the witnesses included five Papuan teachers and three medical assistants.

Father Gill told me, as he has told others, of the first sighting of the bright light. He had just *had* dinner, and as he came out the front door of the mission house he glanced up at the sky and saw Venus, but in addition to Venus he saw a bright white light, somewhat above Venus. Part of the sighting was made under an overcast sky, with the objects ascending and descending through clouds, casting bright haloes on clouds as they passed through!

Blue Book labeled the sighting "stars and planets." But how could this have been possible? In all my career as an astonomer, I have yet to observe stars or planets appearing to descend through clouds to a height of less than two thousand feet, illuminating the clouds as they did so. In addition, Father Gill estimated the height of the disc to be three to four hundred feet, and its apparent diameter about five inches at arm's length. Teacher Stephen said that if he put his hand out closed, it would cover about half of it. I have yet to see Venus appearing larger than my fist.

Father Gill's account continues:

> As we watched it, men came out from this object and appeared on the top of it, on what appeared to be a deck on top of the huge disc. There were four men in all, occasionally two, then one, then three, then four: we noted the various times the men appeared. And then later on all those witnesses who were quite sure that our records were right, and that they agreed [they] saw the men at the same time that I did were able to sign their names as witnesses of what we assumed to be human activity or beings of some sort on the object itself.

The next night was even more interesting! One of the natives, Annie Laurie Borowa, ran into Father Gill's study in great excitement and asked him to come outdoors. The sighting he made then rules out Venus even more completely. Gill's first notes were at 6:02 P.M. when the sun, close to the equator, would not yet have set, although it would have been behind the mountains. Under no circumstances would Venus have been bright enough in the daytime sky to have caused all that excitement among the natives. Again we have Gill's own words:

> . . . We stood in the open to watch. Although the sun had set (behind the mountains), it was quite light for the following fifteen minutes. We watched figures appear on top—four of them—there was no doubt that they were human. This is possibly the same object that I took to be the "mother ship" last night. Two smaller UFOs were seen at the same time, stationary, one over the hills, west, and one overhead. On the large one, two of the figures seemed to be doing something in the center of the deck—they were occasionally bending over and raising their arms as though adjusting or setting up something. One

figure seemed to be standing, looking down on us (a group of about a dozen).

Now comes the climax. Father Gill stretched his arm above his head and waved. To his surprise, the figure waved back. One of his companions waved both arms over his head and then the two outside figures did the same. There was more waving and now all four of the beings seemed to wave back!

> There seemed to be no doubt that our movements were answered. All the mission boys made audible gasps.
>
> As dark was beginning to close in, I sent Eric for a torch and directed a series of long dashes towards the UFO. After a minute or two of this, the UFO apparently acknowledged by making several waving motions back and forth (in a sideways direction, like a pendulum). The waving by us was repeated and this was followed by more passes with the torch and then the UFO began to become slowly bigger, apparently coming in our direction. It ceased after perhaps half a minute and came on no further. After a further two or three minutes, the figures apparently lost interest in us for they disappeared below deck.

Father Gill also indicated that the whole group had begun to shout and to make beckoning motions to the men to descend, but there was absolutely no response, other than that already noted. Finally, there were no sounds whatever emanating from either the beings or their machine.

What Father Gill's notes state next has caused much controversy. At 6:30 P.M., he went in to dinner. How is it, skeptics ask, that in the midst of all this commotion, a person could calmly go in to dinner? One would really have to know Father Gill to understand this. He is a calm man—a man who takes things in his stride; furthermore, this was the second night of apparitions and he had watched for four and one-half hours the night before. When I spoke with Father Gill in Melbourne, I did, however, ask him about this. His response was: "Looking back, I sometimes wonder about this myself. I thought, too, that it might be just a new device of you Americans."

According to his notes, he came out from dinner at 7 P.M. and the UFO was still present, although it appeared somewhat smaller. Then, everyone went into church for evensong. This fact also seems incredible to skeptics; but, for the Boianai group, going in to dinner and to evensong was a part of a rigid daily routine, something one did without question.

I am reminded of a letter I received from an English schoolboy many years ago, describing a typical Daylight Disc, which he stated came down in a sort of "falling leaf motion." It apparently came down too slowly, for he wrote: "And then it was time for tea"—and he went inside, leaving the disc to its own devices. Perhaps we shall never be able to account for human behavior, especially the British!

After evensong, the visibility was poor, the sky was covered with clouds, and no UFOs were in sight. At 10:40 P.M., Gill's notes read: "A terrific explosion just outside the mission house. Nothing seen." According to Crutwell's account, the explosion made Gill jump out of bed and gave him a tremendous shock. Remembering the UFO, he rushed out to see what had happened, but saw nothing unusual. The explosion, however, had awakened everyone on the station. Whether this "penetrating, ear-splitting" explosion had anything to do with the UFO is obviously conjectural. It was just one additional item to be added to the bizarre catalogue of events.

The five dozen or so separate events in Papua in 1959 perhaps lie too far back in time for any reliable documentation now. Undoubtedly much data of potential scientific value was lost by the refusal of the military to conduct any sort of scientific investigation when the events were fresh.

There is, however, one humorous sidelight: At precisely the same time that the events were occurring at Boianai on the 26th, a trader from Samurai, Ernie Evenett, saw an object approach from the north and heading northeast. It was greenish and very bright, with a trail of white flame behind it. It looked like a shooting star.

It descended quite close to me, appearing larger and larger and slowing down until it hovered about five hundred feet above me at an angle of about forty-five degrees. The light on it faded out except for the portholes which were brightly illuminated. The object had a silhouette of a rugby football, and had a kind of ring or band around it with four or five semi-dome portholes below the band on the side I could see.

On the next day, Mr. Evenett crossed over to Boianai on business and the natives asked him if he had seen the American Air Force last night. They said, "We did at Boianai."

Apparently others besides Father Gill felt that the Americans had something to do with what they had observed (and thus it was safe to go to dinner). Unfortunately, the Air Force cannot take credit for having a craft that can hover a few hundred feet above the ground, close enough for observers to make out individual men—and yet be completely silent!

The Socorro Case

For this next case I was sent by Blue Book to Socorro, New Mexico, as an official investigator. Despite my strong desire to find a natural explanation for the sighting (I was still unconvinced about the reality of CE-IIIs), I could find none; the case is therefore listed in the Blue Book files as "Unidentified."

The Socorro case was basically a single-witness sighting (although several other more distant witnesses to the object were reported), but the witness was a policeman whose character and record were unimpeachable. Physical traces were left on the ground; and, as I personally observed, some of the greasewood bushes in the immediate vicinity had been charred. Even Maj. Quintanilla, then head of Blue Book, was convinced that an actual physical craft had been present. He attempted, however, to establish that it had been some sort of test vehicle, perhaps a lunar landing module. All of his efforts (and they were indeed considerable) failed to give any indication that a man-made craft had landed at Socorro on the afternoon in question.

The event took place on the afternoon of April 24,

1964. By the time I arrived in Socorro, several days had passed and curiosity-seekers had played their part; but fortunately, the very early investigators, on the scene within hours, had placed small rocks around the four "landing marks," so I was able to examine them in much their original form.

By a happy train of circumstances, an FBI agent was in the police station on some other business when the incident was reported. He called the executive officer at White Sands Proving Grounds, who in turn called Capt. Holder, the up-range commander of the installation. The presence of the FBI agent probably spurred the Socorro police and the White Sands personnel to treat the matter seriously from the start. Lonnie Zamora, the police officer who was the principal witness, was immediately interviewed and a report written by one o'clock the next morning. Photographs were taken and measurements made with a tapemeasure.

There was very little more that I could do technically, so I concentrated my efforts on exploring the human side of the matter, checking out as closely as I could (then and during several later visits) the character and relationships of the persons involved. I was rather hoping, at the time, that I could somehow invalidate Lonnie Zamora's testimony, but I was completely unable to do this. He came through as a solid citizen, generally well liked and of a practical, down-to-earth nature, thus making his participation in a hoax seem extremely unlikely.

Of all the Close Encounters of the Third Kind, this is the one that most clearly suggests a "nuts and bolts" physical craft along with accompanying noises and propulsion. Zamora's statement, made within a few hours of the sighting, was as follows:

About 5:45 P.M., April 24, 1964, while in Socorro Two police car, I started to chase a car due south from west side of the courthouse. Car was apparently speeding and was about three blocks in front. At point on Old Rodeo Street, near George Murillo residence, the chased car was going ahead towards the rodeo grounds. Car chased was a new black Chevrolet. . . .

At this time I heard a roar and saw a flame in the sky to the southwest some distance away—possibly one-half mile or a mile. Came to mind that a dynamite shack in that area had blown up, decided to leave chased car go. Flame was bluish and sort of orange, too. Could not tell size of flame. Sort of motionless flame. Slowly descending. Was still driving car and could not pay too much attention to the flame. It was a narrow type of flame. It was like a "streamed down"—a funnel type—narrower at the top than at bottom. Flame possibly three degrees or so in width—not wide.

Flame was about twice as wide at bottom than top, and about four times as high as top was wide. Did not notice any object at top, did not notice if top of flame was level. Sun was to west and did not help glasses. Could not see bottom of flame because it was behind the hill.

No smoke noted. Noted some "commotion" at bottom—dust? Possibly from windy day—wind was blowing hard. Clear, sunny sky otherwise—just a few clouds scattered over area.

Noise was a roar, not a blast. Not like a jet. Changed from high frequency to low frequency and then stopped. Roar lasted possibly ten seconds, I was going towards it at the time on a rough gravel road. Saw flames same color as best I recall. Sound distinctly from high to low until disappeared. Windows both were down. No other spectators noted—no traffic except the car in front. Car in front might have heard it but possibly did not see it because car in front was too close to hill in front to see flame.

After the roar and flame, did not note anything while going up the somewhat steep, rough hill—had to back up and try again, two more times. Got up about halfway first time, wheels started skidding (roar still going on), had to back down and try again before made the hill. Hill about sixty feet long, fairly steep and with loose gravel and rock. While beginning third time, noise and flame not noted.

After got to top, traveled slowly on the gravel road westwardly. Noted nothing for a while—for possibly ten or fifteen seconds. Went slow, looking around for the shack—did not recall exactly where the dynamite shack was.

Suddenly noted a shiny type object to south about one hundred fifty to two hundred yards. It was off the road. My green sunglasses over prescription. At first glance, stopped. It looked at first like a car turned upside down. Thought some kids might have turned it over. Saw two people in white coveralls very close to object. One of these persons seemed to turn and look straight at my car and seemed startled—seemed to quickly jump somewhat.

At this time I began moving my car towards them quickly with the idea to help. Had stopped only about a couple of seconds. Objects were like aluminum—was whitish against the mesa background, not chrome. Seemed like oval in shape and I, at first glance, took it to be an overturned white car. Car appeared turned up like standing on radiator or trunk, at this first glance.

The only time I saw these two persons was when I had stopped for possibly two seconds or so, to glance at the object. I don't recall noting any particular shape or possibly any hats or headgear. Those persons appeared normal in shape—but possibly they were small adults or large kids. Then paid attention to road while driving. Radioed to sheriff's office, "Socorro Two to Socorro. Possible 10-40 [accident]. I'll be 10-6 [busy]." Out of car, checking the car down in the arroyo.

Stopped car, was still talking on radio, started to get out; mike fell down, reached back to pick up mike then replaced mike in slot and got out of car. Hardly turned around from car when heard roar (was not exactly a blast), very loud roar—at that close, it was real loud. Not like a jet—know what jets sound like. Started low frequency quickly, then rose in frequency (towards higher tone) and in loudness—loud to very loud. At same time as roar, saw flame. Flame was under the object. Object was starting to go straight up—slowly up. Object slowly rose straight up. Flame was light blue and at bottom was sort of orange-colored. From this angle, saw what

might be the side of object (not end as first noted).
Difficult to describe flame. Thought, from roar, it
might blow up. Flame might have come from underside of object, at middle, possibly a four feet area—
very rough guess. Cannot describe flames further
except blue and orange. No smoke except dust in
immediate area.

Object was oval in shape. It was smooth—no
windows or doors. As roar started, it was still on or
near the ground. Noted red lettering of some type.
Insignia about two and a half feet wide, guess. Was
in middle of object like drawing. Object still like
aluminum—white.

Can't tell how long saw object second time (the
"close" time). [Zamora was at this time seventy-five
to one hundred feet from the object itself.] Possibly
seconds—just guess—from time got out of car, glanced
at object, jumped over edge of hill, then got back
to car and radioed as object disappeared.

As my mike fell as I got out of the car, at scene
area, I heard about two or three loud thumps, like
someone hammering or shutting a door hard. These
thumps were possibly a second or less apart. This was
just before the roar. The persons were not seen when
I got up to the scene area.

As soon as saw flames and heard roar, turned
away, ran from object but did turn head towards
object. Bumped leg on car, back fender area. Car
facing southwest.

After fell by car and glasses fell off, kept running
towards north with car between me and the object
(for protection in case object exploded). Glanced
back a couple of times. Noticed that subject arose
to about level of car, about twenty to twenty-five feet
(guess). (Car was appreciably above object which
was in a gully.) Took, I guess, about six seconds
from when object started to rise and I glanced back.
I guess I ran about halfway to where I ducked down,
just over edge of hill. I guess I had run about twenty-
five feet when I glanced back and saw the object
about level with the car and it appeared directly
over the place where it rose from.

I was still running and I ducked just over the hill

—I stopped because I did not hear the roar. I was scared of the roar, I had planned to continue running down the hill. I turned around towards the ground, covering my face with my arms. Being that there was no roar, I looked up, and I saw the object going away from me in a southwest direction. When the roar stopped, heard nothing. It appeared to go at the same height and in a straight line, possibly ten to fifteen feet from the ground, and it cleared the dynamite shack by about three feet. The shack was about eight feet high. Object was traveling very fast. It seemed to rise up and take off immediately cross-country. I ran back to my car and as I ran back, I kept an eye on the object. I picked up my glasses (I left the sunglasses on the ground), got into the car, and radioed to Ned Lopez, the radio operator to "look out of the window to see if you can see an object." He asked, "What is it?" I answered, "It looks like a balloon." I don't know if he saw it. If Ned looked out of his window which faces north, he couldn't have seen it. I did not tell him at the moment which window to look out.

As I was calling Ned, I could still see the object. The object seemed to lift up slowly and to get small in the distance very fast. It seemed to just clear Box Canyon or Six Mile Canyon Mountain. It disappeared as it went over the mountains. It had no flame whatsoever as it was traveling over the ground and made no smoke or noise.

Just before Sergeant Chavez got to the scene, I got my pencil and drew a picture of the insignia. . . .

Several days later, Zamora and I went to the site alone, and he kindly re-enacted the entire train of events. He showed me just how he had run from the scene, where he had hit the car and knocked off his glasses, and how he had crouched with his arm across his eyes, glancing backward to see what was happening.

I examined the site carefully and took photographs. I also made a point of wandering pretty far afield to see if I could spot similar "landing marks" in the area. If there had been any, they might have indicated that the marks were attributable to cattle or some other "natural" cause. But there were no other similar marks anywhere. The marks themselves were only two or three inches deep, sandy, clayed, and hard-packed, and they appeared to be scooped out, as though a heavy mechanical device had slid rather gently into position.

Maybe there *is* a simple, natural explanation for the Socorro incident, but having made a complete study of the events, I do not think so. It is my opinion that a *real, physical* event occurred on the outskirts of Socorro that afternoon of April 24, 1964.

Because close encounters of the third Kind *are* so odd-sounding I suppose it is tempting to dismiss the many hundreds that have been reported as hoaxes or hallucinations. But there is very little evidence to support this contrived solution and much more evidence to indicate that we are dealing with a most real phenomenon of undetermined origin.

UFOTOS: A PICTURE IS NOT NECESSARILY WORTH A THOUSAND WORDS

This is not a trick photograph, because I don't know how yet.
> *—from a young boy's letter to Blue Book*

There are hundreds of photographs of purported UFOs in the declassified files of Project Blue Book, but not one that the Air Force was ever willing to admit as evidence that UFOs were real. A photograph, of course, is just a UFO report, but in a different form, and like a written report depends entirely on the credibility of the persons offering it. And just as the Air Force refused to accept any written report as evidence of a "genuine UFO," regardless of the credibility of the witness, so they refused to consider seriously any purported UFO photograph.

The majority of the photographs in the Blue Book files are indeed obvious hoaxes or misidentifications. Some look remarkably like hamburgers, padres' hats, inverted teacups and saucers and plates tossed into the air, lenticular clouds, chicken brooders with light bulbs or halved Ping-Pong balls attached to their undersides, and a whole host of other familiar (and some not so familiar) objects. In many cases that is exactly what they are—photographs of familiar objects tricked up by hoaxers to make them appear to be strange-looking "flying saucers."

There are other photographs in the files that are not deliberate fakes. They are real photographs of real objects. However, in many cases, the real objects photographed were aircraft, balloons, meteors, stars, double exposures of the moon, a living-room light fixture, streetlights, or auto headlights which the photographer honestly mistook for

UFOs at the time the film was shot, or after it was developed and the UFOs were "discovered."

There are still other photos of UFOs in the Blue Book
files that are . . . well, what *are* they? One can only
judge for one's self. While the Air Force could not prove
that all UFO photographs it received were fakes (this was
particularly true of those taken by military personnel on
duty), double exposures, scratches or chemical blobs on
negatives, light reflections from birds, balloons, aircraft or other objects, neither could anyone prove to
the Air Force's satisfaction that the photographs they
had taken were anything out of the ordinary.

Which Craft in Salem, Massachusetts?

One classic "UFO" photograph that has made the
rounds in just about every magazine and book on the
subject (including a fall 1976 pulp magazine, and a book
on Project Blue Book published in late 1976) is the famous
Salem, Massachusetts, UFO lights, taken in 1952 by an
official Coast Guard photographer. Unfortunately, not one
of these publications has, to my knowledge, provided any
significant details on the circumstances surrounding the
photograph, other than that it was taken at a Coast Guard
station by a Coast Guard photographer.

The following is the report of the investigation into the
photograph, made by R.G. Eastman, Treasury Department, U.S. Coast Guard, dated July 17, 1952:

> This investigation was predicated on information re-
> ceived from the CO, Coast Guard Air Station, Salem,
> Massachusetts, concerning unidentified airborne ob-
> jects sighted near the Air Station.
>   —— (292-624) SN, official photographer for the
> Air Station, was interviewed at 0845, 17 July 1952,
> in the photo lab at the Air Station.
> Statement enclosed.
>   —— (273-206) HMI, was interviewed in the
> sick bay at the Air Station at 0930, 17 July 1952.
> Statement enclosed.
>   The above are the only known eyewitnesses to

subject objects. No factual information could be learned concerning the size, shape, altitude, speed, sound or direction of motion, of the objects.

All personnel interviewed or questioned were informed that any information concerning the objects was "SECRET" and should not be discussed with anyone without permission of the CO.

/s/————

Blue Book's findings were as follows:

On 16 July 1952 a photograph of four objects was taken by the USCG station photographer at Salem, Massachusetts. The photograph was submitted to ATIC for analysis and the analysis was completed on 1 August 1952. Analysis was made from the original negative which was returned to the Coast Guard at their request. The results of this analysis indicated that the photo was a hoax. Extensive photographs were taken under similar conditions. Failure of the light source to cast reflections on the highly polished cars below indicated that the light was not outside and it was assumed by the analyst at the time that the photo was a double exposure and for this reason a hoax. A subsequent examination of this photo was made in October 1963 and the following analysis is indicated as a more probable cause.

The photo was taken through a window with a 4/5 Busch Pressman Camera (135 MM F4.7 Raptar lens with Rapax shutter, loaded with 4/5 Super XX cut film). The photographers observed several lights which seemed to be wavering. He observed the lights for 5 or 6 seconds and grabbed the camera, which had been on a nearby table. The focus was adjusted to infinity. The photographer pulled the slide in preparation for the picture when he noticed that the lights had dimmed. He assumed at the time that the object he saw was a reflection. He ran out of the room to get an additional witness, and upon returning noticed that the lights were again brilliant. When they went to the window the lights were gone. He again stated that perhaps some sort of refraction or ground reflection could possibly account for the lights.

The following points are deemed pertinent to analysis. The camera was focused on infinity and the picture taken through a window. As the witness approached the window, the objects dimmed, as he returned to his point of initial observation and at the second observation as he re-entered the room the lights were again brilliant. The objects as photographed appear fuzzy and out of focus. The cars and buildings outside are sharply outlined. The window frame inside the building is out of focus. All four objects have the same outline and general configuration, in spite of the blurring.

Conclusion: It is believed that the photos represent light reflections from an interior source (probably the ceiling lights) on the window through which the photo was taken. With the camera set on infinity the window would be more out of focus than the lights. The lights would still be out of focus since the distance from the lights to the window and back to the camera lens would still be shorter than the distance required for a clear picture with the lens setting on infinity. The objects outside the building would be in focus. The apparant [sic] brightness of the reflection would decrease as the photographer approached the window. The initial photo analysis indicating the magnitude of the light and substantiation of fact that the light source was not external is correct. There is no indication of any attempt to perpetrate a hoax. The photo received is similar to many others taken through windows which have been confirmed as reflections of an interior light source. Had the camera been focused for a shorter distance, the outline of the interior light source would have been sharper. It is believed that there is sufficient evidence to substantiate the evaluation of this photo as reflections of internal light sources.

My opinion on this widely publicized case may surprise you: I'd agree with Blue Book's evaluation—that the photograph was nothing more than misidentification of a light reflection in a window of the photo lab at the Coast Guard Station. But for some unknown reason, Blue Book *never publicized its findings*. This was a great chance to capitalize on their "it can't be, therefore it isn't" theory; yet they chose not to. Why?

We may never know. But one thing we *can* learn from this particular case is that photographs of lights purported to be UFOs *cannot* be taken at face value. Indeed, in my opinion, they cannot be taken at *any* value as UFO evidence without meeting the harshest criteria.

As a scientist, I have been extremely suspicious of any "UFO photographs" that have been submitted to me. I am doubly wary of those in the Blue Book files, since the circumstances surrounding many of them were never investigated by Blue Book at all. The adage "a picture is worth a thousand words" simply does not apply when it comes to proving the reality of UFOs based on photographs in the Blue Book files.

In my book, *The UFO Experience*, I set down my own criteria for judging UFO photographs. They bear repeating here. A purported photograph of a UFO (particularly a Daylight Disc, because they are quite simple to fake) should not be taken seriously unless the following conditions are satisfied: (1) there are reputable witnesses to the actual taking of the picture, and those witnesses also sighted the object visually at the time; (2) the original negative(s) is available for study, since no adequate analysis can be made from prints alone; (3) the camera is available for study; and (4) the owner of the photograph is willing to testify under oath that the photograph is, to the best of his knowledge, genuine, that is, that the photograph shows what it purports to—a UFO. (The last condition need not apply if the photograph in question is accompanied by several independently taken photographs, preferably from significantly different locations.)

It is important to remember that in the case of UFO photographs, the photograph is no more reliable than the photographer. Thus, even when all of the above conditions have been met, the most positive statement that one can make about such photographs is that while the probability is quite high that they are genuine, the physical reality of the UFO(s) photographed cannot be established with absolute certainty.

There are no cases in the Blue Book files which meet the above stringent conditions. What we *do* find in the files are several cases that meet *nearly* all of the conditions. Let's examine some of them.

Navy vs. Air Force

Officer Delbert C. Newhouse, a Navy chief photographer with over one thousand hours of aerial photography missions under his belt, was driving his wife and two children from Washington, D.C., to Portland, Oregon, on July 2, 1952. They had just driven through Tremonton, Utah, a small town north of Salt Lake City, when Mrs. Newhouse spotted a group of unusual objects in the sky. Alerted by his wife, Newhouse pulled to the side of U.S. Highway 30S, parked his car, and got out to take a better look. It took him only seconds to realize that he was witnessing a most remarkable sight: A dozen or more disc-shaped objects were cavorting around in the sky in loose formation at about 10,000 feet, and they were like no aircraft he had ever seen or photographed before.

Grabbing his 16mm Bell & Howell movie camera from his car, Newhouse quickly shot 1,200 frames of film of the shiny objects (about 75 seconds in duration), managing to get a clear shot of one of the objects departing to the east, as the others in the group disappeared over the western horizon.

Probably no UFO photographs ever underwent more rigorous and extensive analysis and evaluation by the military. (Even so, as we shall see, there were serious gaps in their investigation.) The U.S. Navy photographic laboratory at Anacostia, Maryland, invested more than 1,000 man-hours analyzing every facet of the films, and the Air Force photo lab at Wright-Patterson Air Force Base—home of Project Blue Book—also subjected them to careful study and evaluation. The Navy analysts concluded they were photographs of intelligently controlled vehicles —not aircraft—but stopped short of describing them as space vehicles. Ultimately, the Air Force claimed the film images might have been light reflected from a flock of seagulls; they classified the Tremonton UFOs as "possible birds."

How probable was the seagull theory? According to the

following Memorandum for the Record of February 11, 1953, from Blue Book files, not very probable at all. This memo is interesting from another standpoint in that it reflects, once again, the Air Force's fear of public disclosure that its investigations of UFOs were not always conducted with the greatest scientific care. Here is the memo:

1. During a trip to Washington, D.C., on 29 January 1953 Capt. Ruppelt was informed that the press had learned about the Tremonton, Utah, movies and that Mr. Al Chop of the Office of Public Information, Department of Defense, Col. Teabert of AFOIN-2, and others believe that the movies should be released in accordance with the promise made this summer to the press that no information on the subject of Unidentified Flying Objects would be withheld. Capt. Ruppelt agreed with this point and it was decided that the factual data on this incident would be sent to Capt. Harry B. Smith, AFOIN-2A2, who would pass it on to Mr. Chop who in turn would write the release. The telecon also requested that the release be forwarded to ATIC for coordination. The subject telecon is TT15, 5 Feb 53, Item 2.

2. On 9 Feb 1953 Mr. Chop called that he had written the release and showed it to Col. Smith of AFOIN-2A. They believe that there would be a question asked as to the findings of the Air Force and Navy photo labs and that these reports would have to be released. If they weren't released, the press would begin to thisk they contained some "hot" material and that the ATIC concurred that this could happen, and that if it did happen it could create a great deal of excitement.

3. The Air Force lab analysis concludes that:

a. They are reasonably certain that the brightness of the images on the film exceeds that of any bird.

b. The objects are not spherical balloons.

c. The objects could be aircraft. (Note: the absence of sound almost rules out aircraft. Aircraft in a "dogfight" can be heard at almost any altitude. In addition, the area of the sighting was not a restricted air space area and it is doubtful that such flying would be carried out in the airways.)

The Navy report says the objects are:

a. Self-luminous or light sources.

b. Could not be aircraft or balloons.

c. No bird is known to reflect enough light to cause the images shown on the film.

It can be noted that the Navy people deduced this on each frame. This required about 1,000 man-hours. It was brought out by two astronomers who heard a Navy briefing on the analysis of the movies that the method used to measure the brightness of each spot was wrong, therefore, the results of the entire study were wrong.

4. The subject of the release was discussed with Lt. Col. Johnston and Col. McDuffy and it was decided that the movies would be released without comment as to what they were *and hope that no questions were asked about the Navy report. This is a "calculated" risk of another big "flap."* [Italics added.]

5. The other alternative is to quickly get more data on the subject. Several things can be done and are listed below in the order of how soon they could be accomplished:

a. As far as gulls are concerned the big question is, how much light will be reflected? Can you see a gull reflecting light and not recognize that it is a gull? To check this it would be necessary to go to a location where you have a lot of gulls and bright sunlight and take movies with a 3-inch lens. It would be necessary to know how far the gulls were away each time a movie was taken. At this time of the year Florida is the only place where sunshine and gulls can be assured.

b. Using special funds, have General Mills release a group of pillow balloons arranged in the same sequence as the objects are in the movies and measuring the distance at which the movies were taken.

c. Have two aircraft do maneuvers at various altitudes and photograph them.

d. Request that the Navy re-do the study using the

methods of density measurement that are prescribed
by the astronomers.

Conclusion

6. If it is deemed advisable to release the movies
quickly, state that the Air Force cannot positively
identify the objects but they are reasonably sure that
they are balloons or gulls, consequently no further effort is going to be put into the incident. If the Navy
and Air Force reports are requested, state that due to
the meager data they used, the reports must be discounted. *It would be rather poor policy to state that
the Navy had made an error in the beginning of their
analysis.* [Italics added.]

7. If it is too much of a risk to do this (suggestion
in paragraph 6) immediately go ahead with items a,
b, and c of paragraph 5 on a high-priority basis.

Recommendation

8. It is recommended that the above plan be given
to AFOIN-2A2 and let them confer with the Director
of Intelligence on the subject of a release.

The recommendation that additional tests be undertaken
to determine whether the UFOs could possibly have been
seagulls or aircraft was never followed up; the case was
dropped, and the possibility of seagulls or aircraft left
wide open.

What *were* the UFOs Newhouse photographed? In this
case a paragraph from p. 224 of Capt. Ruppelt's book is
worth one picture:

After I got out of the Air Force I met Newhouse
and talked to him for two hours. I've talked to many
people who have reported UFOs, but few impressed
me as much as Newhouse. I learned that when he and
his family first saw the UFOs they were close to the
car, much closer than when he took the movie. To
use Newhouse's own words, "If they had been the
size of a B-29 they would have been at 10,000 feet

altitude." And the Navy man and his family had taken a good look at the objects—they looked like "two pie pans, one inverted on top of the other!" He didn't just *think* the UFOs were disk-shaped; he *knew* that they were; he had plainly seen them. I asked him why he hadn't told this to the intelligence officer who interrogated him. He said that he had. Then I remembered that I'd sent the intelligence officer a list of questions I wanted Newhouse to answer. The question "What did the UFOs look like?" wasn't one of them because when you have a picture of something you don't normally ask what it looks like. Why the intelligence officer didn't pass this information on to us I'll never know.

Later on, the Condon Report concurred with Blue Book's "seagull" theory. While its analysis of the Tremonton film quoted Ruppelt in several places, the above comment made by him was neither mentioned nor considered. The substance of Newhouse's observation, as related to Ruppelt, *was* included in the Condon Report, but it was written off on the basis that there was no such detail in the Blue Book files and this evidence was made known only after Newhouse had become associated with NICAP (the independent investigating group considered by the Air Force as its arch enemy) around 1955.

The Tremonton, Utah, case is one in which the Air Force had the testimony of a reliable and credible witness (not to mention an expert in aerial photography), a second adult witness (his wife), and motion pictures of the UFOs observed, but still could not or would not seriously consider a conclusion that the UFOs observed and photographed were real.

Bear Mountain UFO

Sometimes the Air Force described a photograph as a hoax even if there was no proof that a hoax had been perpetrated. The following case, involving the sighting and photographing of a UFO at Bear Mountain State Park, sixty miles north of New York City, on December 18, 1966, was one in which I was prompted to challenge the official Blue Book evaluation of "Hoax." First, the details as reported in the investigating officer's questionnaire:

A. Description of the Object(s):
1. SHAPE: Long object with hump on its back.
2. SIZE COMPARED TO A KNOWN OBJECT: Unknown except very big. Kept shape.
3. COLOR: Goldfish—silver to brown.
4. NUMBER: One.
5. FORMATION, IF MORE THAN ONE: N/A.
6. ANY DISCERNIBLE FEATURES OR DETAILS: Long with hump on back.
7. TAIL, TRAIN, OR EXHAUST, INCLUDING SIZE OF SAME COMPARED TO SIZE OF OBJECT(S): None.
8. SOUND: if heard, describe sound: None.
9. OTHER: pertinent or unusual features: No wings —flat.

B. Description of Course of Object(s):
1. WHAT FIRST CALLED ATTENTION OF OBSERVER(S) TO THE OBJECT(S): Unknown, observer just looked up and saw it.
2. ANGLE OR ELEVATION AND AZIMUTH OF OBJECT(S) WHEN FIRST OBSERVED: 45° moving northeast.
3. ANGLE OR ELEVATION AND AZIMUTH OF OBJECT(S) UPON DISAPPEARANCE: 45° angle.
4. DESCRIPTION OF FLIGHT PATH AND MANEUVERS OF OBJECT(S): It appeared to wobble.
5. HOW DID THE OBJECT(S) DISAPPEAR: Went over and behind fire tower located on a 1,320-foot hill.
6. HOW LONG (WERE) THE OBJECT(S) VISIBLE: five to seven seconds.

C. Manner of Observation:
1. GROUND—visual.
2. OPTICAL AIDS: Camera. Included are two pictures and a negative.
3. N/A

D. Time and Date of Sighting:
1. ZULU TIME-DATE GROUP OF SIGHTING: 2140Z. 18 December 1966.
2. LIGHT CONDITIONS: Dusk.

E. Location of Observer(s): On shore of Lake

Tiorati, Bear Mt. State Park, New York. On the
east end of lake looking west.

F. Identifying Information on Observer(s):

   1. MILITARY OR CIVILIAN: Civilian.

   2. NAME: Mr. ———

   3. AGE: 23.

   4. MAILING ADDRESSES: c/o ——— Bronx, N.Y.
     10465

   5. OCCUPATION: Labor Foreman.

   6. ESTIMATE OF RELIABILITY: I consider Mr. ———
     a reliable source.

G. Weather and Winds—Aloft Conditions at Time
and Place of Sightings:

   1. OBSERVER(S) ACCOUNT OF WEATHER CONDI-
     TIONS: Clear.

   2. REPORT FROM NEAREST AWS OR U.S. WEATHER
     BUREAU OFFICE: Windy +48°F at 1400L.

   3. CEILING: Clear.

   4. VISIBILITY: Unlimited.

   5. AMOUNT OF CLOUD COVER: N/A

   6. THUNDERSTORMS IN AREA AND QUADRANT IN
     WHICH LOCATED: N/A.

   7. VERTICAL TEMPERATURE GRADIENT: N/A.

H. Any Other Unusual Activity or Condition: None.

I. Interception or Identification Action Taken: None.

J. Location, approximate altitude, and general direction of flight of any air traffic or balloon in the
area which might possibly account for the sighting:
Called in too late to check with FAA/First Air
Force.

K. Position, title and comments of preparing officer:
1st Lt. Thomas A. Knutson, UFO Officer, 5713
Defense Systems Evaluation Squadron, Stewart
AFB, New York.
The initial interview was by telephone. The pictures were received 1–1/2 weeks after the call. A
second interview (personal) was conducted after
receipt of photographs and Mr. ——— furnished
the negative. IAW Paragraph 12c of AFR 80-17,
request that the negative and photographs be returned to Mr. ——— upon completion of necessary studies, analysis and duplication by the Air
Force. Mr. ——— is married and employed by

his father. He is quite interested in the object and has given these pictures to the newspapers. The only thing that can make the sighting valid is the negative which is enclosed. Mr. ——— and his brother developed the photographs.

L. Existence of physical evidence such as materials and photographs: Two photographs and one negative. Both attached.

Photograph: (The following information is required for all photographs forwarded with this form.)

Type and make of camera: Fiesta Kodak (Kodak Starlite Camera).

Type, focal length, and make of lens: N/A

Brand and type of film: 127 Verichrome Pan Black

Shutter speed used: 7

Lens opening used, that is, "f" stop: No "f" stop.

Filter used: None.

Was tripod or solid stand used: Hand held.

Was "panning" used: No.

Exact direction camera was pointing with relation to true north, and its angle with respect to the ground: Few degrees.

Additional Comments:

No focusing necessary with the camera. No flash bulb used. One observer claimed that it was about 1/2 mile to fire tower on distant hill so observer claims object is much closer.

The official Air Force Photo Analysis Report of February 20, 1967, concluded that the photograph was of "poor to fair" quality but appeared genuine. The analysis of the photo by Douglas M. Rogers, Intelligence research specialist, stated:

Examination of the negative has negated double exposure and/or retouching. The photographs appear genuine insofar as content is concerned, however no satisfactory explanation could be made of the unidentified object. The object appears to be circular in planform, basically flat in cross section with a domed "superstructure." The object appears to be situated beyond the foreground trees, indicating a diameter in excess of eight inches, and the relative clarity indicates it to be substantially nearer than the background trees. The object could have a diameter as great as two or three feet. No attempt at "panning" was indicated as is evidenced by the sharpness of the general scene. The object exhibits some small degree of blurriness indicating motion, the direction of which could not be ascertained.

The official Blue Book record card on this UFO photo contained the following "conclusion" about the case, with absolutely no valid justification for how such a conclusion was reached: "Photo hoax. Photo does not substantiate the witnesses' description of alleged UFO."

In the face of this completely unfounded and unjustified conclusion, I sent the following letter to Maj. Hector Quintanilla, then Chief of Project Blue Book:

Dear Major Quintanilla:

On re-examination I find no substantiation for the evaluation of hoax, particularly in view of the photo-analysis report, No. 67-10, dated 20 February 1967, which contains no information upon which a hoax can be based. To the contrary, the report stated that close examination of the negative has negated double exposure and/or retouching. The photographs appear genuine insofar as content; however, no satisfactory explanation of the unidentified object could be made. The lack of a satisfactory explanation of the unidentified object does not constitute sufficient reason to declare a hoax. Further, the interviewer considers the witness to be a reliable source.

After examination of the print by myself and by Mr. Beckman of the University of Chicago, we feel that the original negative should be requested for further examination. Mr. Beckman, a qualified photo-analyst, disagrees with the photo analysis presented in the report as to the distance of the object. He points out that the depth of field extends much farther than indicated in the report. It will be noted, from the print, that the focus is poor in the entire periphery of the picture regardless of the distance; only in the center of the picture is the focus good, and this good focus extends essentially to infinity. Consequently no judgment can be made as to the real size of the object, if this judgment is based on the quality of focus.

My recommendation is, therefore, that the evaluation be changed from hoax to unidentified.

Sincerely yours,
J. Allen Hynek

Blue Book ignored my recommendation and maintained a file on the Bear Mountain photograph with the "Hoax" label intact; not really fair to either the scientific method or the character of the witness.

While I acknowledge the possibility that the Bear Mountain photograph *could* have been that of an identifiable object, I don't think so. It is certainly unlikely that this was something small and conventional, tossed into the air by a tourist, because it was wintertime and Bear Mountain State Park is relatively quiet then. Had it been summertime, when numbers of tourists were likely to be in the area, such a consideration would be possible—but only if one accepts the Air Force's estimation of the size of the object, which is decidedly different from the witness's testimony.

The fact is, the Air Force was just not interested in finding out all of the possible facts—or a more thorough investigation might have been conducted. As usual, it was much easier for Blue Book to simply label this one "Hoax."

The Misleading Letter to McMinnville

Perhaps the most interesting unidentified UFO photo case of all, and one which the photo analyst for the Condon Committee all but declared a real UFO, involved two photographs taken by a farmer in McMinnville, Oregon, in 1950. William K. Hartmann, the photo-analyst who evaluated the McMinnville UFO photos for the Condon

Committee, concluded: "This is one of the few UFO reports in which all factors investigated, geometric, psychological, and physical, appear to be consistent with the assertion that an extraordinary flying object, silvery, metallic, disk-shaped, tens of meters in diameter, and evidently artificial, flew within sight of the two witnesses."

Hartmann's work has been recently re-examined, greatly extended, and fully substantiated by Dr. Bruce Maccabee. He concludes from a detailed photogrammetric study that the McMinnville object could not have been a small object close to the camera but that it was at a considerable distance and hence not a fake.*

Yet the following letter, from the Blue Book files, was sent on March 10, 1965, to a Mr. Case (apparently a civilian) by Lt. Col. John F. Spaulding, Chief of the Civil Branch of the Community Relations Division, Office of Information of the Air Force:

Dear Mr. Case:

Your letter to the Department of Science has been referred to this office as a matter pertaining to the Air Force.

The Air Force has no information on photographs of an unidentified object taken by Mr. & Mrs. Trent of McMinnville, Oregon.

In this regard, it should be noted that all photographs submitted in conjunction with UFO reports have been a misinterpretation of natural or conventional objects. The object in these photographs have [sic] a positive identification.

Signed/ John F. Spaulding
Lt. Col. USAF

There are two glaring untruths in this letter—one, Spaulding's statement that the Air Force had "no information" on the photographs; two, that the Air Force had positively identified all UFOs in photographs submitted for evaluation.

*Proceedings of the 1976 UFO Conference, Center for UFO Studies, Evanston, Illinois 60202.

The Brazilian UFO Photos

One of the most highly celebrated and controversial series of photos in the Blue Book files are those taken by an official photographer aboard the Brazilian Navy survey ship, *Almirante Saldanha,* off Trindade Island, some 600 miles east of Rio de Janeiro.

The Blue Book reporting officer's concluding statement makes a mockery of the case: "It is the reporting officer's private opinion that a flying saucer sighting would be unlikely at the very barren island of Trindade as everyone knows Martians are extremely comfort-loving creatures."

Other comments by the same officer were filled with ridicule of the Brazilian government and its military. Frankly, I was astonished that these disparaging statements were not edited by the Air Force prior to their release. Such bias and flippancy have no place in scientific investigations.

Because this case has received so much attention over the years, and has been the subject of so much controversy, the full office of Naval Intelligence Information Report from the U.S. Naval Attaché at Rio to Project Blue Book follows:

Date of Information: Serial No.
21–27 Feb 1958   39–58
                             Date of Report
From: 11 March 1958
U.S. Naval Attache,   Contact
Rio de Janeiro   Press   Evaluation
                               303

Subject:
BRAZIL—Navy—Flying Saucer Photographed from ALMIRANTE SALDANHA
Encl: (1) Set of 4 Brazilian Navy photographs of subject
   1. *Announcement.* On 21 February, two of the leading newspapers in Rio de Janeiro printed photographs showing alleged flying saucer photographed from Brazilian naval ship, ALMIRANTE SALDAN-HA, at approximately midday on 16 January 1958

while the ship was anchored off Trindade Island some 600 miles east of Rio de Janeiro. The ship at the time was engaged in research as part of Brazilian Navy participation in the International Geophysical Year.

2. *Photographer.* The photographs themselves were taken by a freelance [?] photographer, Almiro Baruna, using his Rolleiflex camera set at speed 125., lens opening 8, and were developed in a laboratory in ALMIRANTE SALDANHA. This gentleman has a long history of photographic trick shots and is well known for such items as false pictures of treasure on the ocean floor. Another time he prepared a purposely humorous article, published in a magazine, entitled "A Flying Saucer Hunted Me at Home," using trick photography. Baruna, after the release of his latest "flying saucer" photographs, told the press that the Navy secret service had interrogated him for four hours concerning his photos. "The negatives were projected in large size on a screen. If there were any trick, the gigantic projection would have revealed it. After questioning by officers of the Estado-Maior, the Chief of the Secret Service, the senior officer present said to me, 'I am going to ask you a few questions. Don't be offended because I don't doubt the authenticity of your photos but I need to hear from you. If you were going to make a flying saucer appear on a negative, how would you proceed?' 'Commandante, I am an able photographer specialized in trick photography but not one would withstand close and accurate examination.' "

3. *Brazilian Navy Stand.* Immediately after the photographs of the flying saucer were publicized, the Brazilian Navy refused to make any official statement confirming or denying the incident. However, proofs from the original negatives were sent to the other armed forces and the President via an officer-messenger who related the complete story. According to the press, the narration so impressed Mr. Kubichek that he became convinced of the veracity of the happening.

On 24 February, three days after the photos were first publicized in the press, the Navy Ministry finally made an official statement: "With reference to the reports appearing in the press that the Navy is opposed to divulge the facts concerning the appearance of a strange object over Trindade Island, this Cabinet declares that such information has no basis. This Ministry has no motive to impede the release of photographs of the referred to object taken by ————— who was at Trindade Island at the invitation of the Navy, and in the presence of a large number of the crew of ALMIRANTE SALDANHA from whose deck the photographs were taken. Clearly, this Ministry will not be able to make any pronouncement concerning the object seen because the photographs do not constitute sufficient proof for such purpose."

4. *Statements of* SALDANHA *Personnel.* On the morning after the photos of the flying saucer were published in the press (February 22), the ALMIRANTE SALDANHA departed Rio to continue its mission in connection with the IGY. Two days later, however, the ship docked at Santos (February 24) for voyage repairs and this was the first chance that newspapermen had an opportunity to interview officers and men aboard. The Assistant Naval Attaché was in Santos at this time in connection with the visit of USCGS WESTWIND (Aluena Rio IR 36-58 of 10 March) and had an opportunity to visit aboard. The commanding officer, Capitao-de-Mar-e-Guerra (CAPT) Jose Santos Saldanha de Gama, had not seen the object and was noncommittal. The executive officer also had not seen it but, arriving shortly thereafter, had formed the opinion that those on deck had seen it. The captain had reported that his secretary, a LCDR, had seen it but this officer when personally questioned avoided discussing the matter. Later, it was learned that the photographer was accompanied to the darkroom by an officer who waited outside the door while Baruna developed the negative alone.

At the time of the official visit of the commanding officer of WESTWIND to ALMIRANTE SALDANHA, Capt. Saldanha de Gama freely discussed the flying saucer and showed the original proofs to the callers but again did not commit himself.

5. *Publicity.* The press reports after the publication of the photographs covered a great deal of news-

paper space for about a week, tending to prove or disprove the authenticity of Baruna's photographs DIARIO CARICCA reported that personnel of SALDANHA were under rigid orders of silence. O GLOBO published a story with photographs by photographer ——— of flying saucers (china) taken at Cabo Frio.

Federal Deputy Sergio Magalhaes sent a note to the Navy Ministry on 27 February protesting the Navy's failure to secure sworn statements of witnesses. "For the first time in flying saucer history, the phenomenon was attended by large numbers of persons belonging to a military force which give these latest photographs an official stamp. Threats to national security require official attention and action," said the Deputy. In the middle of all the publicity, other "flying saucer" sighting reports came out including a naval officer who saw a flying saucer a month before sighting from SALDANHA off the coast of Espirito Santo. CO and crew of ATA TRIDENTE said flying saucer several days before SALDANHA sighting but kept information secret.

Preparing Officer's Comments:

1. Most flying saucer stories are not worth wasting much time or effort, but this story apparently substantiated by official Navy photographs taken in the presence of large number of Navy personnal under closely controlled and almost ideal circumstances should have absolutely proved the existence of an unidentified flying object. Unfortunately, further investigation provided only frustration at every turning. A number of Brazilian Navy officers profess to believe the story implicitly but whether they have more information than we is unknown.

2. There appear to be only two explanations for this peculiar incident:

(a) Some overwhelming power has told the Brazilian Navy not to officially verify this incident (which they should easily be able to do, if it occurred) nor to deny it (which they should easily be able to do, if it is a fake). I personally do not believe that anyone has told the Brazilian Navy to keep quiet about it because there has been no hint of such suppression in either Brazilian or U.S. circles; and also because I doubt their control of the individual officers and men is good enough to hold the line.

(b) The whole thing is a fake publicity stunt put on by a crooked photographer and the Brazilian Navy fell for it. This seems like the most likely considering Brazilians' love for sensationalism and gossip, their well-known propensity for never letting the truth stand in the way of a good story, and general bureaucratic inefficiency.

3. In addition, the photographs furnished by the Brazilian Navy are unconvincing. Details of the land are extremely sharp but the disc is hazy and has little contrast and shows no shadow effect. It also appears that the object was inverted in photograph 2 compared to 1 and 3. Also the papers have mentioned extremely high velocities and there appears to be no lateral blurring as would occur with any reasonable shutter speed.

4. It is the reporting officer's private opinion that a flying saucer sighting would be unlikely at the very barren island of Trindade, as everyone knows Martians are extremely comfort-loving creatures.

Prepared and forwarded:
S/M. Sunderland
Capt. USN.

The Blue Book files on this case also contain a United Press dispatch from Rio de Janeiro of February 25, 1958, which stated that the Brizilian Navy Ministry confirmed the UFO sighting and photos as real. The dispatch stated:

The Brazilian Navy Ministry vouched today for the authenticity of the photographs of a "flying saucer" taken recently aboard the Navy survey ship, *Almirante Saldanha.*

Navy Minister Adm. ——— said after meeting with President Kubichek in the summer presidential palace at Petropolis, that he also vouched personally for the authenticity of the pictures.

"The Navy has a great secret which it cannot divulge because it cannot be explained," the minister
said.

One would think that our own government would have
enough diplomatic contacts in Brazil to confirm or deny
officially the authenticity of the photographs. In any case,
the Brazilian UFO photos remain in the Blue Book files
under the listing of "Hoax." Perhaps only the Brazilian
government will ever know for sure.

The Mariana-Go-Round

This final case was the subject of intensive review
and investigation by the Condon Committee and to this
day remains highly controversial.

At 11:25 A.M. on August 5 or 15, 1950 (the exact date
has never been determined), Nicholas Mariana, general
manager of the Great Falls (Montana) Electrics baseball
team, was inspecting the local baseball stadium with his
secretary when he looked toward the smokestack of the
Anaconda Copper Company to the northwest and saw
two stationary bright lights in the sky. After a short period
of observation he determined he could not be watching
aircraft, and ran some fifty feet to his car to get his 16mm
movie camera. While he was filming, the lights moved
from a stationary position toward the southwest against
the wind and continued until they faded away. During the
filming the objects passed behind a water tower, thus
providing a frame of reference for measuring distance,
size, altitude, azimuth, and time duration (thus the speed
of the objects could also be approximated).

So much has already been written about the Great Falls
UFO films that one might well devote an entire book to
the various theories that have been advanced about them.
Furthermore, there is still a controversy over whether
thirty-five of the first frames of the film originally submitted to the Air Force were withheld by the Air Force,
as Mariana claimed, or whether they ever existed to begin
with. At any rate, Mariana stuck firmly to his position
that those frames were submitted, and that they showed
the objects as silvery in appearance with a notch or band

at one point on their periphery and having a rotating motion in unison.

These films were reviewed several times by the Air Force (according to Ruppelt, they were rejected as images of two F-94 aircraft that were known to be in the area), by the Robertson Panel convened by the CIA, by the Condon Committee, by the Douglas Aircraft Corporation, and as the subject of a documentary film about UFOs produced by Green-Rouse Productions in 1956. The most detailed analysis of the film was made by Dr. Robert M. L. Baker, Jr., for Douglas Aircraft. The in-depth papers on this case written by Dr. Baker can well be considered as the basis for validating the study of UFOs at least as anomalistic phenomena.

Since the end of Blue Book, new techniques similar to those used in the analysis of photographs taken by space probes have been applied to the study of UFO photographs with considerable success. These techniques, involving sophisticated computer analysis of picture elements, have shown that a number of photographs formerly considered fake just might be genuine evidence that UFOs exist.

11

THE AIR FORCE NUMBERS GAME

> *He uses statistics as a drunken man uses lamp-posts, for support rather than illumination.*
> —*Andrew Lang*

Over the years, the Pentagon played loosely with statistics to support their position that *all* UFOs are misidentifications of natural phenomena—or outright hoaxes. Often statistical information was not fairly presented.

An outstanding example of the Air Force use of statistics to support rather than to illuminate is their own Blue Book Special Report 14 (see pp. 272), the results of which, properly and fully presented,* would have seriously conflicted with the Air Force position. Instead, the statistical results of that report were never presented. The study, commissioned by the Air Force, was circulated internally, with only a limited number of copies; in 1955 it was made available for public inspection but still was not generally published. Carefully worded press releases were the only contact the public had with the report, and these dealt only with generalities and did not mention the specific results of the study. They stated that because of the subjectivity of the data "the results of these tests are inconclusive since they neither confirm nor deny that the UNKNOWNS are primarily unidentified KNOWNS," carefully avoiding the fact that a proper mathematical interpretation of the tests indicated that the chance that the "Unknowns" were the same as the "Knowns" was less than one in a billion! It seems certain that had the results

---

*See "Scientific Investigation of Unidentified Flying Objects," Dr. Bruce Maccabee; available through the Center for UFO Studies, Evanston, Illinois.

of the tests indicated that the "Unknowns" *were* the same as the "Knowns," there would have been no mention whatever of the subjectivity of the data!

Since the Blue Book files are now open, we can assemble our own statistics and draw our own conclusions. It would be difficult, of course, to match the extensive work done for Special Report 14, especially since we now have three times as many reports to consider, but let's do the best we can.

The reader will note that our total number of Blue Book reports and Blue Book "Unidentifieds" (a faithful reflection of the complete contents of the Blue Book microfilms) does not exactly tally with previously published figures in Air Force press releases. Our totals are somewhat larger, while our number of "Unidentifieds" is somewhat smaller. This can probably be attributed to the fact that from time to time the Blue Book files of earlier years were reviewed and revised; an "Unidentified" of one year could easily become an "Identified" in a later year if an ambitious new officer felt that he could "improve" the situation, or, if, legitimately, new information came to light on an old case and justified a change in its status. In addition, in 1952, a banner year for UFO sightings, the flow of reports was so great that case evaluations had to be cursory and final evaluations left for much later. As I recall, the summary sheets for 1952 were not completed until several years later, and many cases hurriedly labeled "Unidentified" at first, were later declared "Identified."

Our tally shows that the total number of *all* the various categories of reports is 13,134. As the following graph (Fig. 11.1) illustrates, the number of reports varied greatly from year to year. These reports, of course, include both the "Unidentifieds" (the UFOs) and the "Identifieds" (the IFOs—Identified Flying Objects).

What accounts for the higher total of reports in some years? For some reason, UFO reports sometimes occur in bunches, or "flaps" as they have come to be known. The Air Force experienced three of these, in 1952, 1957, and 1966. (The United States experienced another in 1973, four years after the Air Force and the Condon Committee had supposedly put the whole UFO question to rest.) Why flaps occur just may be more of a problem for the psychologist than for the physical scientist; perhaps they

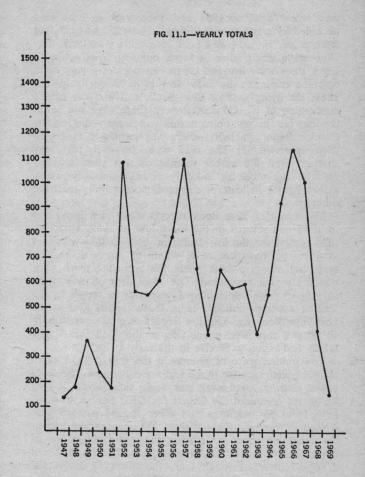

FIG. 11.1—YEARLY TOTALS

are triggered by awakening of public interest that follows one or two well-publicized, spectacular sightings.
But this explanation for the 1952 "flap" is too simple.

Unlike the others, which seemed to consist mostly of
an increased number of IFOs, the "flap" of 1952 was the
only one to represent a genuine increase in the total number of "Unidentifieds." The 1952 flap is unique in another

way: the "flaps" of 1957 and 1966 were in each case preceded by a two-year "buildup." The 1957 wave started from a low in 1954 and built to a climax in 1957. The 1966 wave was similar in form, building from a low in 1963. Each wave dropped off in two steps of a year each, reaching minimum in 1959 and 1968, respectively. (In 1969, the dying year of Blue Book, and the year of the publication of the Condon Report, there were still fewer reports, but in my opinion this was largely due to the Condon Report publicity—there was nothing to UFOs, so why report them?) The 1952 wave, however, rose very sharply; even the earlier months of that year had few reports. The wave hit suddenly in June and July. Then, as the figures indicate, it subsided more rapidly than the other two.

The graph of Blue Book reports starts at a low point in 1947 and returns to the same low in 1969. One possible reason for the low figure in 1947 is that witnesses may not yet have known to whom to report anomalous aerial sightings; in later years the reporting mechanism was fairly well publicized. The 1969 drop-off was probably due to the reluctance of witnesses to report in the face of adverse publicity. Thus, those reports filed in the post–Blue Book and Condon Report days are particularly significant; they were made despite the "bad press" that UFOs had begun to receive in the early 1970s!

The sudden wave of reports in the fall of 1973 came as a complete surprise to me and my colleagues. Then, because nothing whatsoever was being done about it officially, we organized the Center for UFO Studies to serve as a focus for scientists and other trained persons who wished to learn more about the UFO phenomenon and to do something about it. In addition, a monthly review of current UFO events and investigations, *The International UFO Reporter*, of which I am the editor, is now available through the Center for UFO Studies.

The Air Force Admits There Are Unidentified Flying Objects

The Air Force never officially used the term UFO. Blue Book did, however, use the term "Unidentified," and nearly six hundred of these are listed in the files. Bear in

mind that all statistics cited so far, and those which immediately followed, refer to *Air Force evaluations*, not
to the re-evaluations performed by the Center for UFO
Studies which are discussed later in this chapter. These
statistics can therefore be expected to be heavily influ-
enced by the assumption "It can't be, therefore it isn't."

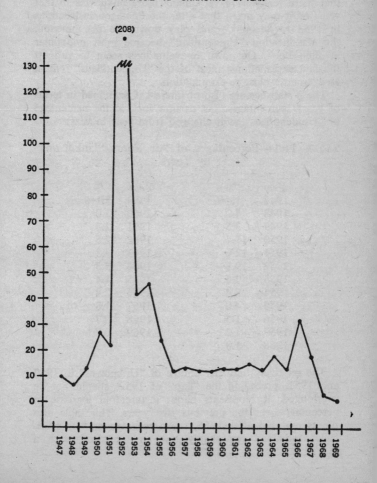

FIG. 11.2—AF "UNKNOWNS" BY YEAR

Let us see how the number of recognized Air Force "Unidentifieds" fluctuated over the years.

Figure 11.2 represents the yearly distribution of the 587 Air Force "Unidentifieds." This graph shows that the number of Blue Book "Unidentifieds" remained at a roughly constant low level over the years except for 1952, when it reached a record high of 208. The existence of the one true "flap" of unknowns in 1952 can mean that there really *were* very many more unknowns in that year; or it may mean that after the Pentagon instructions in 1953 to "debunk" and play down the phenomenon, the classification "Unidentified" became most unpopular at Blue Book. Our own re-evaluations seem to support the first explanations; most of the "Unidentifieds" remain so even after close re-examination.

These statistics are also of interest if examined in terms of yearly percentages. Let us now look at the percentage of "Unidentifieds" as it changed from year to year:

TABLE 11.1—Percentages of Air Force "Unknowns" by Years

Year	%	Year	%
1947	7.4%	1959	3.1%
1948	4.0	1960	2.0
1949	3.5	1961	2.3
1950	11.4	1962	2.5
1951	12.6	1963	3.3
1952	19.3	1964	3.3
1953	7.5	1965	1.4
1954	8.4	1966	2.8
1955	4.0	1967	1.8
1956	1.5	1968	0.7
1957	1.2	1969	0.7
1958	1.8		

The relatively high percentage of "Unknowns" in 1950 and 1951, preceding the "flap" of 1952, should not be overlooked. It represents about a threefold increase in percentage over the previous two years. This table also points out that after 1955, the percentage of "Unidentifieds" remained remarkably low and constant—with a mean of 2.0 percent. To some extent this was due to the "crackdown" on "Unidentifieds" as recommended by the Robertson Panel (p. 20) in 1953. But to a greater extent the low figures represent "unfair" statistical processes. All cases evaluated as "Insufficient Information" were considered by Blue Book to be "Knowns"; all cases evaluated as "Possible Balloons" or "Probable Aircraft" were considered in the statistics *as* balloons and aircraft—the qualifying words "possible" or "probable" were dropped. Clearly, the "Insufficient Information" cases should have been excluded from the statistical computations altogether. Instead, these cases were treated statistically as if they had been solved! Thus, if the insufficient information cases are removed from the 1952 total, the percentage of unknowns rises to 23 percent.

The following table shows the percentages of various known stimuli for reports of sightings that were listed by Blue Book as "Identified."

TABLE 11.2—Total Numbers of IFOs

Type of IFO	Number	Percentage
Astronomical[1]	3,421	26.0%
Aircraft	2,237	17.0
Balloons	1,223	9.3
Radar Phen.[2]	152	1.2
Psychological[3]	63	0.5
Hoax	116	0.9
Meteorological[4]	44	0.3
Birds	85	0.6
Insufficient Information	2,409	18.3
Other	2,807	21.4

[1]of which meteors made up 56%, or 9.5% of the total number of Blue Book cases
[2]such as anomalous propagation, weather returns, malfunctions
[3]also includes unreliable reports
[4]clouds, light phenomena, sundogs, etc.

It is astonishing to note that nearly a fifth of the cases received by Blue Book were assigned to the category "Insufficient Information"! While some of these undoubtedly proceeded from old reports or unreliable witnesses, clearly not all of these reports could be ascribed to these causes. This data makes it clear that Blue Book, too often, took the easy way out.

The table also shows that most witnesses were said to have misperceived astronomical objects—twinkling stars (with motion attributed to them by autokinesis), the setting moon and sun, bright planets, and most often, meteors. Astronomical objects, aircraft, and balloons together make up nearly 53 percent of the total number of reports submitted to Project Blue Book.

Another interesting fact that emerges is that despite the Air Force claims, less than 2 percent of the reports were "Psychological" in nature or the result of hoaxes. Yet, consider the following excerpts from a Department of Defense Office of Public Information Press release dated December 27, 1949:

> The Air Force said that all evidence and analyses indicate that reports of unindentified flying objects are the result of:
> 1—misinterpretation of various conventional objects
> 2—a mild form of mass hysteria
> 3—or hoaxes.

There were only sixty-three cases labeled "Psychological" in the entire Blue Book file and 116 hoaxes, most of which were quite easily detected and dismissed!

UFOs for All Seasons

Apart from the variation in yearly totals of UFO reports, are there "seasons" for UFO reports? Well, as it turns out, there are seasons for UFO reports but not for "Unidentifieds." Figure 11.3 plots the total number of UFO reports received by the Air Force as a function of month of the year and also the total number of Air Force "Unidentifieds" as a function of month.

The graph shows that more reports are made during the months of July and August than during the rest of the year.

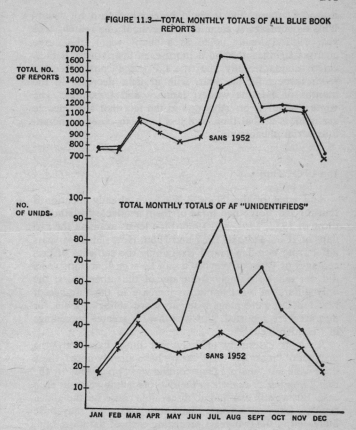

FIGURE 11.3—TOTAL MONTHLY TOTALS OF ALL BLUE BOOK REPORTS

TOTAL NO. OF REPORTS

SANS 1952

NO. OF UNIDS.

TOTAL MONTHLY TOTALS OF AF "UNIDENTIFIEDS"

SANS 1952

JAN FEB MAR APR MAY JUN JUL AUG SEPT OCT NOV DEC

Actually, this is quite logical and should be expected; during the summer months, a greater percentage of the population is outdoors, and since UFOs are an outdoor phenomenon, more people are likely to see them then. Also, it is likely that during the summer months there are more conventional objects around to misinterpret! However, the Southern Hemisphere also has most reports in July—when they are having winter!

The second graph in Figure 11.3 looks at the total number of Air Force "Unidentifieds" by month. At first glance, it would appear that there is indeed a season for "real" UFOs—once again, summer. However, if one removes the year 1952 (already noted as a "flap" year), the curve changes significantly and a more even distribution is indicated. Fundamentally, the true UFO is a constant occurrence throughout the year, with a slight decrease in the months of extreme winter, January and December. The winter "slide" is probably due to the fact that most people are indoors at that time, and less likely to observe anomalous aerial phenomena.

The UFO "Flap"

And what of the "flaps"? We have already mentioned that the Air Force had three of them available for study—those of 1952, 1957, and 1966. First let us examine the two flaps of IFOs, those of 1957 and 1966. How did these years differ from non-flap years? Examining the statistics of percentages of types of reports, it can be seen that both years did not differ strikingly from any of the other years; the only difference was simply an increase in the number of raw reports. Percentage-wise, no more stars, balloons, or aircraft were reported. Nor was there a greater percentage of "Unidentifieds."

It seems extremely unlikely that these flaps were the product of "mass hysteria." As we have already noted, these flaps were not "sharp"; their coming was "predicted" by the rising number of reports in the two preceding years in each case. But we still can find no discernible cause for the added reports. One can suppose that public awareness may have increased in the two years preceding each of the flaps, and, as a result, more people went out and "looked" for UFOs. But this is only a guess.

Now, let us turn to the flap of 1952. This flap was genuine in that it certainly did consist of a higher number of "real" UFOs, even by Air Force standards. Table 11.3 illustrates the month-by-month breakdown of UFOs versus IFOs.

TABLE 11.3—THE GREAT "FLAP" OF 1952

	Total	Identified	Unidentified	%	Insuff. Information
Jan.	14	12	1	8	1
Feb.	18	11	2	15	5
Mar.	24	15	4	21	5
Apr.	84	51	21	29	12
May	71	51	12	19	8
Jun.	124	64	40	38	20
Jul.	366	231	55	19	80
Aug.	218	134	28	17	56
Sep.	105	57	27	32	21
Oct.	51	31	13	30	7
Nov.	44	30	8	21	6
Dec.	47	38	3	7	6
	1,166	725	214	23	227

Total minus Ins. Infor. = 939

The year clearly started out slowly, with an average number of UFOs and IFOs. However, the months of June, July, August, and September were distinguished by a far greater number of "Unidentifieds."

What happened during 1952? All one can say is that if ever there was a UFO phenomenon, it certainly existed during that year. Both the revised statistics and the Air Force data show a sudden surge in the number of observations of Daylight Discs and Nocturnal Lights during the summer of 1952. Even the overzealous attempts of the Air Force to find conventional solutions could not dismiss the excellent cases that occurred in that now famous summer which features the seriously discussed Washington, D.C., radar-visual cases (see p. 122).

At present we cannot explain flaps any more than we can presume to say we understand the entire UFO phenomenon. The only scientifically justifiable statement that can be made is that they exist.

The Revised Blue Book Statistics—
What Really Was Going On?

A member of the staff of the Center for UFO Studies

and I have comprehensively re-evaluated all the cases which comprise the ninety-four reels of microfilmed Project Blue Book records. Despite Blue Book's inadequate follow-up and investigation of the bulk of these cases, it was possible for us to form some sort of judgment as to whether or not the Air Force conclusions were, in each case, valid. In many cases we agreed with the Air Force—and in many we did not. So, let us now examine how things change when one grants the assumption that there may indeed be some sort of unidentified aerial phenomena, source and nature unknown, which may have been, for the most part, accurately reported by over sixteen thousand witnesses.

The following table illustrates the *revised* number of "Unidentifieds" for each of the twenty-two years of open Air Force involvement.

TABLE 11.4—Revised Unidentifieds

Year	Number	Year	Number
1947	10	1959	14
1948	16	1960	17
1949	18	1961	14
1950	31	1962	2
1951	22	1963	4
1952	242	1964	9
1953	44	1965	7
1954	46	1966	36
1955	26	1967	19
1956	21	1968	4
1957	25	1969	1
1958	15		

What these statistics tell us is that out of 13,134 cases reported to the Air Force, of which 10,675 received a classification other than "Insufficient Information," a full 5.8 percent remain unidentified even after re-examination many years later. Over six hundred cases, over as long a period as twenty-two years, is still a number to be reckoned with. And how many of the cases which are classified as "Insufficient Information" might actually have been placed in the "Unidentified" category had further investigation been made?

Now let us see what *kind* of UFOs we are dealing with. The reader is by now well acquainted with the classification scheme utilized in this book, and it is of interest to examine the 640 *revised* "Unknowns" to see how they divide themselves into these classes.

TABLE 11.5—Types of Revised Unknowns

Type	Number	% of Unknowns
Nocturnal Lights	243	38%
Daylight Discs	271	42
Radar-Visual	29	5
Radar	10	2
Close Encounters of the First Kind	46	7
Close Encounters of the Second Kind	33	5
Close Encounters of the Third Kind	8	1
	640	100%

What is extremely surprising here is the great number of *Daylight Disc* cases reported. These cases, from Blue Book files alone, and neglecting the wealth of information from the civilian UFO organizations around the world, involve many hundreds of witnesses, the majority of them with Air Force or some other technical background (sometimes scientific). It is rather surprising that Nocturnal Lights do not lead the list, as they do in most other studies.

Less surprising is the fact that far fewer "high strangeness" cases were reported to the Air Force, or to be exact, reached the Blue Book desks.*

A check of cases available in the open literature, not including the unpublished files of APRO and NICAP,

---

*We have ample evidence, not only from the reports received by the Center for UFO Studies, which is a relatively new organization, but from the two oldest civilian UFO fact-gathering organizations, the Aerial Phenomena Research Organization and the National Investigations Committee for Aerial Phenomena, that a large number of "high strangeness" cases have, in fact, occurred—particularly Close Encounter cases of all three types.

shows that, conservatively, at least five times as many high strangeness cases did not reach the Blue Book list as did. Probably the figure is closer to ten times the cases than five. I surmise that the factor was larger in the late years of Blue Book because by that time the "all is nonsense" approach of the Air Force was well known and it had become clear to the general public that reporting strange UFO events to the Air Force was not only pointless as a serious scientific matter, but was apt to bring ridicule to the reporter.

There is another reason which we touched on in an earlier chapter. Even if reported, cases of "high strangeness" would have had a tough time making it through channels and finally arriving at Blue Book. Reports of humanoids and of strange physical, physiological, or electromagnetic effects would almost always be "solved at local level," and not even be brought before a panel of consultants.

We have seen this "screening" process at work at our own Center for UFO Studies. The center operates a toll-free hot line, used exclusively by police and other official agencies to relay UFO sightings to the Center, where these reports are then investigated and analyzed. But though the Center does receive reports of high-strangeness cases—involving humanoids and the like—it very rarely gets these through the hot-line facility. When queried about this after the fact, the police departments who initially received the cases but did not report them almost invariably stated: "Oh, we wouldn't bother you with stuff like that!" Apparently, "stuff like that" is too far out to be possible; or perhaps the police feel less "threatened" by reports of discs undergoing gyrations in the daytime sky or by strange lights in the night! At any rate, it seems likely that a similar "screening" process took place at Project Blue Book.

One important question arises upon examining these "Revised Unknowns"—namely, what were they *before*? Do these represent the cases that the Air Force had labeled "Psychological" or "Hoax"? Have we finally caught the Air Force pulling a fast one?

Unfortunately for those who want to hold to the idea that the Air Force threw its best cases into the "Psychological" and "Unreliable Witness" bin, the answer is no. Indeed, very few of the cases classified by the Air

Force as "Psychological" had their classifications reversed the second time around on the basis of Blue Book evidence alone. Instead, the classifications most often reversed were "Aircraft" and "Balloons." (Aircraft that made right-angle turns at high speed and balloons that caused electromagnetic effects!) There does seem to have been a slight tendency for the Air Force to classify CE-IIIs as "Psychological"; but with only eight cases reported, we can hardly draw any certain conclusions.

Most of the Air Force "Unidentifieds" held up under scrutiny of the re-evaluation investigators, although some of them were re-evaluated as conventional objects (several turned out to be balloons, aircraft or meteors). Conversely, many of the Air Force evaluations of conventional objects had to be reascribed as "Insufficient Information" whenever it was clearly evident that the Air Force percentages quoted previously for the various categories of IFOs still held, even after re-evaluation.

The "Where" of UFOs

We have answered the question of when UFOs appear; now let us consider *where* they appear. Breakdowns of the "*revised*" Unidentifieds according to geographical distribution appear in Table 11.6 and in Figure 11.4.

While the map shows pretty much what one might expect (namely concentrations toward the states of greatest area and population) there are a few surprises. One of these is the great number of reports in the state of New Mexico and the District of Columbia. While moderately large in area, New Mexico has a low population; yet it evinces a fair number of bona fide unidentified sightings. Also, the District of Columbia, minuscule in area, has six "Unidentifieds" to its credit.

These results only serve generally to corroborate a study carried out by Dr. David Saunders of the Center for UFO Studies. Dr. Saunders examined the cases in the Center's computer data bank, UFOCAT, for evidence of a correlation of frequency of all sightings with population and area of counties. As might be expected, the counties with larger areas and larger populations showed the greatest number of UFO reports, all told.

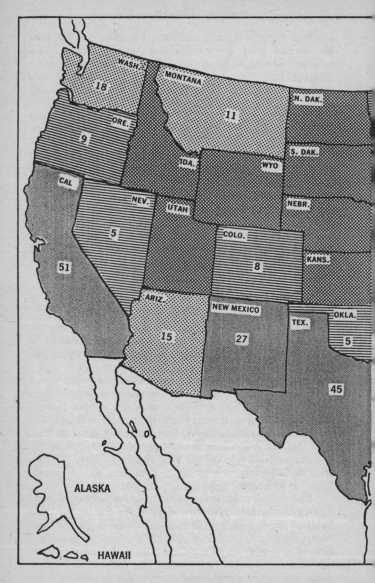

FIGURE 11.4—GEOGRAPHICAL DISTRIBUTION

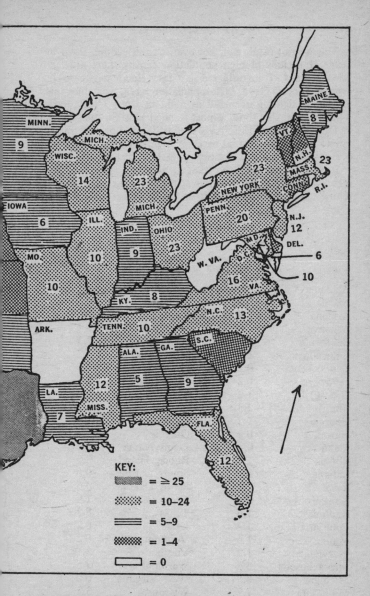

KEY:

	= ≧ 25
	= 10–24
	= 5–9
	= 1–4
	= 0

OF REVISED UNIDENTIFIEDS

This overall result can, however, be misleading. Even in states or regions of high population density there are isolated regions. I investigated a Close Encounter case in Washington, D.C., a high population area, yes, but this particular sighting occurred at night in Rock Creek Park which was, at that time, a most isolated spot! So the studies of Dr. Saunders and the revised statistics do not necessarily vitiate the statement that cases of high strangeness tend to occur in isolated areas, away from human habitation.

It would seem from the statistics that one is more likely to see a genuine UFO (whatever that may turn out to be) if one lives in the Southwest or the Northeast. What this

TABLE 11.6—Geographical Distribution of Revised Unidentifieds

State	% of Total	State	% of Total
Alabama	1.0%	Montana	2.1%
Alaska	0.8	Nebraska	0.4
Arizona	2.9	Nevada	1.0
Arkansas	0.0	New Hampshire	0.4
California	9.9	New Jersey	2.3
Colorado	1.6	New Mexico	5.2
Connecticut	0.2	New York	4.5
Delaware	0.2	North Carolina	2.5
Dist. Col.	1.2	North Dakota	0.8
Florida	2.3	Ohio	4.5
Georgia	1.7	Oklahoma	1.0
Hawaii	0.2	Oregon	1.7
Idaho	0.4	Pennsylvania	3.9
Illinois	1.9	Rhode Island	0.0
Indiana	1.7	South Carolina	0.6
Iowa	1.2	South Dakota	0.6
Kansas	0.4	Tennessee	1.9
Kentucky	1.6	Texas	8.7
Louisiana	1.4	Utah	0.2
Maine	1.6	Vermont	0.2
Maryland	1.9	Virginia	3.1
Massachusetts	3.5	Washington	3.5
Michigan	3.5	West Virginia	0.0
Minnesota	1.7	Wisconsin	3.7
Missouri	1.9	Wyoming	0.2

fact may be telling us about the nature of UFOs is unknown at the present time.

The People Who See UFOs

While examining the cases in Project Blue Book, my colleagues and I kept careful records of the occupations of witnesses (with special attention paid to the military and trained technicians of all kinds). The correlation between occupation and what was perceived—or misperceived—is extremely interesting, and appears below:

TABLE 11.7—Witness Reliability as a
Function of Occupation

Occupation	% of Misidentification
Military pilot	
(single witness)	88
(multiple witness)	76
Commercial pilot	
(single witness)	89
(multiple witness)	79
Radar technicians	
(multiple witnesses)	78
Technical person	
(single witness)	65
(multiple witness)	50
Other	
(multiple witness)	83

It would seem that, as a rule, the best witnesses are multiple engineers or scientists; only 50 percent of their sightings could be classified as misperceptions. Surprisingly, commercial and military pilots appear to make relatively poor witnesses (though they do slightly better in groups).

What we have here is a good example of a well-known psychological fact: "transference" of skill and experience does not usually take place. That is, an expert in one field does not necessarily "transfer" his competence to another one. Thus, it might surprise us that a pilot had trouble identifying other aircraft. But it should come as no surprise that a majority of pilot misidentifications were of *astronomical* objects.

As one might expect, the statistics do show that multiple witnesses are slightly better than single witnesses, since it is unlikely that a group of people would misperceive the same stimulus, group pressure notwithstanding.

Blue Book Special Report Number 14

The great "flap" of 1952 was, as far as we can judge from statistics, a "real" flap and not the result of mass hysteria. Its reverberations in the Pentagon were sufficiently great to have the Air Force commission the Battelle Memorial Institute in Columbus, Ohio—a private, highly regarded industrial research organization—to examine this prime question: Do "Unidentifieds" differ in basic characteristics from "Identifieds"? That is, if one considers these two main classifications separately, and examines each in terms of reported colors, number of objects, shapes, duration of observation, speed, and light brightness (when applicable), does one find similar descriptions reported for both groups? If so, one might deduce that "Unidentifieds" and "Identifieds" belong to the same statistical "universe," to use the statistician's term, and, therefore, that "Unidentifieds" are really *all* misidentifications of ordinary things, perhaps seen under unusual circumstances. If, on the other hand, descriptions of "Unidentifieds" and "Identifieds" differ significantly, then one could make a stronger case for the existence of "real" UFOs.

In statistical theory there is a time-honored method of determining the *probability* (statistics deals with probabilities, not certainties) that one set of things is truly different from another set. This is the "chi-square" test, which one can find described in any standard text on statistics and probability theory. If you were examining, for instance, two crates of apples (but didn't know they were apples), the chi-square test on sizes, weights, numbers of objects, etc., would tell you that the probability was very high that the same sort of things were in the two crates. But if one crate contained apples and the other tennis balls, the chi-square test would tell you that the probability that both crates contained the same thing was extremely small—not zero, but very small!

The Battelle report showed that when six characteristics

(color, shape, number, duration of observation, speed, light brightness) were given the chi-square test, the results were as follows:

Probability that "Unidentifieds" Are the Same as Identifieds

COLOR: Probability *less than 1%*
DURATION OF OBSERVATION: Probability *very much less than 1%*
NUMBER: Probability *very much less than 1%*
LIGHT BRIGHTNESS: Probability greater than 5%
SHAPE: Probability *less than 1%*
SPEED: Probability *much less than 1%*

Now any statistician will tell you that statistical tests are not infallible. He will also likely tell you that examining any *one* characteristic, such as color, might involve subtle subjective differences, or purely unknown causes that could negate the results. But he will definitely tell you that it is *most* unlikely that *all six* of the characteristics examined by the Battelle study could be subject to the same sorts of errors, leading to an erroneous result. A quick calculation shows that the probability of all six UFO-characteristic chi-square tests giving the same results by chance (and thus making the conclusions drawn from the tests wrong) is much less than one chance in a billion.

Yet, the conclusion of the Battelle report completely disregards the results of these tests—almost brazenly, as if they did not exist. How else can one explain this conclusion: "The results of these tests are not conclusive since they neither confirm nor deny that the UNKNOWNS are primarily unidentified KNOWNS, although they do indicate that relatively few of the UNKNOWNS are astronomical phenomena."

Further, the press release on Special Report No. 14 went on to state: ". . . it is considered to be highly improbable that any of the reports of unidentified aerial objects examined in the survey represent observations of technological developments outside the range of present-day scientific knowledge."

Well, okay. Those who cry "Air Force cover-up"—there's all the evidence you need. But, hold on, look at that statement again. Notice that it never denies that, as the chi-square tests show, "Unidentifieds" are truly different from "Identifieds"; it merely sidesteps the question by saying that Unidentifieds do not represent *technological development.* Well, suppose Unidentifieds turned out to be *something outside the realm of technological devices?* Suppose they weren't "nuts and bolts" hardware after all, but holographic images or projections from the human mind or from some intelligence far off? The Pentagon would then be safe in having made the statement they did. And since the Air Force's job *is* military, and deals with defense problems arising from possible enemy use of technological devices, they can always claim to have fulfilled their obligation to the public.

The following quotation, from the final section of the report, summarizes its general tone and its conclusions:

> A critical examination of the distributions of the important characteristics of sightings, plus an intensive study of the sightings evaluated as UNKNOWN, led to the conclusion that a combination of factors, princi-pally the reported maneuvers of the objects and the unavailability of supplemental data such as aircraft flight plans and balloon launching records, resulted in the failure to identify as KNOWN most of the reports of the objects classified as UNKNOWNS.

This conclusion is utterly incredible in view of the re-sults of the chi-square tests—all six criteria tested showed that it was irrelevant whether aircraft flight plans or bal-loon launching records were available.

Perhaps it is no wonder that Battelle did its very best to keep this project a secret. Although Blue Book was, according to Pentagon press releases, completely unclassi-fied, the Battelle project was considered top secret. On many occasions I was reminded by Project Blue Book offi-cers that under no circumstances must the name of the research organization be mentioned. The report was not published until 1955 (I was never given a copy) and only about one hundred were distributed on a "for Official use only" basis. The Pentagon press releases which subsequently appeared were not only ambiguous, they were untrue. And this UFO report becomes the one blight on the record of an otherwise flawless scientific research organization.

A further falling from scientific grace can be noted. The report states: "All records and working papers of this study have been carefully preserved in an orderly fashion suitable for ready reference." A few years ago I personally visited Battelle Memorial Institute and asked to see those "carefully preserved" records. I was told they had been destroyed. It is hardly good scientific practice to destroy original data, which can easily be preserved on microfilm.

However, little blame can be laid on the Battelle group, which went about its business in very rigorous, scientific fashion. In many ways the study itself was a model of scientific procedure and certainly rates far higher than the Condon Report in this respect.

Battelle used as its time base the period from June 1, 1947, to December 31, 1952, thus including the flap of 1952. The reports studied were primarily those received through military channels, but the panel of scientists that was used to evaluate this body of data included persons from many different fields. I was not invited to be a part of the panel, perhaps because of my close association with Blue Book; Battelle wished, quite legitimately, to have an independent look at the subject.

Out of the approximately 4,000 reports, some 799 were found to be so nebulous or sketchy in nature that few "facts" could be extracted from them; this left 3,201 cases. Since some of the reports were duplicates, this finally came down to 2,199 individual cases to work with.

The procedure used in dealing with these cases was as rigorous as the anecdotal nature of the original reports would allow. First, as many discrete facts were extracted from each report as possible, taking care "to insure against the deduction of discrete facts not warranted by the original data."

Next they dealt with the observer's credibility and the self-consistency of the report itself, that is, the absence of contradictions within the report and its general consistency, part by part. The observers were rated in a complex way according to age, training, "attitude," fact-reporting ability, occupation, etc. Reports were then subdivided on the basis of all the above into *Excellent, Good, Doubtful,* and *Poor* (remember that almost 800 of the poorest had already been eliminated from further consideration).

Now came the actual evaluation of the report as to its most probable cause. There were ten possible categories:

Balloon
Astronomical
Aircraft
Light Phenomena
Birds
Clouds, Etc.
Insufficient Information
Psychological
Unknown
Other

Assignment to these categories was certainly not haphazard; in fact, there were several stages involved in the process. First the report was set forth onto a "worksheet," and a primary evaluation was made. Next the "identification panel," unaware of what the first evaluation was, made theirs. The identification was accepted if both of these matched, and if they were not "Unknown." Disagreement meant further consideration until a consensus was reached. If the evaluation was "Unknown," Report No. 14 states that the entire panel had to be brought in and "a group decision was necessary on all reports finally recorded as UNKNOWN, regardless of what the preliminary identification had been." In cases where a group decision was not made in a reasonable time, the report was put aside and later submitted to certain members of the panel of consultants for their opinions. If, after this, the disagreement continued to exist, the report of the sighting was labeled "Unknown."

It is especially important to note the great care that was taken, especially with "Unknowns," because Battelle's results in this particular category brought some interesting information to light. One would intuitively expect that more "Unknowns" would be generated by the *less* reliable observers, and that, therefore, we should find the highest percentage of "Unknowns" among the *Doubtful* or *Poor* reports. (Condon and others had indeed indicated that unexplained sightings came invariably from poor observers.)

Quite the opposite proved to be the case: out of 970 *Excellent*- and *Good*-rated reports, 259, or 27 percent were

DR. J. ALLEN HYNEK

classified "Unknown." But out of 1,229 *Doubtful-* and *Poor*-rated reports, 175 or 14 percent were classified "Unknown." If one limits oneself to the *Excellent* versus the *Poor* sightings (213 and 435 sightings, respectively) one finds that the "Unknowns" make up 33 percent of the *Excellent* reports and only 17 percent of the *Poor* reports. In tabular form we have:

Reliability Rating of Report	% Unknown	Total Number of Reports
Excellent	33.3	213
Good	24.8	757
Doubtful	13.0	794
Poor	16.6	435
		2,199

The Battelle study further differentiated between military observers and civilians and found nearly 38 percent of the *Excellent* reports turned in by military observers were "Unknowns" while only 21 percent of the military reports rated *Poor* were "Unknown."

More simply stated, the most reliable reports contained about twice as many "Unknowns" as did the poorer reports! This surprising and significant result was nowhere mentioned in the report conclusions or in the later press releases. It *was* buried in the report itself, but how many reporters and media people bothered to dig it out? None, to my knowledge.

That it was the prior intent of the Pentagon to use the Battelle report—whatever its results—to support the recommendations of the Robertson Panel that UFOs be "debunked," seems quite clear. This is further supported by a letter to Gen. Watson from Capt. Hardin, then head of Blue Book, dated February 1956.

A review of recent books on Unidentified Flying Objects appearing in the New York *Times* issue of 22 January 1956 is highly complimentary to our Special Report 14. Written by Jonathan N. Leonard, a science editor and author of *Flight into Space*, it gives considerable credence and support to our UFO position. It would appear from this review that the downgrading and subsequent release of Special Report 14 is serving well *the purpose for which it was intended.* [Italics added.]

Science writer Leonard apparently missed the message of Special Report 14, for he writes in the same issue of *The New York Times,* ". . . the Air Force released the results of a massive, intelligent, painstaking and detailed analysis of all flying saucer reports. It employed excellent scientists and used elaborate apparatus. The conclusion is negative . . . the scientists found no evidence whatever that even the few surviving 'unknowns' were likely to have come from space."

First of all, since when does 22 percent of reports studied in Blue Book No. 14 constitute a "few surviving 'unknowns' "? Table 8 in that Air Force report shows that of the 2,199 reports that the Battelle scientists studied, 434 were classed as "Unknowns," and 240 were classed as having "Insufficient Information" to allow study. Thus 22 percent of all cases for which sufficient data were available for study in the "massive, intelligent, painstaking and detailed analysis" were classed as *"Unknowns."* Hardly "a few."

Second, the statement "were unlikely to have come from space" is irrelevant. The Battelle study was directed toward finding out whether a new unknown phenomenon *existed—* not to designate its origin. It is first important to determine whether or not a phenomenon exists; only then should one consider possible origins.

The conclusions of the Battelle report and the material in the Pentagon press releases that followed were clearly designed to give the impression that science had administered the *coup de grâce* to UFOs (the summary of the Condon Report, some years later, was fashioned to give the same impression)—except, of course, it wasn't science at all; only shamefully biased interpretation of statistics to support a preconceived notion. Once again, statistics which could have been used to illuminate were used instead to debunk the UFO phenomenon.

12

BLUE BOOK END GAME:
THE CONDON REPORT

*This unusual sighting should therefore be assigned to
the category of some almost certainly natural phenomenon which is so rare that it apparently has never
been reported before or since.*

—from the Condon Report

The released files of Project Blue Book contain little that
is specific about the events that led to the demise of Project
Blue Book, particularly the role played by the Condon Report and its complete endorsement by the National Academy of Sciences, an endorsement which, in my opinion,
will come back to haunt this prestigious body just as the
fall of meteorites came back to haunt the French Academy
of Sciences more than a century ago.

The events which led to the abandonment of Project
Blue Book are, however, certainly an integral part of the
Blue Book story—and deserve to be told. It was no secret
to those on the Blue Book staff in Dayton, Ohio, that the
Air Force had been seeking, for several years, an honor-
able way out of processing UFO reports. Project Blue
Book had become more and more of a public relations
burden to the Air Force, and as long as its methodology
and attitudes remained unchanged, this burden was likely
to increase.

In 1965, paralleling the attempts to get Blue Book off
the Air Force's back, there was, oddly enough, an effort
being made within Blue Book itself to improve their procedures. I had made one of my periodic attempts in this
direction, and, earlier that year, had sent a letter to Maj.
Gen. E.D. LeBailly, strongly suggesting that a scientific
panel from outside the Air Force be set up to review Blue
Book procedures and that, unlike previous panels, these

men come "prepared to do their homework." It was with considerable personal pleasure that I noted in a letter of Maj. Gen. LeBailly's, to the military director of the Scientific Advisory Board of the Air Force, dated September 28, 1965, that some of my suggestions were used; he asked that "a working scientific panel . . . review Project Blue Book and advise the Air Force as to any improvements that should be made . . . to carry out the Air Force's assigned responsibility." He went on to note that I would be ready to fully assist such a committee. But my services were never requested.

General LeBailly's letter did, however, lead to the formation of the O'Brien Committee which met in February 1966 and recommended that: "A UFO program be strengthened to provide opportunity for scientific investigation of selected sightings in more detail and depth than has been possible to date." The committee then made a most important recommendation which, had it been carried out, would very likely have led to quite a different result than the one achieved by the Condon Committee. It recommended that the Air Force negotiate contracts "with a *few selected universities* to provide selected sightings of UFOs." [Italics added.] It went on to specify that a single university should coordinate the teams which, together, should study perhaps a hundred sightings per year, devoting an average of ten man-days to each investigation and the resulting report. These recommendations were put forth by the committee in the hope that such investigations would·"provide a far better basis than we have today for our decision on a long-term UFO program."

It is my opinion that those seeking to "get the Air Force out of the UFO business" saw here a chance to turn the recommendations to their own advantage. When, therefore, the notorious Michigan wave of sightings occurred in March 1966 (just a month after the O'Brien recommendations were made), and Congressmen Gerald Ford and Weston Vivian called for a Congressional hearing on the UFO subject, the O'Brien recommendations were implemented, *but with a somewhat different end in view*.

In keeping with the O'Brien recommendation, several independent universities were to examine specific, interesting UFO cases as they occurred, sending competent persons into the field, and to do this on a continuing basis until conclusions could be reached as to whether or not the UFO phenomenon was worthy of scientific study. But note the great difference between "determining whether the UFO phenomenon was worthy of scientific study" and "determining whether we were being visited by extraterrestrial beings." The first was true to basic scientific principles; the second was merely the testing of a given hypothesis.

Although I was at the Congressional hearing that was set up to implement the O'Brien recommendations, I was not privy to the behind-the-scenes action that set them into motion. I was saddened when I later saw the UFO investigation located at one university rather than at several, and placed directly in the hands of one, and only one, prominent scientist. It came to pass that the contract was given to the University of Colorado, specifying that Dr. Edward U. Condon, a member of the Physics Department, be solely in charge. The Condon Committee was in existence from October 1966 to November 1968. The official title of their final report was "The Scientific Study of Unidentified Flying Objects"; but it is more generally known as the "Condon Report."

Almost from the start, the Condon Committee ran into troubles. The foremost of these stemmed from the personalities of the director, Dr. Condon, and his chief administrator, the late Robert Low. These are detailed best in Dr. David Saunders' book, *UFOs: Yes!*, and in less detail in my own book, *The UFO Experience*. The committee never worked as a coherent body and was torn by much internal strife.

The report itself was issued early in 1969. The negative conclusions and recommendations in Dr. Condon's summary chapter were all that the Air Force needed to relieve itself of the Blue Book burden. At a top-level meeting at the Pentagon in March 1969, the fate of Blue Book was decided. From the moment the meeting opened, it was a foregone conclusion that Blue Book was through.

But what of the Condon Report itself? *Was* it actually a negative report? Surprisingly, if one goes past Dr. Condon's summary, and Walter Sullivan's (science editor of *The New York Times*) introduction, and concentrates on the case investigations themselves, one will probably find the Condon Report to be a powerful document *in favor* of the reality of the UFO phenomenon.

I am reminded of a visit I had, about a year after the Condon Report was issued, from Dr. Claude Poher, of the French Committee Nationale Études Spaciaux (CNES) who had been conducting some rocket experiments at Cape Kennedy in Florida. In the course of our conversation, he expressed a very serious interest in the UFO phenomenon and I asked him whence his interest sprang. He replied, "I read the Condon Report." I asked how that possibly could have spurred his interest and he replied in a most serious manner, "If you really *read* the Condon Report and don't stop with Condon's summary, you will find that there is a real problem there." I couldn't agree more.

It is not the province of this book to enter into a critical review of the Condon Report. This has been done quite adequately by several authors, notably Dr. Joachim Kuettner,[1] Dr. Peter Sturrock,[2] David Jacobs,[3] David Saunders,[4] James E. McDonald,[5] and myself.[6]

Nevertheless, a few highlights from various critiques of the Condon Report are, I believe, essential in order for the reader to recognize its true value and the obfuscating nature of Dr. Condon's summary.

A statement by the UFO Sub-Committee of the AIAA reads, "To understand the Condon Report, which is difficult to read, due in part to its organization, one must study the bulk of the report. It is not enough to read summaries such as those by Sullivan and by Condon, or summaries of summaries on which the vast majority of readers . . . seem to rely. There are differences in the opinions and conclusions drawn by the authors of the various chapters and there are differences between these and Condon's summary. Not all conclusions contained in the report itself are fully reflected in Condon's summary. . . . Condon's chapter, summary of the study, contains more than its title indicates: it discloses many of his personal conclusions . . .

[1]Kuettner, Chairman of the American Institute of Aeronautics and Astronautics Sub-Committee on UFOs, November 1970 issue of *Astronautics and Aeronautics*.
[2]Sturrock, "Evaluation of the Condon Report on the Colorado UFO Project."
[3]Jacobs, *The UFO Controversy in America*.
[4]Saunders, *UFOs: Yes!*
[5]McDonald, *The UFO Investigation*, February–March 1969.
[6]Hynek, *Bulletin of Atomic Scientists*, April 1969.

the UFO Sub-Committee did not find a basis in the report for his prediction that 'nothing of scientific value will come of further studies.' Dr. Condon had stated in his summary that further studies of UFOs 'probably cannot be justified in the expectation that science will be advanced thereby.' "

In making such a sweeping statement Condon should have kept in mind the dictum of Sir James Jeans: "It is the unexpected that happens in science." Suppose the early pioneers of science had adopted Condon's attitude and throttled human curiosity at its source whenever something new and unexplained appeared on the horizon. As Dr. Anthony Michaelis, science editor of the *London Daily Telegraph*, once pointed out, "The reality of meteorites, of hypnosis, of the continental drift theory, of germs, of the city of Troy, and of Pleistocene man were in the past dismissed with scorn and laughter. . . ."

How does one know with oracular certainty that any investigation conducted along scientific lines will or will not be productive? To dismiss out of hand the thousands of UFO reports from all over the world, and from basically credible witnesses, on the grounds that one person does not believe any good can come of further investigation, seems to me the very length of tunnel vision.

But let us look at some of the findings buried deep within the Condon Report, and draw our own conclusions. It seems incredible that Dr. Condon could have completely overlooked statements such as the following.

> In conclusion, although conventional or natural explanations certainly cannot be ruled out, probability of such seems low in this case and the probability that at least one genuine UFO was involved appears to be fairly high. (Case #2 p. CR 251.)

Or a statement that a regular staff member on the Colorado Project wrote, in summarizing a case he had been studying:

> This must remain as one of the most puzzling radar cases on record and no conclusion is possible at this time. It seems inconceivable that an anomalous propagation (AP) echo would behave in the manner described even if AP had been likely at the time. In view of meteorological situation, it would seem that

AP was rather unlikely. Besides, what is the propability that an AP return would appear only once and that time appear to execute a perfect ILS (instrument landing system) approach? (Case #21, pp. CR 17-171.)

Or this passage concerning the now famous McMinnville, Oregon, photographs of May 11, 1950 (Case #46, p. CR 407):

This is one of the few UFO reports in which all factors investigated, geometric, psychological, and physical, appear to be consistent with the assertion that an extraordinary flying object, silvery, metallic, disc-shaped, tens of meters in diameter, and evidently artificial, flew within the sight of two witnesses. It cannot be said that the evidence positively rules out fabrication, although there are some factors such as the accuracy of certain photometric measures on the original negatives, which argue against such an assertion.*

With respect to the famous Great Falls, Montana, sighting of August 15, 1950, the Condon Report states:

The case remains unexplained. Analysis indicates that the images on the film are difficult to reconcile with aircraft or other known phenomena, although aircraft cannot entirely be ruled out.

The work of Dr. R.M.L. Baker** fully supports this statement and proves convincingly that the aircraft analysis is untenable.

The above are just a few examples of Condon's blatant disregard of the contents of his own report. It would be

---

*The author of that last comment, Dr. William Hartman, later had some misgivings about so positive a statement and issued, in effect, a retraction. However, recent work by Dr. Bruce Maccabee (Proc. CUFOS Con., pp. 152–163) bears out Hartman's original estimate: the detailed analysis of the original negatives provides strong evidence that the object photographed was at a distance of at least a mile from the camera, thus effectively ruling out a hoax.

**Baker, *Journal of the Astronautical Sciences*, January–February, 1968, Vol. XV, No. 1, pp. 1731–36.

kinder to assume that he never read the report in full
rather than to charge him with being guilty of the unscientific procedure of choosing only those elements of the
report which suited his own purposes.

A more detailed critique of the Condon Report is not
in place here; but it is appropriate to summarize rather
quickly the main reason why the Condon Committee
went astray. Jacobs, in his book *The UFO Controversy in
America*, provides some of the explanation:

> Condon was unable to maintain a continuous
> project staff; out of the original twelve only Low
> (chief administrator) and two other full-time staff
> members remained with the project for its full dura-
> tion. Much of the personal conflict was based on the
> philosophical issue of what assumptions to make
> when investigating cases. Neither of the two groups
> involved saw the primary focus as being to deter-
> mine whether UFOs constituted an anomalous phe-
> nomenon. Instead, one group with Saunders as
> spokesman thought that the committee should con-
> sider the extra-terrestrial hypothesis and other the-
> ories about the origin of UFOs; his group wanted to
> look at as much of the data as possible. The other
> group, with Low as spokesman, thought the extra-
> terrestrial theory was nonsense and believed that so-
> lution to the UFO mystery was to be found in the
> psychological make-up of the witnesses. The main
> conflict was whether UFOs were an extra-terrestrial
> phenomenon rather than whether they constituted
> a unique aerial phenomenon.

Therein lies the fatal mistake. Had they adhered to the
original recommendations of the O'Brien Committee and
examined *not* whether UFOs were visitors from outer
space but whether a *phenomenon existed* (regardless of
origin), which was worthy of scientific study, the final
report might have been worthwhile. As it was, they became embroiled in discussing one specific theory of UFOs,
namely that they were extraterrestrial spacecraft. In so
doing, they broke a cardinal rule of scientific procedure—
get the facts straight first *before* attempting to theorize.

Not only did the Condon Committee address itself to

the wrong problem but it neglected to find a suitable definition for the problem under attack. The definition of UFO used by Dr. Condon led to an inordinate waste of time and money. He defined UFO as "an unidentified flying object . . . which is defined as the stimulus for a report made by one or more individuals as something seen in the sky . . . which *the observer* could not identify as having an ordinary, natural origin." (Italics added.) The sky is *full* of things which many observers find puzzling: bright planets, meteors, advertising planes, twinkling stars, etc. While it is true that the "U" in UFO means unidentified, we must always remember to ask "unidentified *to whom*?" A bright planet such as Venus shining through a cloud cover which is sufficiently thick to blot out the rest of the stars may appear strange and mysterious to a given observer, but it would not be to an astronomer. In my opinion, the definition Dr. Condon *should* have used is: "The reported sighting of an aerial phenomenon (close to or on the ground) which defies explanation not only by the original observer but by those persons technically competent to make an identification in natural terms if possible."

The use of Condon's definition lowered the floodgates to dozens of UFO reports which should not have been eligible for study by the Condon Committee. Lens flares, cloud formations, meteors, balloons, and other IFOs (identifiable flying objects) needlessly squandered the time of the Condon Committee. The Committee should have lived up to the title of its report: "The Scientific Study of Unidentified Flying Objects," and should have limited its survey to truly unidentified reports.

Nonetheless, in spite of the loose definition of UFO used (which therefore greatly increased the chances of identifying the cases they had studied) the Condon Committee still could not identify about one-third of the cases it studied! Had the obvious IFOs been excluded from consideration to begin with, the Condon staff would have been left with the embarrassing situation of not being able to explain the great majority of the cases they examined; which, of course, is the *true* meaning of UFO—cases which remain unidentified even after examination by experts.

A correct interpretation of the Condon Report is thus, it seems to me, diametrically opposed to that which Dr. Condon stated in his summary. The great majority of the truly puzzling cases that the Committee set about to explain remained unexplained, and were therefore by definition, UFOs. Thus, the conclusion of the Committee *should* have been: "The UFO phenomenon is real." Once that was established, there should have been no question as to whether UFOs are a fitting subject for further scientific inquiry.

Had the results of the Condon Report been correctly interpreted, its release would, most probably, have produced some constructive approaches to the UFO problem. But the media handling of the Condon Report, and its resounding endorsement by the National Academy of Sciences, led many to think that UFOs had "had it," and that the problem had indeed been solved.

The endorsement of the report by the National Academy of Sciences is difficult to explain; one can only assume that the very busy men charged with the responsibility of reviewing the Condon Report found it too bulky and burdensome to read in detail and based their endorsement largely on the heretofore solid scientific reputation of Dr. Condon.

The Condon Report, as popularly interpreted by the media, did, however, admirably serve the purposes of the Pentagon. On December 17, 1969, after nearly a year had passed, Air Force Secretary Robert Seamans terminated Project Blue Book. He stated, on the basis of the recommendations of Dr. Condon (and not, to be exact, of the Condon Committee, members of which had widely divergent opinions) that Blue Book could not be continued because it "cannot be justified either on the grounds of national security or in the interest of science."

To the majority of the public this was indeed the *coup de grâce* to the UFO era. Science had spoken. UFOs didn't exist, and the thousands of people who had reported strange sightings (and the probable many thousands more who were reluctant to report) could all be discounted as deluded, hoaxers, or mentally unbalanced.

The UFOs, however, apparently did not read the Condon Report. When, in the fall of 1973, a major wave of

UFO reports occurred in the United States, the cold, clammy hand of the Condon Report was at last lifted by the UFO phenomenon itself.

And in 1977 the reports continue to flow.

EPILOGUE

Since 1947 many peoples of the world have become in-creasingly aware of that bizarre phenomenon we call UFOs—but it has been too strange, too unacceptable, and too uncomfortable for either the scientific world (which should have expressed at least some scientific curiosity about a subject that concerned so large a number of peo-ple) and for the military (which should have been less interested in maintaining its public image of invincibility and omniscience) to accord it more than a passing (and disdainful) glance.

Now that more than a quarter of a century has passed, and the UFO phenomenon is still with us (not having obliged the savants who declared it to be but a passing fad) a call for a reappraisal of the situation is in order. And so let us make one here and now:

Let all who have, either through native interest, through reading, or through personal experience (and there are far more of these than appear in any statistics) a sincere interest in having a thorough and unbiased—and scien-tific—ongoing study made of the entire UFO phenomenon lend their support to bringing such a study into being.

The stage is set for this new adventure into uncharted fields; there exists today a growing number of scientifically and techncally trained persons who are ready to de-vote their time and attention to the whole matter of the nature of UFOs, and to follow wherever the search may lead.

Let us give them our encouragement and our support.

APPENDIX A

For general help in the preparation of this book and for
the following story about Astronaut Slayton, I am indebted to Richard Budelman, former press secretary to
the mayor of Milwaukee, Wisconsin, and currently consultant on local governmental problems. He introduced
the Slayton story in this way: "On numerous occasions
at cocktail parties and other social gatherings, I discussed
the subject of UFOs with numbers of people. Some told
of their own sightings or experiences with these enig-
matic objects; not the least of which was a story told me
as a reporter by Donald K. (Deke) Slayton, of Sparta,
Wisconsin.

"I was a general assignment reporter with the *Milwaukee Journal* at the time and had been assigned to cover a
press conference kicking off the annual Easter Seal drive.
Slayton was honorary chairman of the drive. Following
his press conference, I asked for a separate interview on
the subject of women ever becoming astronauts, my special assignment from my editor.

"During the interview I raised the subject of UFOs. I
asked him whether the astronauts placed any credence in
UFO reports. He said he had never discussed the subject
with them but, after a pause, he calmly told me that he
had once had an aerial encounter with a UFO over St.
Paul, Minnesota. It was 1951 and he was maintenance
officer and test pilot for a P-51 fighter group based in
Minneapolis. A tornado had struck his base, damaging
two full squadrons of P-51 aircraft. It was while flight-
testing one of the aircraft, in bright daylight, that he en-
countered a disc-shaped object, pursued it, but lost it
after it went into a climbing left turn as he closed in on
it."

Budelman told me that he thought he had the news scoop of the year—an astronaut had seen a genuine UFO! But his newspaper refused to print the story, on the grounds that their "science editor did not believe in UFOs"!

Slayton confirmed this story in a letter to me, in which he stated: "During one of these test flights . . . I was cruising at about 10,000 feet. The only reason this number sticks in my mind is because my first reaction upon seeing the object was that it was a kite, and a few seconds later it occurred to me that this could not be the case.

"Upon closer examination the object was obviously at about my altitude and seemed to be coming from the opposite direction, so I continued to watch it until it was directly off my left wing and about 500 feet below. At this point it appeared to be a round balloon of about the size of a weather balloon, and I assumed that was what it was. I decided to make a pass on it and did a 180-degree turn which put me directly in trail of the object. . . . Upon getting in trail, it appeared to be a disc-shaped object rather than round, sitting at about a 45-degree angle with the horizon. The object seemed to be somewhat slower than I at that point, but started to accelerate and went into a climbing left turn as I closed on it. I lost sight of it . . . and returned to home base.

"I did make a report the following day to our intelligence section and have discussed the subject with numbers of people since, but attach no great importance to it. My only conclusion was that it was an unidentified object, at least to me, and I would not speculate as to what it might have been. Since it was a bright clear day, I have discounted its being a weather illusion or an optical illusion."

APPENDIX B

Major Pestalozzi's July 7 Letter to Dr. McDonald:
(See sketch, p. 111)

Dear Jim:

The information you requested several weeks ago concerning a UFO report submitted by me, as reporting officer, to the USAF Project Blue Book, follows:

The intervening years and a very mediocre memory do, of course, preclude my recalling the exact date, report data such as time, meteorological conditions [these obtained later from existing Blue Book records of this case are: Weather clear, visibility 50 miles, temp. 72 deg. F., dew point 50 deg. F., wind calm, sea-level pressure 143 millibars, station pressure 27.310 inches], flight altitude (which must have been about 20,000 feet), names of observers, etc. I will, however, relate the incident to you to the best of my recollection.

While standing on the front entrance steps of the Davis-Monthan Air Force Base Hospital, I observed the approach of two UFOs upon a B-36 flying on a general east-west heading directly over the base. The UFOs appeared, from the ground, to be round in shape and metallic in color (the same color as the B-36). The objects approached the aircraft from the northeast at a speed about three or four times that of the aircraft.

The two objects appeared to be about the same size when first observed. One object appeared to gain altitude as it approached the aircraft because it seemed to grow smaller. It stationed itself, at the

B-36 speed, just behind and to the port side of the B-36. The second stationed itself between the pusher-type prop spinners and the leading edge of the starboard elevators. The air crew, which landed the aircraft at DMAFB, and were interrogated by me, confirmed the ground-observed stationing of this object in this extremely close proximity to the aircraft.

I can no longer remember the length of time of the observation, but all of the air crew members, except one who flew the aircraft during the entire incident, were able to get to the starboard observation port to see the UFO.

The objects were reported to be symmetrically convex top and bottom, about 10 or 12 feet thick from top to bottom at the middle and quite sharp at the edge. (The crew gave an approximate figure in inches which I cannot remember.) The object was reported by the crew, as I remember, to be about 20 or 25 feet in diameter. (It fit rather snugly between spinners and elevator.)

Some of the air crew members reported seeing a pale band of red color about halfway between the top and the edge of the object. All members did not see this color band, however. Upon questioning, the pilots denied that the objects interfered with either the flying characteristics of the B-36 or the navigation or radio equipment.

Upon departure from the aircraft the UFO lost altitude, crossed under the aircraft, joined the other object, and the two departed at extremely high speed in a southerly direction. (Aircraft altitude, airspeed, heading, UFO headings, approximate speeds and exact size estimates are in the original report, but I cannot remember them.) [What a loss not to have the original detailed report! One can only wonder how it disappeared.] During the close proximity of the object the pilots did not try evasive action.

The aircraft and crew were from Carswell AFB, Texas, and were on a flight to March AFB, Cal. It is possible that this report is filed in Blue Book archives under either of those base names. [Unfortunately, it is not].

I hope this report and the diagram are of some help, Jim.

Signed,
[Maj. Pestalozzi]

APPENDIX C

Selfridge Sighting: Officer's Narrative Report

On the night of 9 March 1950, our radar station was in operation monitoring night flying by units of the 56th Fighter-Interceptor Group, Selfridge AFB, Mich. I came on duty approximately at sundown, relieved 1st Lt. Mattson at the PPI scope (of the AM/CPS-5 Radar Sight), and established contact with the F-80s already airborne. Lt. Mattson, Sgt. McCarthy, and Cpl. Melton, who made up the rest of our crew for this night, mentioned to me at this time that an aircraft had been picked up intermittently on the HRI scope of the ANC/CPS-4 height finder radar at 45,000 feet and over. I knew the highest assigned altitude of the F-80s was 24,000 feet; the target was not at that time visible on either radar scope, so I attributed the report of the high-flying aircraft to interference, crew inexperience, or both. Over the next fifteen minutes the rest of the crew, mentioned above, repeatedly reported this high-flying target at apparently rapidly changing altitudes without my being able to turn around rapidly enough from my monitoring of the F-80s in the area to observe for myself. Finally, however, I saw this target which was a very narrow and clear-cut presentation on the NRI scope. It was at approximately 47,000 feet about seventy (70) miles out, and the indication was definitely not that of a cloud or atmospheric phenomenon. I checked pilots in the area by VHF and was assured by F-80 pilot at the highest assigned altitude that he was at 24,000 feet. The clarity, narrowness, and definition of the presentation was definitely that of an aircraft. The target gave a similar presentation to that given by an F-80, and if anything, narrower. It was definitely at this time not presenting a very large reflecting surface toward our station and I could not at this time pick up the target on the CPS-5, ruling out B-36 or other large aircraft. Further indications of this aircraft were picked up intermittently but with increasing regularity for the next 45 minutes or an hour, and entries were made of these occurrences in the controller's log; though relatively fairly correct, [they] are inaccurate, due to the extreme inaccuracy of Sgt. McCarthy's watch. During this period, approximately 1945 to 2030 (7:45 to 8:30 P.M.), this target seemed to stay in the area in which our fighters were flying, sometimes approximating their courses, but 20,000 feet above them. During this same 45-minute period, Lt. Mattson and other members of the crew reported, both from the HRI scope of the ANC/CPS-4 and another PPI scope of the AN/CPS-5, that the target hovered in one position and also that it progressed from a position given as 270°, 78 miles at 45,000 feet to a position at 358°, 53 miles at roughly the same altitude in 4–5 minutes. This would give it a speed upwards of 1,500 miles per hour for this run. I cannot substantiate this speed. Coverage of target during this run was reportedly intermittent and the times were not to my knowledge accurately tabulated at actual instances of radar pickup during this run. Subsequent individual questioning I undertook with members of the crew bears out the possibility of inaccuracy in timing during this run. I knew only that the target was very fast. I observed during this period, by momentarily turning around and watching the HRI scope, several extreme instances of gaining altitude and losing altitude. I was not able at this time to take down the actual figures, but observed it losing and gaining up to 20,000 feet very rapidly.

I was able, at 2046 (8:46 P.M.) EST, to identify this aircraft on my PPI scope (AN/CPS-5) and simultaneously on the HRI scope. The only actual timing and figures I took down on this target I did during the six minutes from 2046 to 2052 (8:46 to 8:52 P.M.), during which time this aircraft was giving indications on both scopes without fade. I took down the range and azimuth on the minute for this period and Sgt. McCarthy took down the altitudes. (Sgt. McCarthy's times were off as aforementioned but in this case, due to the fact that we were both following the same target, I have reconstructed these times into my own, which were taken in grease

pencil directly on the scope head, and later transcribed.)
Information recorded is as follows:

Time	Azimuth	Range in miles	Altitude in feet
2046	1,560	45	25,000
2047	1,510	49	29,000
2048	1,460	56	35,000
2049	1,420	60	33,000
2050	1,390	67	36,000
2051	1,360	73	38,000
2052	1,330	79	33,000

These figures, although not as spectacular as some of
the climbs and speeds I observed, show definitely the erratic speed and altitude changes. The differences in speed
from one minute to the next were apparent to me as were
the climbs and dives. At 2052 the aircraft faded from the
PPI scope and was picked up for periods of one and two
minutes up to 120 miles. It appeared to hover for two
minutes at approximately 110 miles distant. It faded at
120 miles for the last time. The height-finder carried the
aircraft past the six minute period listed above to a 1,230,
87 miles, 31,000 feet where it faded for the night from
the CPS-4.

*The CPS-5 was very accurate on this particular night
which was supported by F-80 pilots' agreement with many
geographical positions given them off the CPS-5.* The
AN/CPS-4, though a more erratic piece of equipment,
could not, through any known or prevalent weakness in
its operation, account for this manner of extreme changes
in altitude. I went over all possible errors which could
be induced by AN/CPS-4 error exhaustively with my
technical personnel.

We are continuing investigation at this station.

I have been a rated pilot since 12 April 1943, and have
been assigned to controller duties for aproximately 2½
years.

S/Francis E. Parker
1st Lt. USAF

APPENDIX D

Revised Statistics—Final

Year	NL	DD	RV	R	CE I	CE II	CE III	Total
1947	0	9	0	0	0	1	0	10
1948	3	10	1	0	1	1	0	16
1949	3	12	0	0	0	1	2	18
1950	2	21	2	2	4	0	0	31
1951	7	9	1	0	4	1	0	22
1952	103	117	7	5	4	5	1	242
1953	19	17	2	2	2	2	0	44
1954	19	17	3	1	3	3	0	46
1955	10	11	0	0	3	1	1	26
1956	10	6	2	0	2	1	0	21
1957	7	9	4	0	2	3	0	25
1958	2	7	3	0	1	1	1	15
1959	7	5	0	0	1	1	0	14
1960	12	4	0	0	1	0	0	17
1961	5	4	0	0	2	1	2	14
1962	1	1	0	0	0	0	0	2
1963	2	1	0	0	1	0	0	4
1964	3	3	0	0	1	1	1	9
1965	0	1	1	0	2	3	0	7
1966	18	6	1	0	7	4	0	36
1967	8	1	1	0	5	1	0	16
1968	1	0	1	0	0	2	0	4
1969	1	0	0	0	0	0	0	1
Total	243	271	29	10	46	33	8	640
%	38.0	42	5	2	7	5	1	

Total No. 640

BIBLIOGRAPHY

Bowen, C., ed.: *The Humanoids,* Chicago: Henry Regnery, 1969.

Condon, E.J.: *The Scientific Study of Unidentified Flying Objects,* New York: Bantam Books, 1968.

Fuller, J.G.: *Incident At Exeter,* New York: G.P. Putnam's Sons, 1966.

Hynek, J.A.: *The UFO Experience,* Chicago: Henry Regnery, 1972.

Hynek, J.A. & Vallee, J.: *The Edge of Reality,* Chicago: Henry Regnery, 1975.

Jacobs, D.: *The UFO Controversy in America,* Bloomington: Indiana University Press, 1975.

Maccabee, B.: *The Scientific Investigation of Unidentified Flying Objects* (to be published).

Ruppelt, E.J.: *The Report on Unidentified Flying Objects,* New York: Ace Books, 1956.

Sagan, C. & Page, T.: *UFOs: A Scientific Debate,* New York: W.W. Norton & Co., 1972.

Saunders, D.R. & Harkins, R.R.: *UFOs? Yes!,* New York: The World Publishing Co., 1968.

Sturrock, P.A.: *Report on a Survey of the Membership of the American Astronomical Society Concerning the UFO Problem.* Plasma Research Laboratory, Stanford University, 1977.

Symposium on Unidentified Flying Objects—Hearings before the Committee on Science and Astronautics, U.S. House of Representatives, 90th Congress, July 29, 1968 —U.S. Government Printing Office, Washington, D.C.

Valle, J.: *Anatomy of a Phenomenon,* Chicago: Henry Regnery, 1965.

Webb, D.: *1973: Year of the Humanoids,* Evanston: Center for UFO Studies, 1976.

ACKNOWLEDGMENTS

Many persons helped me in the preparation of this book which involved detailed examination of ninety-four reels of microfilm. One person to whom I am especially indebted and to whom much credit for this book must go has requested anonymity for valid personal reasons. My thanks and deep appreciation nonetheless.

To another, Richard Budelman, I am indebted for his loyal assistance in searching out relevant intelligence matters, for the culling of photographic material, and for submitting valuable material, large portions of which I have incorporated in partially revised form.

I wish also to thank Marilyn Weigand for assistance in research, and Charles Schaughnessy and the staff of the Modern Military Branch of the National Archives for assistance in obtaining usable copies of photographic material.

My special thanks also to Allan Hendry, Managing Editor of *The International UFO Reporter* for his excellent art work.

J. Allen Hynek